An Introduction
to the Heidelberg
Catechism

Texts and Studies in Reformation and Post-Reformation Thought

General Editor
Prof. Richard A. Muller, Calvin Theological Seminary

Caspar Olevianus, A Firm Foundation: An Aid to Interpreting the Heidelberg Catechism, translated and edited by Lyle D. Bierma.

John Calvin, The Bondage and Liberation of the Will: A Defence of the Orthodox Doctrine of Human Choice against Pighius, edited by A. N. S. Lane, translated by G. I. Davies.

Law and Gospel: Philip Melanchthon's Debate with John Agricola of Eisleben over Poenitentia, by Timothy J. Wengert.

Martin Luther as Prophet, Teacher, and Hero: Images of the Reformer, 1520–1620, by Robert Kolb.

Melanchthon in Europe: His Work and Influence beyond Wittenberg, edited by Karin Maag.

Reformation and Scholasticism: An Ecumenical Enterprise, edited by Willem J. van Asselt and Eef Dekker.

The Binding of God: Calvin's Role in the Development of Covenant Theology, by Peter A. Lillback.

Divine Discourse: The Theological Methodology of John Owen, by Sebastian Rehnman.

Heinrich Bullinger and the Doctrine of Predestination: Author of "the Other Reformed Tradition"? by Cornelis P. Venema.

Architect of Reformation: An Introduction to Heinrich Bullinger, 1504-1575, edited by Bruce Gordon and Emidio Campi.

An Introduction to the Heidelberg Catechism: Sources, History, and Theology, by Lyle D. Bierma, with Charles D. Gunnoe, Jr, Karin Y. Maag, and Paul W. Fields.

An Introduction to the Heidelberg Catechism

Sources, History, and Theology

With a Translation of the Smaller
and Larger Catechisms of Zacharias Ursinus

Lyle D. Bierma
with Charles D. Gunnoe Jr.,
Karin Y. Maag, and Paul W. Fields

Baker Academic
Grand Rapids, Michigan

Published by Baker Academic
a division of Baker Publishing Group
P.O. Box 6287, Grand Rapids, MI 49516-6287
www.bakeracademic.com

Printed in the United States of America

Library of Congress Cataloging-in-Publication Data
Bierma, Lyle D.
    An introduction to the Heidelberg Catechism : sources, history, and theology : with a translation of the smaller and larger catechisms of Zacharias Ursinus / Lyle D. Bierma ; with Charles D. Gunnoe, Karin Maag, Paul W. Fields.
        p.   cm. — (Texts and studies in Reformation and post-Reformation thought)
    Includes bibliographical references.
    ISBN 0-8010-3117-6 (pbk.)
    1. Heidelberger Katechismus. 2. Reformed Church—Catechisms—History and criticism. I. Gunnoe, Charles D., 1963– II. Maag, Karin. III. Fields, Paul W., 1953– V. Ursinus, Zacharias, 1534–1583. Catechesis minor. English. V. Ursinus, Zacharias, 1534–1583. Catechesis maior. English. VI. Title. VII. Series.
BX9428.B54 2005
238'.42—dc22   2005045345

Table of Contents

Contributors   7
Series Preface   9
Preface   11

Part 1: Historical Introduction

1. The Reformation of the Palatinate and the Origins
    of the Heidelberg Catechism, 1500-1562
        Charles D. Gunnoe Jr.   15

2. The Purpose and Authorship of the Heidelberg
    Catechism
        Lyle D. Bierma   49

3. The Sources and Theological Orientation of the
    Heidelberg Catechism
        Lyle D. Bierma   75

4. Early Editions and Translations of the Heidelberg
    Catechism
        Karin Y. Maag   103

5. Bibliography of Research on the Heidelberg
    Catechism since 1900
        Paul W. Fields   119

Part 2: Translations of Ursinus's Catechisms

Introduction
    Lyle D. Bierma   137

The Smaller Catechism   141

The Larger Catechism   163

Contributors

LYLE D. BIERMA (Ph.D., Duke University) is Professor of Systematic Theology at Calvin Theological Seminary, Grand Rapids, Michigan, and editor of the *Calvin Theological Journal*.

PAUL W. FIELDS (M.L.S., Syracuse University) is Theological Librarian and curator of the H. Henry Meeter Center for Calvin Studies at Calvin College and Calvin Theological Seminary, Grand Rapids, Michigan.

CHARLES D. GUNNOE JR. (Ph.D., University of Virginia) is Associate Professor of History and chairperson of the Department of History, Aquinas College, Grand Rapids, Michigan.

KARIN Y. MAAG (Ph.D., University of St. Andrews) is director of the H. Henry Meeter Center for Calvin Studies at Calvin College and Calvin Theological Seminary and Associate Professor of History at Calvin College, Grand Rapids, Michigan.

Series Preface

The heritage of the Reformation is of profound importance to the church in the present day. Yet there remain many significant gaps in our knowledge of the intellectual development of Protestantism in the sixteenth century, and there are not a few myths about the theology of the Protestant orthodox writers of the late sixteenth and seventeenth centuries. These gaps and myths, frequently caused by ignorance of the scope of a particular thinker's work, by negative generations, or by an intellectual imperialism of the present that singles out some thinkers and ignores others regardless of their relative significance to their own times, stand in the way of a substantive encounter with this important period in our history. Understanding and appropriation of that heritage can occur only through the publication of significant works—monographs and sound, scholarly translations—that present the breadth and detail of the thought of the Reformers and their successors.

Texts and Studies in Reformation and Post-Reformation Thought proposes to make available such works as Caspar Olevianus's *Firm Foundation*, Theodore Beza's *Table of Predestination*, and Jerome Zanchi's *Confession of Faith*, together with significant monographs on traditional Reformed theology, under the guidance of an editorial board of recognized scholars in the field. Major older works, like Heppe's *Reformed Dogmatics*, will be reprinted or reissued with new introductions. These works, moreover, are intended to address two groups: an academic and a confessional or churchly audience. The series recognizes the need for careful, scholarly treatment of the Reformation and of the era of Protestant orthodoxy, given the continuing literature as well as the recent interest in reappraising the relationship of the Reformation to Protestant orthodoxy. In addition, however, the series hopes to provide the church at large with worthy documents from its rich heritage and thereby to support and to stimulate interest in the roots of the Protestant tradition.

Richard A. Muller

Preface

Both parts of this book were inspired by the work of Dr. Fred H. Klooster (1922-2003), Professor of Systematic Theology at Calvin Theological Seminary from 1956-1988 and one of the world's leading authorities on the Heidelberg Catechism. Prof. Klooster began teaching a seminar on the HC in 1963, and his interest in the subject eventually led to a sabbatical research year in Heidelberg (1968-1969), several journal articles, a 468-page unpublished manuscript on "The Heidelberg Catechism: Origin and History" (1981), a collection of introductory adult education presentations entitled *A Mighty Comfort: The Christian Faith according to the Heidelberg Catechism* (1990), and a magisterial 2-volume commentary, *Our Only Comfort: A Comprehensive Commentary on the Heidelberg Catechism* (2001). In the 1980s he and one of his students also produced an unpublished English translation of two major sources for the HC, the Smaller and Larger Catechisms of Zacharias Ursinus.

Several years ago Prof. Klooster asked me if I would take responsibility for getting his historical volume and translation of Ursinus's catechisms into publishable form. The latter proved easier than the former. Because of difficulties encountered in reworking his history of the Heidelberg Catechism, it was agreed that I and a small team of scholars would write an entirely new historical introduction, with Klooster's manuscript as one of our resources. Therefore, besides my own chapters and revised translation of Ursinus's catechisms, I am pleased to include contributions by historians Charles Gunnoe and Karin Maag and theological librarian Paul Fields. In honor of Prof. Klooster and his forty years of outstanding work on the HC, we dedicate this book to him.

Special thanks are due the administration and trustees of Calvin Seminary for granting me a six-month sabbatical leave in 2003 to complete this book. I also wish to thank my colleague at Calvin Seminary, Richard Muller, for his encouragement throughout this project and for offering to include it in the series *Texts and Studies in Reformation & Post-Reformation Thought*. Finally, I am grateful to freelance editor Jan Ortiz for her careful work in copyediting and formatting the text.

A few paragraphs in Chapter 2 were first published in my article "Olevianus and the Authorship of the Heidelberg Catechism: Another Look," *The Sixteenth Century Journal* 13, no. 4 (1982): 17-27, and in my chapter "*Vester Grundt* and the Origins of the Heidelberg Catechism," in *Later Calvinism: International Perspectives*, ed. W. Fred Graham (Kirksville, Mo.: Sixteenth Century Journal Publishers, 1994), 289-309, and are reprinted here with permission.

Lyle D. Bierma
Calvin Theological Seminary

Part 1:
Historical Introduction

1

The Reformation of the Palatinate and the Origins of the Heidelberg Catechism, 1500-1562

Charles D. Gunnoe Jr.

The city of Heidelberg is famed for its romantic setting along the Neckar River and especially for its impressive castle ruins, which loom over the old city— a large part of which was built during the Reformation period. As the home of the oldest university within the current boundaries of Germany and of scholarly luminaries such as Max Weber and Karl Jaspers, it is also rightly renowned as an intellectual center. The famous fossil remains of a hominid known as Heidelberg Man (*homo heidelbergensis*) were found a few kilometers southeast of Heidelberg in 1907. The city was also one of the few German towns to escape World War II relatively unscathed, and over the last decades, thousands of Americans have come to know Heidelberg as the headquarters of the U.S. Army in Europe.

For Reformed Protestants, however, the city is chiefly famous for lending its name to the Heidelberg Catechism. While the HC is a defining confessional document of Reformed Protestantism, when seen from the broader perspective of central European history, the story of the catechism's origin is more appropriately reckoned to that of an important signpost in the tragic sequence of events that would eventually lead to the Thirty Years' War. In this chapter, I will attempt to outline the political, cultural, and social milieu that gave birth to the Heidelberg Catechism (HC). Dynastic rivalries, shifting imperial power blocks, a tradition of openness to innovative ideas, a latent impulse toward religious reform, and especially growing pressure from below were some of the factors that went into the mix that ultimately gave birth to a document that has proven itself to be an enduring and inspiring monument to the Reformed faith.[1]

---

1. The following works offer broad coverage of Palatine history in the late medieval and early modern periods and have been used extensively in this chapter: Henry J. Cohn, *The Government of the Rhine Palatinate in the Fifteenth Century* (Oxford: Oxford University Press, 1965); Volker Press, *Calvinismus und Territorialstaat: Regierung und Zentralbehorden der Kurpfalz 1559-1619*, Kieler Historische Studien, vol. 7 (Stuttgart: Ernst Klett Verlag, 1970); and Meinrad Schaab, *Geschichte der Kurpfalz*, 2 vols. (Stuttgart: Kohlhammer, 1988, 1992). These shorter works offer compelling analytical overviews of the period: Volker Press, "Die 'Zweite Reformation' in der Kurpfalz," in *Die reformierte Konfessionalisierung in Deutschland* (Schriften des Vereins fur

Origins of the Rhineland-Palatinate

The context for the HC was the Palatinate, one of the leading principalities of the Holy Roman Empire in the early modern period. In the sixteenth century, the Palatinate consisted of two major components, the Rhenish "Lower Palatinate" with its capital in Heidelberg and the North Bavarian "Upper Palatinate." The territories of the Lower Palatinate were widely dispersed on both banks of the Rhine alongside those of the bishoprics of Worms, Speyer, and Mainz. The territory's ruler, the Elector Palatine, enjoyed the highest place of honor among all the secular princes of the empire. However, the Palatinate's aspirations to greater glory generally exceeded the resources of its modest territorial base. To understand the Palatinate's basic predicament, one must turn to the territory's origin in the High Middle Ages.

The first oddity of Palatine history is that the title of the officeholder, "count palatine,"[2] came into existence before the southwest German territory known as the "Palatinate" (*Pfalz*). As the title suggests, a count palatine was originally a palace official, and the position originated at the Merovingian court in the early Middle Ages. In the high medieval period the count palatine of Lotharingia established a territorial base in the upper Rhine region along the borders of the older "stem" duchies of Swabia and Franconia. As the original stem duchies broke apart, the Palatinate was one of the new territorial states, alongside Württemberg, that rose to prominence. The powerful Wittelsbach family received the Palatinate from the Hohenstaufen Emperor Frederick II in 1214. In the Treaty of Pavia (1329) the Wittelsbach family divided its holdings. The elder branch of the dynasty assumed possession of a geographically divided state consisting of the Rhine territories, known as the Rhine Palatinate or Lower Palatinate, and the North Bavarian territory, henceforth known as the Upper Palatinate. The younger branch of the family continued to rule the remaining Bavarian districts.

Reformationsgeschichte, 195), ed. Heinz Schilling (Gutersloh, 1986) 104-29; Anton Schindling and Walter Ziegler, "Kurpfalz, Rheinische Pfalz und Oberpfalz," in *Die Territorien des Reichs im Zeitalter der Reformation und Konfessionalisierung: Land und Konfession 1500-1650*, vol. 5, Der Südwesten, ed. Anton Schindling and Walter Ziegler, 8-49 (Münster: Aschendorff, 1993); Eike Wolgast, *Reformierte Konfession und Politik im 16. Jahrhundert: Studien zur Geschichte der Kurpfalz im Reformationszeitalter* (Heidelberg: Universitätsverlag C. Winter, 1998). For treatment extending into the seventeenth century, see Charles D. Gunnoe Jr., "The Palatinate," in *The Oxford Encyclopedia of the Reformation*, ed. Hans J. Hillerbrand (Oxford: Oxford University Press, 1996); and idem, "Palatinate," in *Europe 1450-1789: Encyclopedia of the Early Modern World*, ed. Jonathan Dewald (New York: Scribner's, 2004), 4:373-75.

2. Latin, *comes palatinus*; German, *Pfalzgraf*. Sometimes rendered as "Palsgrave" in English from the Old Dutch *Paltsgrave*. After receiving the electoral dignity, the count palatine was known as the "elector palatine," and the territory referred to the "Electoral Palatinate" (*Kurpfalz*). The leaders of the collateral branches of the Wittelsbach family would also bear the title of "count palatine" while only the ruler of the Electoral Palatinate was known as the "elector palatine." See below.

Over the coming centuries, the Bavarian Wittelsbachs, who controlled a larger, contiguous, and more compact territory, would prove formidable rivals for their Rhenish cousins, the Palatine Wittelsbachs.[3]

The late medieval period (ca. 1250-1500 A.D.) was a traumatic time in the political history of the Holy Roman Empire. The medieval Holy Roman Empire encompassed the modern-day countries of Germany, Austria, the Netherlands, Belgium, Luxembourg, Switzerland, and the Czech Republic in addition to large portions of Italy, France, and Poland. While in the tenth and eleventh centuries the Holy Roman Empire had been the most powerful centralized state in Western Europe, the long struggle with the papacy and the rising power of regional princes gradually undermined the position of the emperor. The denouement of the long struggles of the Hohenstaufen dynasty against the pope and his Italian allies came with the execution of the young Conradin, the last heir of the Hohenstaufen house, in 1268. After enduring a long interregnum in the late thirteenth century, in which there was no universally recognized reigning monarch, the Holy Roman Empire stabilized as an elected monarchy in the fourteenth century. The signal moment in this consolidation was the proclamation of the Golden Bull by Emperor Charles IV in 1356. The Golden Bull recognized the right of three ecclesiastical and four secular electors to take part in imperial elections.[4] In bestowing other special privileges and obligations upon these electors (*Kurfürsten*), the Golden Bull raised these princes above their peers in the empire. The Elector Palatine (a.k.a. "count palatine on the Rhine") was one of the elevated princes—much to the chagrin of the Bavarian Wittelsbachs.[5] The Elector Palatine also enjoyed the ceremonial status of imperial steward (*Erztruchseß*) and acted as imperial vicar (*Reichsvikar*), along with the duke of Saxony, in the case of a vacancy of imperial office.

Solidified by the provisions of the Golden Bull, the Palatine Wittelsbachs played an impressive role in the imperial history in the fifteenth century, and even placed one of their members, Ruprecht (r. 1400-1410), on the imperial

---

3. The lingering hostilities between the Wittelsbachs are outlined in Volker Press, "Bayerns wittelsbachische Gegenspieler—Die Heidelberger Kurfürsten 1505-1685," in *Um Glauben und Reich: Kurfürst Maximilian I.*, ed. Hubert Glaser (Munich: Hirmer Verlag; Munich/Zürich: R. Piper & Co. Verlag, 1980), 24-48.

4. The ecclesiastical electors were the bishops of Trier, Cologne, and Mainz. The secular electors were the king of Bohemia, the duke of Saxony, the margrave of Brandenburg, and the count palatine on the Rhine.

5. The Golden Bull did not create the process of electing the Holy Roman Emperor but formalized the procedures and definitively settled the question of which princes had the right to take part. Earlier, the Wittelsbach emperor Louis IV "the Bavarian" had envisioned alternating the voting right between the two branches of the Wittelsbach family. With the Golden Bull, Charles IV undermined his Bavarian Wittelsbach rivals by bestowing this important privilege on the relatively weaker Palatine Wittelsbachs. For a general discussion of the terms of the Golden Bull and its significance, see Geoffrey Barraclough, *The Origins of Modern Germany* 2d ed. (New York, Capricorn Books, 1963), 316-21; and F. R. H. Du Boulay, *Germany in the Later Middle Ages* (London: Athlone, 1983), 39-42.

throne.[6] However, like most Germanic dynasties in this period, the Wittelsbachs did not practice strict primogeniture but tended to divide their territories among their heirs.[7] This is why when we come to the late-medieval era we do not find one Saxony, Bavaria, or Austria but two or more. Ruprecht divided his holdings among his many heirs and thus created an abundance of cadet lines—all of which bore the title of "count palatine on the Rhine and duke in Bavaria." At the height of this splintering in 1618 there were some eleven branches of the Palatine house, and of course all this time there was the second Wittelsbach line who actually held Bavaria.[8] The Electoral Palatinate nevertheless continued its upward momentum, especially during the reign of Elector Frederick I the Victorious (r. 1449-1476). Around the turn of the sixteenth century, the Palatinate appeared poised to emerge as the dominant power in southwest Germany.

The decisive development that upset this train was the Bavarian War of Succession (*Landshuter Erbfolgekrieg*, 1503-1505). In brief, Georg the Rich, the last duke of Bavaria-Landshut, attempted to pass his holdings on to his daughter Elizabeth and her husband, Ruprecht, the son of the Elector Palatine Philip the Upright (r. 1476-1508). Because this plan flew in the face of accepted legal principles (in the absence of a male heir, lands were to revert to the Bavarian Wittelsbach house) and ran counter to the interests of the Emperor Maximilian I and Duke Albrecht IV of Bavaria, the Palatinate faced a powerful coalition of rivals in implementing Georg's will. Upon Georg's death in 1503, Elizabeth and Ruprecht sought to claim what they thought to be their rightful inheritance with the backing of Elector Philip, "who was foolish enough to believe," in the words of Henry Cohn, "that he could augment his territories at the expense of all his neighbors simultaneously."[9] This was an imprudent decision for Philip; the Palatinate and its allies generally faired the worse in the ensuing war. Not only did he fail to secure the lower Bavarian lands for the Palatine house, but he was also forced to surrender some of the Rhenish holdings to his rivals. The Bavarian Wittelsbachs emerged strengthened; they were able to reunify upper and lower

---

6. "Ruprecht I" as German king (or "King of the Romans"), "Ruprecht III" as Elector of the Palatinate (r. 1398-1410). Because Ruprecht never received imperial coronation in Rome, he is known as king rather than as emperor. While Ruprecht's reign is certainly a high point in the dynastic history of the Palatinate, it is considered a low point in the history of the late medieval empire as his limited *Hausmacht* made him a rather weak ruler. He nevertheless used his position effectively to advance the material basis of the Electoral Palatinate.

7. The Golden Bull had sought to eliminate divisions of the electors' core territories, but these provisions were not widely observed until the sixteenth century and after. Cohn, *The Government of the Rhine Palatinate*, 17-19.

8. Cohn, *The Government of the Rhine Palatinate*, 6-7, 17-19, 22-23, 41; Schaab, *Geschichte der Kurpfalz*, 1:145-60. Cf. the genealogical tables in Schaab, *Geschichte der Kurpfalz*, 1:220-25 and 2:253-55. While there were many individuals who bore the title "count palatine" (the appellation had also been revived as a minor rank that the Emperor could bestow upon a member of the lower nobility or a recently ennobled commoner), only the leader of the Palatine Wittelsbachs could claim the title of Elector Palatine.

9. Cohn, *The Government of the Rhine Palatinate*, 15.

Bavaria by incorporating most of Duke Georg's holdings.[10] The Cologne Arbitration of 1505 created the small principality known as Pfalz-Neuburg as a settlement for Georg's heirs, but the Palatinate was the real loser of the war.[11]

The defeat of the Palatinate in the Bavarian War of Succession set up the basic political challenge that the Palatinate faced in the early years of the Reformation. Many of the territories to the south, gained in the previous century, were lost, and the diplomatic setting was precarious. The Bavarian Wittelsbachs had won a major victory at the Palatinate's expense, and sought to complete their triumph by securing the long-desired electoral dignity. Other local rivals such as Hesse and Württemberg had also gained in the Palatinate's loss. For the Palatinate, the safest strategy for the coming years would be one of careful consolidation working in close alliance with the reigning Habsburg dynasty.[12]

While the Palatinate could afford no experiments on the political front, the intellectual-religious milieu seems to have provided a well-disposed environment for Martin Luther's fledgling movement. Heidelberg had been a leading center of the Northern Renaissance, at one time hosting a circle of humanists including the likes of Jacob Wimpfeling, Johann von Dalberg, Rudolf Agricola, Johannes Reuchlin, Johannes Trithemius, and Conrad Celtis.[13] Interestingly, the University of Heidelberg proved largely resistant to the Humanists' leavening influence.[14] While most of the elder generation of humanists remained loyal to Catholicism after the advent of the Reformation, they did provide an important initial audience for the reception of Luther's attack on indulgences, and many of their younger comrades went over to the Protestant cause.[15]

The Palatinate also possessed a healthy domestic tradition of anticlericalism, and the Palatine electors had long usurped the rights of the responsible bishops in administering their churches in the region under their control.[16] Also in favor of a ready reception of the Reformation in the Palatinate was the close connection

10. Emperor Maximilian of Austria's assistance did have its price and the Bavarians surrendered some Alpine territory to the emperor.

11. Schaab, *Geschichte der Kurpfalz*, 1:213-19. This principality was a remnant of the former duchy of Bavaria-Landshut, along with some lands from Bavaria-Munich and the Upper Palatinate. It bore the title Pfalz-Neuburg or *Junge Pfalz* as its rulers were from the Palatine Wittelsbach line in Heidelberg. Because Ruprecht and Elizabeth died in 1504, the new principality was intended as compensation for their sons Philip and Ottheinrich. This small Swabian principality would be the political, cultural, and religious laboratory of Ottheinrich, the future elector palatine.

12. Schaab, *Geschichte der Kurpfalz*, 2:13-14.

13. Henry J. Cohn, "The Early Renaissance Court in Heidelberg," *European Studies Review* 1 (1971): 295-322.

14. Eike Wolgast, *Die Universität Heidelberg, 1386-1986* (Berlin: Springer, 1986), 23. Cohn notes, however, that humanists did occasionally take up posts at the university. Cohn, "The Early Renaissance Court in Heidelberg," 302-3.

15. See Bernd Moeller, "The German Humanists and the Beginnings of the Reformation," in *Imperial Cities and the Reformation: Three Essays*, trans. H. C. Erik Midelfort and Mark U. Edwards (Philadelphia: Fortress, 1972), 19-38.

16. Cohn, *The Government of the Rhine Palatinate*, 140-52. This trend continued under Ludwig V. Press, *Calvinismus und Territorialstaat*, 173.

between the Palatine Wittelsbachs and the electoral Saxon court.[17] We thus encounter the basic matrix of Palatine church history for the first three decades of the Reformation era. Reforming ideas found numerous avenues to penetrate the territory and many elements of the populace were open to the message; however the political leadership had been schooled by past overreaching and desperately wanted to maintain cordial relations with the ruling Habsburgs.[18]

The "Pre-Reformation"

The traditional view of the church history of the Palatinate is that the territory more or less remained loyal to the Roman Catholic church during the early phase of the Reformation, except for a fleeting flirtation in the 1540s, only to embrace Lutheranism in 1556, and then swing to full-blown Calvinism in 1563. Such a picture is a gross oversimplification that downplays the strands of continuity in the development of Palatine religious history. The Reformation in the Palatinate underwent the longest incubation phase of any major German territory. German historians conventionally refer to this period as the "Pre-Reformation" of the Palatinate, because, while the territory did not officially embrace Protestantism, the evangelical cause made important inroads into the Palatinate that facilitated its official move into the Protestant camp at mid-century.

When the German Reformation began in 1517, Ludwig V (r. 1508-1544) reigned as Elector Palatine, though in theory he shared power with his starry-eyed brother, Count Palatine Frederick (later Elector Frederick II) who was frequently occupied as a Habsburg representative in the early decades of the century. Contemporary observers as well as modern historians have not been particularly impressed by Ludwig. Volker Press commented that he was one of the most colorless figures among the princes of the first decades of the Reformation and also suggested that "cautious" or "hesitant" might be more appropriate adjectives to describe this prince often hailed as "the peaceful" (*Pacificus*).[19] The problems of the Palatinate were not of his making, however, and he labored under both financial exigency and strategic weakness. His shortage of funds—huge debts were a chief inheritance of his more open-handed forebears—had a deleterious impact on the cultural life of the Palatinate.[20] The Palatinate was no longer a major center of German humanism, and the famed University of Heidelberg went into decline. The general lack of cultural patronage was also a matter of priorities.

---

17. The chief figure here was Pfalzgraf Wolfgang who served as honorary rector of the University of Wittenberg in 1515. See Walter Hensß, "Frühe Spuren der Reformation in Kurpfalz (1518-1528/29)," *Blätter für Pfälzische Kirchengeschichte und religiöse Volkskunde* 50 (1983): 5-42.

18. The Palatine house effectively used its vote for Charles V in the imperial election of 1519 to consolidate its position and secure imperial authorization for a number of privileges. See Walter Müller, *Die Stellung der Kurpfalz zur lutherischen Bewegung von 1517 bis 1525* (Heidelberg: Carl Winter's Universitätsbuchhandlung, 1937), 8-17; Schaab, *Geschichte der Kurpfalz*, 2:15-16.

19. Press, *Calvinismus und Territorialstaat*, 170-71.

20. Ludwig's ambitious plan to transfer his debts to the Palatine estates fell on deaf ears in the spring of 1517. Cohn, *The Government of the Rhine Palatinate*, 197-99.

Not unlike most of his peers, Ludwig was much more interested in hunting than in poetry. "A good humanist education," commented Meinrad Schaab, "later showed few effects."[21] The only cultural endeavor that captured his imagination was the expansion of the Heidelberg Castle.[22] (Luther himself enjoyed a personal tour of the castle during his famous visit in 1518.)

It is nearly obligatory to begin a discussion of the Reformation of the Palatinate with a retelling of Luther's appearance before the chapter of the Augustinian Hermits in Heidelberg in April 1518. Hosting this "Heidelberg Disputation" and giving birth to Philip Melanchthon are the two bragging points of the Palatinate's otherwise humble place in early Protestant history. The Heidelberg Disputation was a defining moment in the evolution of Lutheran theology. In his *Heidelberg Theses*, Luther asserted a Christocentric "theology of the cross" which he contrasted with the "theology of glory" of the medieval schoolmen.[23] It must be conceded from the outset, however, that the Heidelberg Disputation had a modest immediate impact on the Palatinate itself. The Heidelberg Disputation was like a wave whose initial pass hardly disturbed the status quo, but whose long-term reverberations in the region shook the foundations of the established ecclesiastical powers. Rather than converting any ruling princes or theology professors, Luther's chief success was with the young clerics and students who attended the convocation. Chief among the converts were Martin Bucer, Johannes Brenz, and Martin Frecht, each of whom would do much to plant Protestantism in upper Germany and, especially in the case of Brenz and Bucer, have a significant lasting impact on the Palatinate.[24]

While Ludwig displayed no attraction to Luther's evangelical theology, he did play something of a pro-Protestant role at the Diet of Worms (1521), which had everything to do with political calculations and perhaps nothing at all to do with Luther's gospel message. Ludwig was closely allied with Frederick the Wise of Saxony at this point, so, in general, he was inclined to support Saxon diplomatic aims. Perhaps Ludwig's major contribution to the Protestant Reformation was serving as a voice against the setting aside of Luther's safe conduct pledge for travel to the diet—thereby preventing a situation similar to the betrayal of Jan Hus at the Council of Constance. It is even rumored that he got into a fistfight with Elector Joachim of Brandenburg over the issue. Likewise, after Luther's dramatic appearance before the imperial estates, Ludwig abstained from the vote at Worms that placed Luther under the imperial ban. He and Frederick the Wise left the diet before the promulgation of the Edict of Worms, which prohibited the spread of Protestant teaching in the empire. Moreover, the Palatinate did not

---

21. Schaab, *Geschichte der Kurpfalz*, 2:14.

22. Wolfgang Eger, "Kurfürst Ludwig V. der Friedfertige (von Wittelsbach) Pfalzgraf bei Rhein," in *Der Reichstag zu Worms von 1521: Reichspolitik und Luthersache*, ed. Fritz Reuter (Worms, 1971), 352-68; See especially p. 355. Müller, *Die Stellung der Kurpfalz*, 10-12.

23. For the text of the theses, see Martin Luther, *Luther's Works: American Edition*, ed. Helmut T. Lehman, vol. 31, ed. Harold J. Grimm (Philadelphia: Muhlenberg Press, 1957), 37-70.

24. Walter Henß, "Frühe Spuren der Reformation in der Kurpfalz," *Blätter für pfälzische Kirchengeschichte und religiöse Volkskunde* 50 (1983): 5-42.

vigorously enforce the Edict of Worms, and for a season Ludwig was even regarded as a protector of the Protestant faith in the contemporary pamphlet literature.[25]

There is ample evidence from the region surrounding the Palatinate that the Reformation was genuinely a popular movement that made deep inroads into every level of society: from prominent local knights such as Franz von Sickingen, to the townspeople in the neighboring upper German cities, to the "common" men and women who subsequently risked all in the tragic Peasants' War.[26] As a leading university town in the environs of so many prominent imperial cities that eagerly embraced the Reformation, it is hardly surprising that a vigorous reform-minded circle took root in Heidelberg in the 1520s.[27]

The university itself remained officially Catholic—especially in theology—although there is evidence that a majority of students had evangelical convictions. A number of prominent Protestants, including Frecht, Brenz, and Theobald Billicanus, served on the faculty, and the popularity of their lectures was an irritant to other faculty.[28] Additionally, enrollment at the university suffered with the rise to prominence of Protestant universities such as Wittenberg, Tübingen, and Marburg.

There are a number of indications that Protestant sermons could be heard throughout Palatine territory in this period; Wenzel Strauss, a prominent preacher at the Church of the Holy Spirit (*Heiliggeistkirche*), was such a zealous proponent of the Protestant message that he earned the nickname "the

---

25. Eger, "Kurfürst Ludwig V. der Friedfertige," 352-68; Müller, *Die Stellung der Kurpfalz*, 18-31. Ludwig was somewhat at odds with the curia at that moment due to some squabbles concerning his ecclesiastic brothers. Both he and Frederick the Wise of Saxony were eager to defend the privileges of the Reichsvikar vis-à-vis the emperor. While Ludwig's interests were opposed to those of Charles on the vicariate question, relations with the emperor remained quite cordial at this point.

26. The question of the degree to which the Reformation can be considered a popular movement has been frequently contested in historical scholarship. Regarding these groups in upper Germany, see Bernd Moeller, "Imperial Cities and the Reformation," in *Imperial Cities and the Reformation: Three Essays*, trans. H. C. Erik Midelfort and Mark U. Edwards (Philadelphia: Fortress, 1972), 41-115; Steven Ozment, *The Reformation in the Cities: The Appeal of Protestantism to Sixteenth-Century Germany and Switzerland* (New Haven: Yale University Press, 1975); and Peter Blickle, *The Revolution of 1525*, trans. Thomas A. Brady Jr. and H. C. Erik Midelfort (Baltimore: Johns Hopkins, 1981). The early adherence of the regional nobility to the Protestant faith, such as the Erbach and Landschad families, as well as the Kraichau knights to the south, is a vital part of the history of the Reformation in the Palatinate. Cf. Press, *Calvinismus und Territorialstaat*, 173-78, and idem, "Die Grafen von Erbach und die Anfänge des reformierten Bekenntnisses in Deutschland," in *Aus Geschichte und ihren Hilfswissenschaften*, ed. Hermann Bannasch and Hans-Peter Lachman (Marburg: N. G. Elwert Verlag, 1979), 653-85.

27. Henrik Alting, *Historia de ecclesiis palatinis* (Groningen, 1728), 23-27; Henß, "Frühe Spuren der Reformation in der Kurpfalz," 7-8. In addition to Bucer, Brenz, and Frecht, the following individuals were significant members of the fledgling movement: Theobald Billicanus, Franciscus Irenicus, Johann Isenmann, and Erhard Schepf.

28. Wolgast, *Die Universität Heidelberg*, 26; Press, *Calvinismus und Territorialstaat*, 174.

evangelical trumpet."[29] A Saxon envoy reported that the gospel was preached "loud and clear" in Heidelberg; however, the people did not want to be called Lutherans.[30] Ludwig's desire to maintain the favor with the Roman curia certainly played a role here. The elector had secured numerous benefices for his younger siblings from the church. This was an important part of the overall political-economic matrix of the Palatine Wittelsbachs, and he did not want to endanger it.[31] The early twenties can be characterized as a period of advancing reform "from below" paired with an ambivalent stance toward reform on the part of the Palatine authorities.

Involvement in suppressing the Knights' Revolt (1523) and especially the Peasants' War (1525) pushed Ludwig closer to an anti-Protestant position. Ludwig's forces played a critical role in besieging Franz von Sickingen's castle. Sickingen's close relationship to the Palatine house made his religiously justified rebellion harder to bear. Whereas the Knights' Revolt had not represented a major strategic challenge, the Peasants' War was an uprising on a vast scale that threatened to completely overturn the current social and political order. The program of the "Twelve Articles," a peasant manifesto from upper Swabia, with its wide-ranging assault on feudal lordship, struck a deep chord with the peasants who labored on the left bank of the Rhine. Ludwig proved an effective leader in the campaign to defeat the peasants, and even disbanded some of the rebels through mediation—on one occasion serving a feast to the peasants who had laid down their arms. Like many political leaders, however, Ludwig surmised that religious reform that overran imperial sanction was a dangerous phenomenon.[32] The Palatine leaders also felt threatened by Anabaptists who were apparently present in the Rhine territories in some quantity. Ludwig moved against them forcefully. While the 350 executions in the Palatinate cited in Anabaptist martyrologies is likely exaggerated, many brethren did pay the ultimate price for their faith under Ludwig's reign.[33]

The Pre-Reformation suffered setbacks in the mid-twenties. While important Protestant influences remained in the territory, some of the initial momentum of the movement was lost. Most of the leading lights of the early Protestant circle emigrated to more hospitable environs.[34]

---

29. Müller has a special appendix dedicated to Strauss entitled "Hofprediger des Kurfürsten Ludwig V., insbesondere daten zu Wenzel Strauß," *Die Stellung der Kurpfalz*, 126-29.

30. Henß, "Frühe Spuren der Reformation in der Kurpfalz," 21-22.

31. Müller, *Die Stellung der Kurpfalz*, 8-9; Eger, "Kurfürst Ludwig V. der Friedfertige," 353. By 1529, Ludwig had been able to place brothers on many episcopal sees, including Speyer and Worms.

32. Schaab, *Geschichte der Kurpfalz*, 2:17-18. Cf. also Gunther Franz, *Der deutsche Bauernkrieg*, 11th ed. (Darmstadt: Wissenschaftliche Buchgesellschaft, 1984).

33. Schaab, *Geschichte der Kurpfalz*, 2:24-25.

34. Billicanus, Bucer, and Brenz had all departed from Palatine territory by the end of 1522. Later prominent scholars such as Sebastian Münster and Simon Grynaeus did not remain long due to the woeful salaries. Frecht remained in Heidelberg until 1531. See Wolgast, *Die Universität Heidelberg*, 25-26.

On the political front, a chief influence was Ludwig's experience in the Peasants' War. In his mind, the evangelical movement had clearly helped trigger this unrest, and he was determined to avoid a repeat of these disturbances. However, he had become sympathetic to the peasants' grievances with the old regime. In the coming decades when the Palatine princes sought to address the "abuses" of the old church, rather than the core theological concerns of the Reformers, Ludwig was informed by the issues outlined in the peasants' program.[35] After the war, Ludwig is best characterized as neither actively supporting, nor actively suppressing the evangelical movement. Rather, Ludwig sought to forge a confessionally neutral diplomacy that mediated between the increasingly divided confessional groups. In the immediate aftermath of the Peasant's War, some Protestant-minded pastors were released from their posts.[36] However, Ludwig's regime never actively suppressed the evangelical movement in general. In fact in some ways the Palatine regime was even supportive of Protestantism in this era.

An overview of the career of Heinrich Stoll is illustrative of the often-paradoxical Palatine religious policy. Of all the theologians who labored in Heidelberg during the first generation of the Reformation, Heinrich Stoll was the person who worked the longest to plant the evangelical faith in the Palatinate. After the Peasants' War and the release of a few evangelical firebrands, Ludwig called Stoll to serve as a court preacher. This was a rather curious selection in that Stoll had recently been forced out of Worms for his evangelically oriented preaching. Clearly Stoll's measured vision of reform enjoyed support at court. Stoll also joined the university faculty and was elected rector on three separate occasions. He represented the Palatinate at major religious colloquies and even attended, along with a Catholic colleague from the university, the Council of Trent in 1551. While Stoll no doubt displayed a willingness to compromise and negotiate, he was a committed Protestant who rejected the Interim.[37] The fact that such a vigorous champion of Protestantism could be tolerated through the reigns of the brothers Ludwig and Frederick and into the reign of Ottheinrich

---

35. Albrecht Pius Luttenberger, *Glaubenseinheit und Reichsfriede: Konzeptionen und Wege konfessionsneutraler Reichspolitik 1530-1552 (Kurpfalz, Jülich, Kurbrandenburg)*, Schriftenreihe der Historischen Kommission bei der Bayerischen Akademie der Wissenschaften, 20 (Göttingen: Vandenhoek & Ruprecht, 1982), 130.

36. Henß, "Frühe Spuren der Reformation in der Kurpfalz," 27. These included Wenzel Strauss and the court preacher Johann Geyling. Unfortunately the lack of source materials due to the depredations of the seventeenth century make it hard to flesh out the early history of the Reformation in the Palatinate at the parish level.

37. Gustav Adolf Benrath, "Heinrich Stoll (Stolo) aus Diebach (1489 bis 1557), Pfarrer und Professor in Heidelberg," *Monatshefte für Evangelische Kirchengeschichte des Rheinlandes* 16 (1967): 273-85; Henß, "Frühe Spuren der Reformation in der Kurpfalz," 7; Hans Rott, *Friedrich II. von der Pfalz und die Reformation* (Heidelberg: Carl Winter's Universitätsbuchhandlung, 1904), 92. Because Stoll did not leave printed works behind, his precise theological position is difficult to ascertain. Regarding the Interim, see the discussion below.

speaks volumes for the ambiguity of the Palatine religious posi' relative freedom afforded Protestants. Even in 1535, the Papal nun Vergerio labeled Heidelberg one of the most Lutheran towns in Germany.

The other anomaly of Ludwig's reign is that he tolerated a limited official introduction of the Protestant faith in the Upper Palatinate. This concession came in 1538 when the Upper Palatine estates appealed to the elector to allow the celebration of the Lord's Supper according to Lutheran usages.[39] The north German variety of Protestantism had penetrated the Upper Palatinate both from Saxony and the neighboring imperial city of Nuremberg. Count Palatine Frederick, who early on revealed some inclination to the Protestant camp, had served as governor here from 1518.[40] Frederick helped secure the concession from Ludwig without manifestly going over to the Lutheran side himself. The fact that Ludwig sanctioned these innovations created a situation in which the Upper Palatinate practically became a "bi-confessional land" by the end of his reign.[41]

In short, the only constant in Ludwig's religious policy was its lack of constancy. Ludwig portrayed himself both as a loyal son of the old church and as a fair mediator between the confessional camps, while simultaneously tolerating the wild growth of Protestantism in his lands. Protestantism had not yet won the day, but the Catholic position was weakening—perhaps beyond repair.[42]

Official Reformation and Schmalkaldic War

Perhaps the most˙enigmatic and romantic figure of the Heidelberg Reformation is Ludwig's brother and sometime coregent Frederick II (r. 1544-1556). Years spent at the Habsburg-Burgundian court in Brussels exercised a profound influence on the young Frederick. Here Frederick forged a lifelong bond with the Habsburgs—one that in the end would lead to profound disappointment for both houses. Frederick cut a handsome and athletic figure at court and was a

---

38. Cited in Wolgast, *Reformierte Konfession und Politik*, 18.

39. For the Reformation of Upper Palatinate, see Johann Baptist Götz, *Die religiöse Bewegung in der Oberpfalz von 1520 bis 1560* (Freiburg im Breisgau: Herder, 1914); and Volker Press, "Die Grundlagen der kurpfälzischen Herrschaft in der Oberpfalz 1499-1621," in *Verhandlungen des Historischen Vereins für Oberpfalz und Regensburg* (Regensburg: Verlag des Historischen Vereins, 1977), 31-67. The Upper Palatinate differed greatly socially, politically, and economically from the Lower Palatinate. The mining industry was a cornerstone of the local economy and a key source of princely revenues. In contrast to the Lower Palatinate, it had fairly compact borders and also possessed the tradition of holding a representative assembly of the regional estates. The request for evangelical services was first granted by word of mouth and then officially confirmed in 1539. The economic clout of the estates regarding taxation facilitated winning this concession.

40. In taking up residence in the Upper Palatinate, Frederick satisfied the request of the Upper Palatine estates to have a member of the Palatine household reigning in their midst. Frederick II shifted the administration from Neumarkt, the established seat of the extinguished house of Pfalz-Neumarkt, to Amberg, the largest town in the Upper Palatinate in 1544. Press, *Calvinismus und Territorialstaat*, 181; Press, "Die Grundlagen der kurpfälzischen Herrschaft in der Oberpfalz 1499-1621," 43.

41. Wolgast, *Reformierte Konfession und Politik*, 19.

42. See Schaab, *Geschichte der Kurpfalz*, 2:23.

25

master of the tournament. He drew especially close to Philip the Handsome, son and heir of Emperor Maximilian I. Philip's premature death robbed Frederick of an influential patron. Nevertheless, Frederick did enjoy some favor at court and was especially honored as a foreigner to be elected as a member of the exclusive Order of the Golden Fleece.

While Frederick was perhaps the superior of his Habsburg playmates at the joust, merely having a contestable claim to be coruler of a smallish German principality made him very much their political inferior.[43] The degree to which Frederick's chivalrous dash did not match the power politics of the Habsburgs was brought home when Frederick made a rash effort to woo Philip's daughter, Eleonore of Habsburg, future queen-consort of Portugal and France. Eleonore's brother Charles, the future emperor, uncovered Frederick's intentions toward his sister and took action to quash the politically barren union. Frederick's missives to Eleonore were confiscated by the Habsburg authorities, and he was banished from court.[44]

Frederick did work his way back into Charles's favor, though the emperor considered him something of a lightweight in the political arena. Nevertheless his courtly bearing, skill at arms, and utility as an imperial representative brought him some recognition. He took the field as a prominent officer more than once and was also entrusted with critical diplomatic tasks in the service of Charles V.[45] Frederick's high place in imperial service served the Palatine interests in two ways: It helped maintain goodwill between the Palatine Wittelsbachs and the Habsburgs, and it served to keep Frederick occupied and thus left the administration of the Palatinate largely in the hands of Ludwig. Frederick's and Ludwig's affairs became less entangled when Frederick took up the post of governor of the Upper Palatinate in 1518.[46]

43. Both the agreement that Ludwig and Frederick should jointly rule the Palatinate and especially the understanding that Frederick should stand next in the line of succession to Ludwig (in preference to the young princes Ottheinrich and Philip who were the progeny of Frederick's older deceased brother Ruprecht) were counter to the stipulations of the Golden Bull. There was, however, great precedent for doing so, and this particular arrangement was not challenged by the imperial authorities.

44. Karl Brandi, *The Emperor Charles V*, trans. C. V. Wedgewood (New York, A. A. Knopf, 1939), 77-79.

45. Frederick's military exploits included participation in Emperor Maximilian's campaign against Venice in 1508, leading a major contingent in the relief of Vienna in 1529, and later taking the field as a general against the Turks in Hungary in 1532. His diplomatic-administrative commissions are too numerous to list. In 1521, he was regent of the imperial governing council (*Reichsregiment*) in Nuremberg in Charles V's absence. For his numerous services, he was long denied a Habsburg bride or suitable compensation. Important posts such as viceroy of Naples and even election to the post of "King of the Romans" had been waved before him in the past. Ultimately Charles supplied him with a fat annual subsidy. *Allgemeine Deutsche Biographie* (Leipzig, 1875-1912), 7:603-5; Müller, *Die Stellung der Kurpfalz*, 15. See Schaab, *Geschichte der Kurpfalz*, 2:21.

46. Press, *Calvinismus und Territorialstaat*, 170.

While Frederick was not preoccupied with military or diplomatic duties, he continued to angle for a prominent marriage. He finally achieved his goal of securing a Habsburg bride when at age 53 he married the fifteen-year-old Princess Dorothea of Denmark in 1535. This marriage with the niece of Charles V brought Frederick both a closer bond to the Habsburg house and a rather impracticable claim to the Danish throne. Dorothea's father King Christian II had been deposed in 1534 and was replaced by Christian (III) of Holstein. Regaining the Danish throne for his wife and himself became the chief foreign policy aim of Frederick and would often impinge on other aspects of his diplomacy—especially on the religious front. These designs were rather hopeless from the outset, owing largely to Frederick's relatively humble fiscal position (and his expensive tastes), which earned him the mocking nickname "Freddy with the empty pockets."[47] While considerable energy, imagination, and political capital went into his royal aspirations, Frederick was not a Philip of Hesse or a Moritz of Saxony who might venture to alter the status quo by force. As the great imperial historian Karl Brandi curtly surmised, "Even to attain the crown of Denmark, he mounted no war-horse and set foot aboard no ship."[48]

Frederick's early exposure to Protestantism was extensive; he had even employed Martin Bucer as a chaplain in the early 1520s.[49] His official responsibilities in the Habsburg administration, however—not to mention his great passion for chivalrous pursuits of every sort—seem to have at least outwardly pushed him away from the Protestant movement. Nevertheless, he helped facilitate legalization of Protestant services as governor of the Upper Palatinate. In religious colloquies, he was seen as a fair mediator between the sides, and it is possible that his role as chair of the Colloquy of Regensburg (1541) had some impact on his reconsideration of religious questions in the early 1540s.

Whether out of personal conviction or pressure from the heir-apparent Ottheinrich, his advisors, and the populace, Frederick began to ebb toward the Protestant faith. The first signs of the long-awaited conversion came in 1545, when Frederick and Dorothea celebrated Easter by receiving communion in both kinds.[50] Later that year at Christmas, many prominent courtiers received communion in both kinds in Heidelberg. The year 1546 proved to be the year of Reformation for the Palatinate. A series of edicts and judgments legalized the reform. Frederick sought and received approbation of the religious changes at a special gathering of Palatine nobles in Heidelberg in April of 1546.[51] A Protestant

47. "Friedel mit der leeren Taschen." Press, *Calvinismus und Territorialstaat*, 181.

48. Brandi, *The Emperor Charles V*, 355.

49. Müller, *Die Stellung der Kurpfalz*, 21, 31.

50. News of this development spread quickly as we can see from Martin Luther's letter to Duke Albrecht of Prussia from May 2, 1545. *Luther's Works: American Edition*, ed. Helmut T. Lehman, *Letters* vol. 50, ed. Gottfried Krodel (Philadelphia: Fortress 1975), 252-55.

51. Rott, *Friedrich II*, passim; Adolf Hasenclever, *Die kurpfälsche Politik in den Zeiten des schmalkaldischen Krieges (Januar 1546 bis Januar 1547)* (Heidelberg: Carl Winter's Universitätsbuchhandlung, 1905), passim, especially pp. 29-46. See also works by Press, Schaab, and Sehling [Goeters].

church order was also prepared in 1546; a printed church order appeared in 1547.[52] For once the sovereign had nearly caught up with the popular clamor for Protestantism.

Frederick's disappointment with Charles's empty promises and perhaps some genuine sympathy for the evangelical movement also tempted Frederick to move toward an alliance with the Protestant Schmalkaldic League. He had been a loyal servant of the Habsburgs for decades, but Charles's willingness to ignore Frederick's and Dorothea's claim upon the Danish throne (by agreeing to recognize the legitimacy of the current Danish king), revealed how much a pawn Frederick had been in Charles's larger schemes. In fact, the marriage to Dorothea now seemed to Frederick only a ploy to further bind the Palatinate to the Habsburg cause.

Nevertheless, the diplomatic situation was quite complex, and useful allies for a fiscally and militarily challenged prince were not easy to come by. The Schmalkaldic League was the natural counterpole of attraction, but it had entered into an alliance with Denmark and thus was in no position to support Frederick's Danish aspirations. Likewise the Schmalkaldic League had even been in discussions with the Catholic Bavarians, who were jealously eyeing the Palatine electoral dignity during these years and wary of overweening Habsburg power. Finally, it seems that Philip of Hesse, the most influential prince in the Schmalkaldic League in south-central Germany, was reluctant to risk handing leadership of the league to Frederick.[53]

While the Palatinate did adhere to the Protestantism at this time, it did not join the Schmalkaldic League. The end result of this rather humble political movement forward on behalf of the Protestant cause came swiftly. The Schmalkaldic War broke out in 1546. Frederick sought to remain neutral in the conflict and maintained his personal loyalty to Charles; however, he released a small detachment to assist the duke of Württemberg in honor of a mutual-defense agreement.[54] After the Protestant forces were defeated in the spring of 1547, the folly of Frederick's political machinations was plainly evident. The emperor regarded him as an enemy for allowing his forces to enter the fray against him. Faced with the threat of Charles's transferring the Palatine electoral dignity to the Bavarians, Frederick rode to Schwäbisch Hall to throw himself upon the mercy of the emperor. This led to perhaps the most dramatic scene of his

52. See Sehling [Goeters], *Kirchenordnungen*, 14:20-22, 109-11; Press, *Calvinismus und Territorialstaat*, 191. Martin Bucer may have taken part in the composition of the 1546 church order, as he was in the city in March of that year. The printed version of the church order has been quite a mystery, as it did not have "Kurpfalz" or "Friedrich" on the title page but claimed to be the church order of Ottheinrich from Pfalz-Neuburg. In fact, this church order was largely a reprint of the earlier Pfalz-Neuburg legislation of 1543, but it was printed specifically for use in the Electoral Palatinate. This seems to have been part of Frederick's strategy to promote reform while simultaneously seeking to present himself to Charles V as remaining true to his old beliefs. The Protestant cause in the Schmalkaldic War was already unraveling as the church order was printed.

53. Rott, *Friedrich II*, 14-26; Hasenclever, *Die kurpfälische Politik*, 56-79.

54. Hasenclever, *Die kurpfälische Politik*, 80-96.

dramatic life. Charles berated the elderly elector for his disloyalty.[55] Despite Frederick's kneeling before the emperor three times, Charles still refused to extend his hand to Frederick. Nevertheless, Frederick was spared the worst; the electoral dignity was saved and the punishment for his disloyalty was rather mild.[56] Charles intended to use Frederick once again as a tool for Habsburg interests. Frederick agreed to submit to the emperor's religious policies and to support him at the upcoming diet in Augsburg. The religious settlement that Charles would impose would land a crushing blow on Protestantism in southern Germany.

The Interim (1548) and the Religious Peace of Augsburg (1555)

After Charles's defeat of the Protestant Schmalkaldic League, his forces occupied much of southern Germany, and he was in a position to attempt to dictate a religious settlement in the empire. The arrangement that he imposed on the imperial estates at the "iron-clad" Diet of Augsburg (1547-1548) is known as the Interim (or sometimes the Augsburg Interim) and was meant to be a provisional arrangement until a general council could reach an agreement on disputed issues. Until then, the Interim required the reintroduction of Catholic practices in all Protestant territories of the empire.[57] The major concessions to the Protestants were allowing the laity to receive communion in both kinds and allowing clerical marriage.

Frederick publicly embraced the Interim and allowed it to be proclaimed in his lands, but the Interim was not actively implemented in the Palatinate, and most Protestants retained their posts, though a few left voluntarily. Some university faculty zealously supported the Interim; however, a comedy that mocked the Interim won an enthusiastic audience among the citizens and students of Heidelberg.[58] Even though contemporaries and modern church

---

55. Rott, *Friedrich II*, 79-80; Hasenclever, *Die kurpfälische Politik*, 147-50. Here is a firsthand account of Charles's lecture to Frederick: "Cousin, I am very displeased that in recent years you should have shown enmity towards me, sending troops to support my enemies, you who are related to me through blood and were brought up in my household. In consideration, however, of this and in view of your regret and repentance, and hoping that from now on you will serve according to your duty and will behave in a very different way, I agree to pardon you and forgive what you have done against me. I expect that in future you will endeavor to make amends for the affection with which I restore you to my friendship." Manuel Fernández Alvarez, *Charles V: Elected Emperor and Hereditary Ruler*, trans. J. A. Lalaguna (London: Thames and Hudson, 1975), 140.

56. Karl Brandi, *The Emperor Charles V*, 558-60; Hasenclever, *Die kurpfälische Politik*, 148-49; Press, *Calvinismus und Territorialstaat*, 192. Contemporary witnesses to the encounter were disappointed by Frederick's less-than-heroic composure, but were shocked at Charles's refusal to give him his hand to kiss or show any outward sign of reconciliation. The punishment was the temporary loss of the Boxberg district, which was later recovered by Frederick III.

57. In the event, the Interim was hardly enforced in northern Germany. The Catholic estates bitterly opposed the Interim, and thus it was not binding upon them.

58. Rott, *Friedrich II*, 84-94, 124-25. Rott's researches in the district of Germersheim led him to conclude that it was unlikely that pastoral turnover was heavy as a result of the Interim. Many

historians have generally had a negative appraisal of Frederick's religious policy, his reign proved to be the decisive period in deciding whether the Palatinate would remain Catholic or move toward the Protestant fold. Ironically, it was during the Interim itself that the Palatine administration was arranged in such a fashion that ruled out a return to Catholicism.

The clear direction of Palatine affairs can be observed among the staffing of the highest court officials. During the Interim, Frederick relieved none of his Protestant advisors from their posts. At the same time, only one major voice for the Catholic cause, Wolfgang von Affenstein, remained in the government. As retirements brought further changes in the bureaucratic apparatus, the vacancies were all filled by Protestants, most of whom had studied at leading Protestant universities such as Wittenberg and Tübingen. Frederick also was able to redirect a great deal of income to support the university and other educational institutions at this time, thus laying the roots for the rapid return to prominance of the University of Heidelberg under the Protestant sovereigns Ottheinrich and Frederick III. Ironically Frederick's endowments, which included the closure of numerous monasteries, received papal approbation. With a staunchly Protestant heir in the wings and a fully Protestant administrative apparatus, the return to the Protestant fold appeared to be only a matter of time.[59]

Nevertheless, after the emperor's defeat in the "revolt of the princes" and the ensuing de facto legalization of Protestantism in the Treaty of Passau (1552), Frederick did not publicly return the Palatinate to the Protestant confession. This final act of caution has sealed the judgment of historians on Frederick that political considerations took priority over personal convictions in determining his religious policy. In his defense, he had felt the displeasure of his Habsburg overlord more than enough in his lifetime and had come close to losing the electoral dignity in the aftermath of the Schmalkaldic War. This curious period of Palatine church history was also marked by a vacuum in religious leadership.[60] There was no leading reformer present and no decisive figure in the prince's council. This left most of the decisions in the hand of the elderly prince Frederick who desired no more experiments.

In contrast to the role Charles had forced upon Frederick in the 1547-1548 Diet of Augsburg, the Palatinate diplomatic position at the important imperial Diet of Augsburg in 1555 favored the Protestant cause. This meeting produced the important "Religious Peace of Augsburg" which recognized both Lutheranism, in the form of the Augsburg Confession, and Catholicism as legal confessions in the Holy Roman Empire; Reformed Protestantism was excluded. All secular princes were granted the jus reformandi—the right to determine the religion of their territories. This principle is summed up in the Latin dictum cuius regio, eius religio ("whose region, his religion").

of the evangelical pastors who flourished under Friedrich II continued in place into the reign of Ottheinrich.

59. Press, *Calvinismus und Territorialstaat*, 194-96; Sehling [Goeters], *Kirchenordnungen*, 14:20-22.

60. Press, *Calvinismus und Territorialstaat*, 197.

The *jus reformandi* was not extended to the ecclesiastical territories; if a prince-bishop chose to convert to Protestantism, he would have to step down from his office. Ordinary citizens were also denied the right to determine their faith but were allowed to emigrate if their theological convictions differed with the sovereign's religious policy. The Palatinate was the most vocal supporter of extending the liberty of conscience to subjects. In the wake of the Peace of Augsburg, Frederick took the initial steps to prepare a revised Protestant church order, but he did not live long enough to see this program to fruition. Before he died, Frederick again received communion in both kinds, signaling a final inclination to the path of reform.[61]

Assessment of the Reigns of Ludwig V and Frederick II

While the religious policies of Ludwig V and Frederick II have generally been seen as, at best, noncommittal and, at worst, mercenary, it is possible to give a more positive appraisal of their religious-diplomatic aims.[62] They both pursued a middle path between increasingly antagonistic confessional camps, which included a drive to religious reform but not at the cost of the peace. In a sense, the brothers represented a stance that would later be labeled *politique* during the period of the French Wars of Religion in that they were not willing to sacrifice domestic harmony in limitless pursuit of confessional purity. As Albrecht Luttenberger has surmised, "The religious consensus was functionally constitutive for the maintenance of the peace and order; the internal definition of its contents was basically of secondary consequence."[63] Already in the mid-twenties the Palatine brothers had been willing to make key concessions to the evangelical party such as clerical marriage and communion in both kinds to secure a compromise. Like many others, they continually stressed the need to call a general council to settle the religious strife in the empire. In all this, they apparently lacked the notion of religious truth as having an eternal veracity that compelled their personal assent but rather saw theological truth as a hierarchically determined phenomenon in which one had to accede to the legal norm. In short, there was no "here I stand" in either Ludwig or Frederick.

However, Frederick in particular, in his sensitive appreciation for the stakes involved, perhaps laid some claim to his infrequently employed byname "the Wise." Already in 1525, he feared that without a peaceful generally accepted religious solution "that each individual would want to be considered and called the best and most Christian and suspect the other as being unchristian. From this will awaken discord, strife, and enmity among all classes, and in the end to an

61. Rott, *Friedrich II*, 119-22; Sehling [Goeters], *Kirchenordnungen*, 14:21-22; Press, *Calvinismus und Territorialstaat*, 200-203.
62. Luttenberger, *Glaubenseinheit und Reichsfriede*, 129-39. According to Luttenberger's exhaustive analysis, the Palatine policy was more pragmatic as opposed to drawing on a deeper philosophical-ethical basis. He also sees a marked continuity in approach from the 1520s through the 1550s in Palatine policy.
63. Luttenberger, *Glaubenseinheit und Reichsfriede*, 136.

unheard of shedding of blood and wasting of the land and people, also the destruction of all mercy and good morals."[64] The Palatinate would reap this harvest with particular fury in the Thirty Years' War.

New Directions in German Protestantism

The period from 1548-1555 proved to be a watershed in the history of the Reformation in upper Germany (i.e., southern Germany). Whereas Frederick had not actively enforced the Interim in the Palatinate, military occupation in some of the free imperial cities brought a drastic change in the cities' religious policies. Before the Interim most of these cities had inclined toward a vision of reform commonly referred to as "Upper-German Protestantism" by continental historians.[65] With this expression, historians mean to connote the vision of reform that flourished in southern Germany and was heavily influenced by Huldrych Zwingli's reform of Zurich. Simply put, this was Protestantism with a strong Reformed orientation. The defining marks of the movement according to Bernd Moeller were "the austerity of their divine service, the opposition to images, but above all the opposition of their pastors to the Lutheran doctrine of communion."[66] This vision of reform flourished in numerous prosperous Southern cities, and the most visible theologian of this movement was Martin Bucer in Strasbourg.

The imposition of the Interim shook this movement to its foundations and altered the future climate of German Protestantism well beyond the end of the Interim in 1552. These cities were forced to return to Catholic usages (with the exception of allowing communion in both kinds and clerical marriage), to accept Catholic congregations in their midst, and even to have their constitutions rewritten in such a way as both to disempower the guildsmen who had endorsed the earlier more radical vision of reform and to establish more conservative-minded patrician regimes.[67] When Protestantism was fully legalized again in 1555, the cities had no choice but to adhere to the Augsburg Confession without reservation. The result of these developments was the replacement of the original upper German Protestantism, with its Reformed orientation, with Lutheranism following the north German model.[68] Thus, when we come to the publication of the Heidelberg Catechism in 1563, it will not be as if the Palatine confession had

---

64. Quoted in Luttenberger, *Glaubenseinheit und Reichsfriede*, 133.

65. The *locus classicus* of this description is Moeller, "The Imperial Cities and the Reformation," 90-103.

66. Ibid., 92.

67. Ibid., 103-15.

68. This is especially the case in Strasbourg where Johann Marbach was largely successful in bringing the city into line with the North German form of Lutheranism. According to Moeller, Strasbourg "even tried to disavow its 'Reformed' past." "The Imperial Cities and the Reformation," 111. See Thomas A. Brady Jr., *Protestant Politics: Jacob Sturm (1489-1553) and the German Reformation* (Atlantic Highlands, N.J.: Humanities Press, 1994).

moved away from the common regional understanding of Protestantism. Rather, the regional flavor of Protestantism had altered considerably since the imposition of the Interim.

However, if upper German Protestantism with its traditional Reformed orientation was in retreat at midcentury, north German Lutheranism was also entering a crisis period. The Interim also served as a catalyst in larger territorial states of the north, as there was a tremendous controversy within the Lutheran community regarding whether it was in any way licit to accept either the Augsburg Interim, or the milder, so-called Leipzig Interim that was formulated in Saxony. Melanchthon argued that some Catholic ceremonies, which had been discarded in Protestant services, were mere "adiaphora," or things indifferent, and that one could accept some of them without jeopardizing the core of the evangelical faith. Other Lutherans, such as Matthaeus Flacius Illyricus, rejected this notion and alleged that Melanchthon and his followers were corrupting the purity of the gospel message as it had been discovered by Luther. The Lutherans who wanted to remain absolutely faithful to Luther's own teaching without deviation—especially on the Eucharist—were known as Gnesio-Lutherans. The Lutherans who followed Melanchthon and who were willing to modify some of Luther's formulations were known as Philippists or Melanchthonians.[69] Particularly disturbing to the Gnesio-Lutherans was the suspicion that Melanchthon and his followers, especially in their desire to reach theological accommodation, were nearing the Eucharistic theology of the Reformed. For this reason, the Philippists were often accused of being "Crypto-Calvinists" or "Sacramentarians."

While Melanchthon became the object of much scorn in many corners in the 1550s, he was considered an unparalleled theological authority in the Palatinate; Palatine electors going all the way back to nominally Catholic Ludwig had sought out his advice. Given these facts, it is not surprising that the Philippist faction would be well represented among the pastors, academics, and bureaucrats that the electors had attracted to Heidelberg.

Ottheinrich: "Lutheran" Reformation of the Palatinate (1556-1559)

With Elector Ottheinrich (Otto Henry), we encounter a man who was quite different from both of his uncles. Whereas Ludwig had been hesitant and relatively frugal, Ottheinrich was a spendthrift who threw caution to the wind. Whereas Frederick could apparently bend his religious beliefs to match the political circumstances, Ottheinrich was a committed Protestant who placed himself in an extremely disadvantageous situation. The Palatinate would make its definitive entry into the Protestant communion under Ottheinrich's leadership.

Before turning to Ottheinrich's reform of the Palatinate, it will be useful to briefly outline his personal characteristics and his early career. In intellectual curiosity, physical stature, and *joi de vivre*, Ottheinrich calls to mind the more

---

69. See Karin Maag, ed., *Melanchthon in Europe: His Work and Influence Beyond Wittenberg*, Texts and Studies in Reformation and Post Reformation Thought (Grand Rapids: Baker, 1999).

famous contemporary Henry who ruled England. Ottheinrich may have lacked Henry VIII's power and brutality, but he did not lack his style. Ottheinrich was the son of the unfortunate Ruprecht and Elizabeth who had sought to lay claim to the patrimony of Georg the Rich of Lower Bavaria. He and his brother Philip "the Contentious" jointly ruled their small principality from 1522.[70] In his early years, he developed his wide-ranging tastes for books, art works, occult sciences and especially building.[71] According to Heinrich Bornkamm, Ottheinrich was "the most educated among the German princes of his time."[72] Ottheinrich also possessed a quality that historians find hard to define, much less quantify: He was likeable. Ottheinrich moved toward the Lutheran faith in the late 1530s to early 1540s and introduced Protestantism to Pfalz-Neuburg in 1542.

Ottheinrich's otherwise innovative reign in Pfalz-Neuburg came to an abrupt halt in 1544 when he was forced to leave his dominions because of the crushing weight of his debts. He was given a fairly generous offer; the estates of Pfalz-Neuburg agreed to assume his debts and grant him a large annuity with the proviso that he leave the administration of the territory to them. Pfalz-Neuburg continued Ottheinrich's Protestant orientation in his absence and bore the wrath of Charles V in the Schmalkaldic War for their Lutheran activism. Imperial forces occupied the territory, and Ottheinrich's Renaissance castle was plundered in 1546.[73] The territory continued under imperial administration for the coming years. Unlike Frederick II, Ottheinrich refused a humiliating reconciliation with Charles and remained in exile in Heidelberg and Weinheim. His presence in the Rhine Palatinate was a boon to the pro-Reform party and an increasing annoyance to his temporizing uncle Frederick II. He returned to Pfalz-Neuburg as a ruler after the Treaty of Passau (1552).

Most indications suggest that the Palatine populace welcomed the long-anticipated change in administration and religious policy represented by Ottheinrich upon his accession to the Electoral Palatinate in early 1556. Ottheinrich had finally achieved the post that he had waited most of his life for and wasted little time in making decisive changes. He reintroduced the Lutheran

70. From 1505 to their majority in 1522, Count Palatine Frederick served as the young princes' regent. Ottheinrich and Philip jointly ruled from 1522 while dividing their patrimony in 1535. In 1541, Philip turned over his territories to Ottheinrich. Philip died of stomach cancer in 1548. Schaab, *Geschichte der Kurpfalz*, 2:29-30.

71. The commemorative issue of Ruperto Carola has a number of pieces that illustrate these broad interests. Georg Poensgen, ed., *Ottheinrich: Gedenkschrift zur vierhundertjährigen Wiederkehr seiner Kurfürstenzeit in der Pfalz (1556-1559)*. Ruperto Carola Sonderband (Heidelberg, 1956). See also, Barbara Kurze, *Kurfürst Ott Heinrich: Politik und Religion in der Pfalz, 1556-1559* (Gütersloh, C. Bertelsmann, 1956); and Joachim Telle, "Kurfürst Ottheinrich, Hans Kilian und Paracelsus: Zum pfälzischen Paracelsismus im 16. Jahrhundert," in *Von Paracelsus zu Goethe und Wilhelm von Humboldt*, Salzburger Beiträge zur Paracelsusforschung, 22 (Vienna: Verband der wissenschaftlichen Gesellschaften Österreichs, 1981), 130-46.

72. Heinrich Bornkamm, "Kurfürst Ottheinrich von der Pfalz," in *Das Jahrhundert der Reformation: Gestalten und Kräfte* (Göttingen: Vandenhoek & Ruprecht, 1961), 261.

73. Hasenclever, *Die kurpfälsche Politik*, 104-19. The citizens of Pfalz-Neuburg received a foretaste of the "Spanish fury" under the same Duke of Alva who would lead Spanish forces in the attempt to suppress the Dutch Revolt.

confession with a series of enactments in 1556.[74] The church order of 1556 marked the Palatinate as a Lutheran territory, with a distinct south German stamp because its primary source of inspiration had been the Württemberg church order of 1553 composed by Johannes Brenz. However, the work of Ottheinrich's favorite reformer, Melanchthon, also had an impact on the settlement. There were a few touches that suggested an attempt to bow to Reformed concerns. Not surprisingly, the Palatine church order accepted the Augsburg Confession as its confessional norm. Johannes Brenz's *Landescatechismus* from Württemberg was used for educational purposes.[75]

Ottheinrich did not limit his reforming efforts to the mere legislation of Protestantism; his regime eagerly sought to ensure that the Protestant faith took root at the parish level. He also sought to gain a reformer of note, again calling the favorite Palatine son Melanchthon, but when that failed he then tried to win the services of Melanchthon's chief critic Matthaeus Flacius Illyricus. Ottheinrich authorized a wide-ranging church visitation in 1556. Johann Marbach, now the driving force in the Strasbourg church, served as the leader of this effort. The chaos that the church visitors found in the parishes left them horrified: the ideas of the Anabaptists and Caspar von Schwenkfeld had taken root, few properly trained ministers were available, and many parishioners clung to the traditions of their folk piety. When the visitors concluded their work, Marbach drew up a list of recommendations for reforming the Palatine church.[76] Another characteristic of Ottheinrich's Reformation that mirrored the upper German tradition was state-mandated iconoclasm. In the three short years of his reign, Ottheinrich's officials largely cleared the Palatinate of the material artifacts of late-medieval piety.[77]

74. All of the enactments are printed in Sehling [Goeters], *Kirchenordnungen*, 14:111-264.

75. Sehling [Goeters], *Kirchenordnungen*, 14:13-220; Wolgast, *Reformierte Konfession und Politik*, 25-26. The antecedents of the church order are laid out in the excellent introductions written by J. F. G. Goeters. It has been frequently maintained that the Neuburg church order of 1554 was the chief inspiration for the 1556 Palatine church order. This apparent similarity, however, depends on their joint dependence on the Württemberg order. The Pfalz-Neuburg order also included portions from Melanchthon's *Examen Ordinandorum*; however, the Palatine order of 1556 takes these portions directly from the more recent Mecklenburg *Kirchenordnung* of 1554. Goeters suggests that Ottheinrich's Neuburg councilors Johann Ehinger, Georg Frölich, and perhaps Michael Diller may have been responsible for mildly pro-Reformed touches. Some of the preparatory work for the new church order had taken place during the last months of Frederick II's reign.

76. Walther Koch, "Johann Marbach in seiner Bedeutung für die Pfälzische Kirchengeschichte," *Blätter für pfälzische kirche und religiöse Volkskunde* 22 (1962): 119-20. Marbach's various recommendations are printed in C. Schmidt, *Der Antheil der Strassburger an der Reformation in Churpfalz. Drei Schriften Johann Marbach's mit einer geschichtlichen Einleitung* (Strasbourg, 1856); and Georg Biundo, "Bericht und Bedenken über die erste kurpfälzische Kirchenvisitation im Jahre 1556," *Jahrbuch der Hessischen kirchengeschichtlichen Vereinigung* 10 (1959): 1-40. Like Flacius and Melanchthon, Marbach and Brenz refused Ottheinrich's invitation to lead the Palatine church.

77. Hans Rott, "Kirchen- und Bildersturm bei der Einführung der Reformation in der Pfalz," *Neues Archiv für die Geschichte der Stadt Heidelberg* 6 (1905): 229-54. The order to bring Catholic services to an end (which includes instructions regarding the abolition of images, vestments, etc.) is printed in Sehling [Goeters], *Kirchenordnungen*, 14:111-13.

In addition to definitively establishing the Protestant confession at home, Ottheinrich also became the most aggressive champion of Protestant rights in the empire. Ottheinrich advocated an aggressive agenda at the Diet of Regensburg (1556) that focused on the removal of the "ecclesiastical reservation," which denied the *jus reformandi* of the Peace of Augsburg to ecclesiastical territories. With its close association with the neighboring bishoprics of Mainz, Speyer, and Worms, it was very much in the Palatinate's strategic interest to open the road to reform in ecclesiastical territories. Beyond this, the Palatine representatives also advocated freedom for *all citizens*—not merely the princes—to adhere to either the Lutheran or the Catholic confession. Ottheinrich attempted to force the emperor to accede to the Protestant estates' demands by making payment of aid for defense against the Ottoman Turks (*Türkenhilfe*) dependent on a liberalization of the imperial religious policy. Naturally the Catholic estates were not enthusiastic about this plan; likewise, the north German Lutheran princes were wary of a move that would threaten the status quo, which they found generally tolerable. In the end, this ambitious effort met no success.[78]

Ottheinrich's most enduring contribution proved to be his reformation of the University of Heidelberg (1558). Here Ottheinrich leaned on the expertise of his most trusted theological and academic authority, Philip Melanchthon. Ottheinrich instituted a wide-ranging overhaul of the university's curriculum, with particular impact on the arts faculty. The reformation was further empowered by directing new revenue streams to the university and by recruiting a more prestigious faculty. Perhaps the greatest success was in medicine, wherein Ottheinrich secured the widely learned scholars Jacob Curio, Petrus Lotichius— who is actually more famous as a poet than as a physician—and Thomas Erastus, who both helped usher in the Palatine Reformation and won lasting fame for his views on church discipline. Impressive new recruitments also came to the law, with Christoph Ehem and François Baudouin, and to the arts. Ironically, theology languished somewhat behind the pack because several major players, including Melanchthon himself, refused offers to come to Heidelberg. Melanchthon's student Tilemann Heshusius did eventually join the faculty along with Pierre Boquin. As general superintendent of the Palatine church, Heshusius was by far the most influential person in church affairs.[79]

By bringing into his university a wide range of Protestant views from Zwinglianism (Erastus) to incipient Gnesio-Lutheranism (Heshusius), Ottheinrich either appreciated ability over strict confessional orthodoxy, or he was not a fine connoisseur of theological subtlety. Future conflicts were nearly inevitable; Gustav Adolf Benrath joked of Ottheinrich's faculty that they were a

---

78. These developments are succinctly covered in Horst Rabe, *Reich und Glaubensspaltung: Deutschland 1500-1600*, Neue Deutsche Geschichte, vol. 4 (Munich: C. H. Beck, 1989), 342-45.

79. Bornkamm, "Kurfürst Ottheinrich von der Pfalz," 259-60; and Wolgast, *Die Universität Heidelberg*, 34-40.

"*corps d'espirit*, however they had no espirit de corps."[80] In fact a major controversy over the Lord's Supper had already begun in 1559 that would not be pacified until the accession of Ottheinrich's successor Frederick III.

The Heidelberg Lord's Supper Controversy (1559-1560)

With the death of Ottheinrich, the old electoral Palatine Wittelsbach line died out and Elector Frederick III, the Pious (r. 1559-1576) of Pfalz-Simmern (Wittelsbach), ascended to the throne. [81] The house of Pfalz-Simmern was one of the cadet branches of the Wittelsbach family that had been created in King Ruprecht's partitions in the early fifteenth century. Frederick III had converted to Protestantism through the influence of his wife Maria of Brandenburg-Kulmbach and had demonstrated this conviction through his resistance to the Interim in 1548. Conversion to Protestantism had led to his alienation from his father who refused to extend him the resources to maintain his princely estate. When the childless Ottheinrich began his reign, Frederick stood in line to inherit the Palatinate and took up the normal post of heir-apparent as governor of the Upper Palatinate. As governor, he gladly assisted the implementation of Ottheinrich's Reformation. Upon the death of his father, Johann II of Pfalz-Simmern, in 1557, Frederick introduced the new Palatine church order into the small territory of Pfalz-Simmern.[82] Elector Frederick is generally thought to have possessed Melanchthonian Lutheran theological convictions—not unlike Ottheinrich but rather better informed—on his accession.[83]

80. Gustav Adolf Benrath, "Die Eigenart der pfälzischen Reformation und die Vorgeschichte des Heidelberger Katechismus," in *Heidelberger Jahrbücher* 7 (1963): 16.

81. For Frederick's biography, see August Kluckhohn, *Friedrich der Fromme, Kurfürst von der Pfalz, der Schützer der reformirten Kirche. 1559-1576* (Nördlingen, 1879); idem, "Wie ist Kurfürst Friedrich III. von der Pfalz Calvinist geworden?" *Münchener Historisches Jahrbuch für 1866* (1866): 421-521; Walter Hollweg, "Friedrich III., der Fromme, Kurfürst von der Pfalz: Der Mensch. Der Christ. Eine kritische Untersuchung," in *Neue Untersuchungen zur Geschichte und Lehre des Heidelberger Katechismus* (Neukirchen-Vluyn: Neukirchener Verlag, 1961), 9-85; Owen Chadwick, "The Making of a Reforming Prince: Frederick III, Elector Palatine," in *Reformation, Conformity and Dissent*, ed. R. Buick Knox (London: Epworth, 1977), 44-69. Chadwick's theory is that the rough treatment of Frederick III's brother-in-law, the pugnacious Albrecht Alcibiades (also the stepson of Ottheinrich), by the Lutheran princes led him to mistrust their intentions and began his alienation from the Lutheran fold.

82. Upon inheriting the Electoral Palatinate in 1559, Frederick transferred Pfalz-Simmern to his brother Georg. Ottheinrich's former duchy of Pfalz-Neuburg was given to a member of the house of Pfalz-Zweibrucken. Schaab, *Geschichte der Kurpfalz*, 2:35, 145-47.

83. Barton argues that Frederick was already a "latent Crypto-Calvinist" upon his accession, but most other scholars view him as a Philippist Lutheran at that point. However, Kluckhohn considered him more-or-less a Philippist Lutheran through the Naumburg Colloquy. Peter F. Barton, *Um Luthers Erbe: Studien und Texte zur Spätreformation Tilemann Heßhus (1527-1559)* (Witten: Luther Verlag, 1972), 197; Sehling [Goeters], *Kirchenordnungen*, 14:37; Benrath, "Die Eigenart der pfälzischen Reformation und die Vorgeschichte des Heidelberger Katechismus," in *Heidelberger Jahrbücher* 7 (1963): 20; Chadwick, "Making of a Reforming Prince," 56-61; Press, *Calvinismus und Territorialstaat*, 222-23, 226; Kluckhohn, "Wie ist Kurfürst Friedrich III," 45, passim.

Ottheinrich had assembled a rather volatile mix of personalities and convictions at the University of Heidelberg, and a rather ugly academic dispute erupted upon the eve of his death. The controversy concerned the promotion of the Friesian theology student Stephan Silvius. The church superintendent and theology professor Heshusius had originally determined the content of the theses, to which Silvius objected, as it slandered both Zwinglianism and Catholicism. After Silvius refused to defend the original theses, Heshusius blocked his promotion. Rather than being strictly a Lutheran-Reformed controversy, university faculty saw this as an issue of academic liberty. The Reformed theologian Boquin championed Silvius's cause and was supported by the university rector Erastus. The faculty senate, which probably possessed a Melanchthonian Lutheran majority at this point, agreed with Silvius's claim that he should have the right to choose his own theses. Not only did Heshusius lose the immediate decision, he was also barred from attending future university senate meetings due to his highhanded conduct. Thus, on the eve of Frederick III's ascension, the chief champion of the Gnesio-Lutheran standpoint had already alienated himself from the university.[84] Elector Ottheinrich died on February 12, 1559, in the midst of this controversy.

The controversy over the Lord's Supper was about to turn more acrimonious and attract more public attention when Frederick arrived in Heidelberg in February of 1559. The second round began when Wilhelm Klebitz, a deacon at the *Heiliggeistkirche*, defended distinctly Reformed theses on the Eucharist in seeking a university degree. The superintendent Heshusius had been out of town when the promotion occurred but lost no time in attacking Klebitz from the pulpit on his return. What ensued was something of a pulpit war, which greatly irritated the authorities. Frederick's councilors, and then the elector himself, attempted to mediate the conflict but to no avail. Heshusius sought both to fire and to excommunicate Klebitz, but the prince considered this action too severe. The elector directly intervened in the controversy after Heshusius excommunicated Klebitz a second time and ordered him reinstated to communion. Frederick forbade the ministers' use of the expressions regarding Christ's presence in the Eucharist "in the bread" and "under the bread" because he found the phrases divisive. Of course, these phrases were a standard means for Lutherans to capture both the mystery and the reality of Christ's presence in the Lord's Supper.

Heshusius understandably thought that the elector had gone too far and condemned the prince's decree. By taking such an intractable stand, Heshusius had made himself an absolute liability. While one may sympathize with Heshusius's strength of conviction, no sovereign prince who exercised the *jus*

84. Universitätsarchiv Heidelberg A-160/7, f. 324-36; Eduard Winkelmann, *Urkundenbuch der Universität Heidelberg*, 2 vols. (Heidelberg: Carl Winter's Universitätsbuchhandlung, 1886), 119; Erastus to Abraham Musculus, Nov. 23, [15]77. Zofingen, Nr. 1.53; Ruth Wesel-Roth, *Thomas Erastus: Ein Beitrag zur Geschichte der reformierten Kirche und zur Lehre von der Staatssouveranität* (Lahr/Baden: Moritz Schauenberg, 1954), 18-21; Barton, *Um Luthers Erbe*, 200-201.

reformandi could tolerate such insolence from his church superintendent. Frederick attempted to achieve a just settlement by dismissing both of the agitators on September 16, 1559. The loss of Klebitz hardly crippled the Reformed party, but the dismissal of the leading Lutheran church authority had incalculable long-term impact.[85]

In the aftermath of the dismissals, Frederick sent an emissary to Melanchthon to seek his recommendations for mending the rift in the Palatine church. Melanchthon answered both with a personal letter to Frederick and with a public *Judgment,* that offered further commentary on the current theological climate.[86] In brief, Melanchthon approved of the action that Frederick had taken in releasing both Klebitz and Heshusius. Though Heshusius had been his own student, he rebuked him in the *Judgment* for his presumptuousness. Farther afield, he used the opportunity of the *Judgment* to attack his Gnesio-Lutheran opponents. He eschewed controversial novel formulae and doctrines intended to explain or preserve the notion of Christ's physical presence in the Eucharist. He suggested that all Christians should focus on the Pauline motif (1 Corinthians 10:16) that the bread is a *koinonia* (communion) with the body of Christ.[87]

Not surprisingly, Melanchthon's letter and *Judgment* were well received in Heidelberg. Certainly the elector was gratified to have his actions endorsed by such a prominent authority. What was perhaps surprising, however, was how the parties differed in their response to Melanchthon's *Judgment.* On the one hand, leading Reformed agitators such as Erastus, who embraced the *Judgment,* wanted to make sure it was printed as soon as possible. The Philippists, on the other hand, who were generally the strongest force in the university, did not want to see Melanchthon's *Judgment* misused. Because they no doubt recognized that the Reformed Protestants were eager to exploit Melanchthon's harsh attack on the

---

85. Barton, *Um Luthers Erbe,* 200-217; Chadwick, "Making of a Reforming Prince," 62; Press, *Calvinismus und Territorialstaat,* 227-28; Wesel-Roth, *Erastus,* 18-22; Gustav Adolf Benrath, "Die Korrespondenz zwischen Bullinger und Thomas Erastus," in *Heinrich Bullinger 1504-1575: Gesammelte Aufsatze zum 400. Todestag,* vol. 2, Zürcher Beiträge zur Reformationsgeschichte, vol. 8, ed. Ulrich Gäbler and Erland Herkenrath (Zürich: Theologischer Verlag, 1975), 90; Wim Janse, "Non-conformist Eucharistic Theology: The Case of the Alleged Zwinglian Polemicist Wilhelm Klebitz (c.1533-68)," *Nederlands archief voor kerkgeschiedenis—Dutch Review of Church History* 81 (2001): 5-25.

86. C. G. Bretschneider and H. E. Bindseil, eds., *Philippi Melanthonis opera quae supersunt omnia. Corpus Reformatorum* (Braunschweig: C. A. Schwetschke et filium, 1843-1860), 9:960-63. For a translation of Melanchthon's letter into English, see Lowell C. Green, *Melanchthon in English* (St. Louis: Center for Reformation Research, 1982), 23-28. Melanchthon to Frederick, November 1, 1559: "I therefore approve the plan of the Most Illustrious Elector because he commanded silence on the part of those quarreling on both sides in order that there not be a distraction in the young church and its neighbors." Translation, Green, *Melanchthon in English,* 25. *Opera Philippi Melanchthonis,* CR, 9:961.

87. *Opera Philippi Melanchthonis,* CR, 9:962-63: "Et in hac controversia optimum esset retinere verba Pauli: Panis quem frangimus, κοινωνια εστι του σοματος."

Gnesio-Lutherans, they used their clout at the university to refuse authorization to print Melanchthon's *Judgment*. The Reformed partisans nevertheless had no trouble finding prominent foreign printers to publish Melanchthon's letter.[88]

In retrospect, the arrival of Melanchthon's *Judgment* marked the zenith of Philippist Lutheranism in the Palatinate.[89] Melanchthon died less than six months after writing the letter. Had he lived a few years longer, the confessional history of the Palatinate would probably have evolved much differently. Given the apparent Philippist majority, with the right combination of advice and appointments, Melanchthon might have secured the ascendancy of the Philippist position in Heidelberg. In the vacuum left by Melanchthon's death, the Heidelbergers looked to Zürich and Geneva for advice. In the final analysis, Melanchthon's efforts served to facilitate the Palatinate's entry into the Reformed camp.

The Heidelberg Lord's Supper Disputation (1560)

A distinct Reformed tendency surfaced in the Palatine Reformation during the Heidelberg Disputation of June 1560—sometimes referred to as the "Heidelberg Lord's Supper Disputation" or the "Wedding Debates." While it is likely that a majority of pastors and citizens continued to favor a moderate form of Lutheranism, the Reformed were growing more influential both in the university and at court. The Palatine developments drew the notice of German Lutherans, and, after his expulsion, Heshusius became a vocal critic of confessional changes in the Palatinate. Fearing that her husband was falling under the influence of Zwinglian heretics, the elector's wife Maria expressed her concerns to her son-in-law Duke Johann Friedrich II of Saxe-Gotha.[90] The occasion of the wedding of Frederick's daughter Dorothea Susanne to Johann Wilhelm of Saxe-Weimar was used as an opportunity to stage an in-house disputation over the mode of Christ's presence in the Eucharist. The debate was between Duke Johann Friedrich's theologians and the Heidelberg theologians.

A most colorful report of this disputation from the Reformed side is found in a letter from Caspar Olevianus to John Calvin. According to Olevianus's assessment, the Saxons hoped to use this opportunity to place one of their own clerics in the church superintendent office recently vacated by Heshusius. Clearly, the duke desired to lead the lost Palatine sheep back into the fold, and

---

88. Melanchthon's *Judgment* was printed at least twelve times in 1560-1561 (eight Latin, four German editions; see *Verzeichnis der im deutschen Sprachbereich erschienenen Drucke des XVI. Jahrhunderts* [Stuttgart: Anton Hiersemann, 1983-], 13:418-20). For a discussion of the controversy regarding the publication of Melanchthon's letter in Heidelberg, see Sturm, *Der junge Zacharias Ursin*, 229-30; Wesel-Roth, *Erastus*, 29.

89. The following section on the Heidelberg Disputation of 1560 is an abbreviated version of a chapter of my dissertation, "Thomas Erastus in Heidelberg: A Renaissance Physician during the Second Reformation" (Ph.D. diss., University of Virigina, 1998), 79-85.

90. Son of Johann Fredrich, the nephew of Frederick the Wise, who was married to Frederick III's daughter Elizabeth. Wesel-Roth, *Erastus*, 22. Press, *Calvinismus und Territorialstaat*, 226.

even before the debate, the Saxon court preacher Johann Stoessel insinuated in a sermon that Frederick had been seduced by his councilors.[91] External pressure was mounting for Frederick to eliminate the heretical forces at work in the Palatinate, which ironically served as a catalyst for his definitive move to the Reformed camp.

The ground rules of the disputation stipulated a one-to-one debate between a Saxon theologian and a Palatine theologian. The Saxon court preacher Johannes Stoessel and Pierre Boquin were the chief debaters, though other theologians sat in on different days. Olevianus's account implies that the Lutherans placed no small hope of victory in the fact that Boquin was ill-suited for the task, and Olevianus even suggested that Frederick was tricked into agreeing to the terms of debate. Once the event was proposed, however, he could hardly back out. Both sides were to have a moderator who sat at the same table with the disputants as well as a scribe to record the debate. The event, which was held June 3-7, 1560, was open to the general public, and the princes were seated on a balcony above the disputants. Boquin began the disputation by defending theses that set forth the Reformed interpretation of the Lord's Supper. These theses were very similar to the ones Klebitz had defended in his bachelor's exam.[92] Boquin's presentation pleased the elector but failed to win the sympathy of the audience. According to Olevianus, Boquin lacked the debating skill to ward off Stoessel's heavy-handed tactics. More critically, most of the audience could not understand him because of his thick French accent. Consequently, the boisterous Stoessel easily bettered Boquin.

In the midst of the debate, however, Frederick proposed a change that was to fundamentally alter the psychological impact of the disputation. He summoned the medical professor Erastus, whose Reformed sympathies were well known, and ordered him to sit with Boquin in order to clarify his arguments. Olevianus suggests that Duke Johann Friedrich did not resist this suggestion, which must have sounded more like an innovation for the sake of linguistic clarity than a tactical move. The Saxons, however, quickly lamented their decision to allow Erastus to enter the debate. Erastus both expressed the Reformed case eloquently and deftly eluded Stoessel's rhetorical ploys. Olevianus relates: "When [Erastus] had attended Dr Boquin for about half an hour, and had summarized and elucidated some [of the Reformed] arguments, it was amazing how the empty

91. *Calvini Opera, Corpus Reformatorum*, vol. 18, col. 191. See Erdmann Sturm, *Der junge Zacharius Ursin: Sein Weg vom Philippismus zum Calvinismus (1534-1562)* (Neuenkirchen-Vluyn: Neukirchener Verlag, 1972), 223.

92. Sources for the disputation are printed in D. Seisen, *Geschichte der Reformation zu Heidelberg von ihren ersten Anfängen bis zur Abfassung des Heidelberger Catechismus* (Heidelberg, 1846), 99ff.; and Carl Büttinghausen, *Ergözlichkeiten aus der Pfälzischen und Schweizerichen Geschichte und Literatur* (Zürich bey Drell, 1766-1768), 31-36. Accounts of the disputation are included in Kluckhohn, "Wie ist Kurfürst Friedrich III," 40-44; idem, *Friedrich der Fromme*, 69-73 [which largely repeats Kluckhohn's earlier work verbatim]; Wesel-Roth, *Erastus*, 23-24; and Sturm, *Der junge Zacharias Ursin*, 222-29.

confidence of the adversary was lowered."[93] Stoessel quickly protested that according to the original conditions of debate he was only supposed to be facing Boquin. He refused to continue the debate if Erastus actively participated. Stoessel supposedly pledged that he would first debate Boquin and later have a second debate with Erastus. When it came time for Stoessel to debate Erastus individually, however, he declined saying that the duke did not desire a second debate. Moreover, he added the faint objection that he did not wish to debate with a physician but rather with a theologian.[94]

Even from Olevianus's rather one-sided account, one receives a clear impression that it was exactly the sort of debate in which either side could claim unequivocal victory. No doubt Stoessel had gotten the better of Boquin, but Erastus had embarrassed Stoessel. From the perspective of the Heidelberg Reformed, the debate proved to be an unparalleled success. Frederick was impressed by the simplicity of the Reformed arguments to such an extent that he continued to doubt Christ's physical presence in the sacrament. Whether or not they had actually won the debate, Boquin and Erastus had expressed the heart of the Reformed argument in a manner that the elector found persuasive. Erastus remarked that prior to the disputation "the prince still wavered" with regard to the Lord's Supper, but at the disputation "he learned more correctly. Thus little by little the Reformation had begun."[95] In the coming months, Frederick would find it increasingly difficult to reconcile his growing conviction in the veracity of the Reformed doctrine of the Lord's Supper with his desire to remain true to the faith of the Augsburg Confession.

The Naumburg Princes's Conference (1561)

The Augsburg Confession became a central issue in a conversation among a group of regional princes later that month. Duke Christoph of Württemberg, who was a pious Lutheran and had been especially supportive of Elector Ottheinrich and his reforming efforts, noted that only two of the princes who had signed the Augsburg Confession in 1530 were still alive. From this realization came the idea to gather together all the evangelical princes of Germany to reaffirm their common commitment to the faith of the Augsburg Confession. It was hoped that such a move would serve as a display of unity to the Catholic forces—who were simultaneously meeting at Trent—and might also serve to limit dissension within the Lutheran ranks. The proposed meeting was scheduled for Naumburg in January of 1561.[96]

---

93. *Calvini Opera, Corpus Reformatorum*, vol. 46, col. 193-93: "Is quum hora fere dimidia assedisset D. Bouquino, atque argumenta aliquot collegisset et explicasset, mirum quam deiiceretur adversarii inanis confidentia, adeo perspicue apte et graviter negotium velut in transcursu explicabat."

94. *Calvini Opera, Corpus Reformatorum*, vol. 46, col. 193.

95. Erastus to Abraham Musculus, Nov. 23, [15]77. Autograph, Zofingen, Nr. 1.53. "Princeps tunc nutans adhuc rem, discit rectius. Ita paulatim coepta est reformatio."

96. Robert Calinich, *Der Naumburger Fürstentag 1561* (Gotha, 1870); Kluckhohn, "Wie ist Kurfürst Friedrich III," 48-62; idem, *Friedrich der Fromme*, 79-106; Karl Schornbaum, "Zum Tag

When the princes prepared for their gathering at Naumburg they discovered that their first task was going to be to select *which* text of the Augsburg Confession to accept as authoritative. The basic problem was that, since Melanchthon had authored the original version of the text himself, he felt the liberty to enhance it to meet the changing theological landscape. This led to the existence of basically two Augsburg Confessions: the original of 1530, known as the *Invariata*, and the altered Confession of 1540, known as the *Variata*.[97] In brief, the *Variata* employed language in the article concerning the Lord's Supper that was more acceptable to individuals of Reformed convictions. While one might imagine that the earliest version (i.e., the *Invariata*) would be the natural choice for the princes, making such a determination was difficult, because the *Variata* had been the most widely used version after 1540 and in fact had legal status in the empire as the basis of the Peace of Augsburg (1555). The *Variata* had also been reprinted in official pronouncements and had been the basis for many religious dialogues throughout the empire. As Frederick seemed to occupy a theological position somewhere between Melanchthonianism and full-fledged Sacramentarianism, it is not surprising that he preferred the *Variata*. Frederick recoiled from the German text of the *Invariata* that read: "the true body and blood of Christ under the form of Bread and Wine are present in the Lord's Supper and are there distributed and received." He found this smacked too much of papal doctrine.[98] As anticipated, determining which version of the Augsburg Confession to authorize as the basis of their common faith was the first order of business of the prince's assembly.

At the gathering, the majority of Lutheran princes inclined toward accepting the *Invariata* as the basis of their discussion, but even this decision held an unexpected twist. Neither the original autograph, nor any official copies from the 1530 Diet were at hand. The best substitutes available were the early printed quarto and octavo editions of the Augsburg Confession in Latin, which had been published by Melanchthon in 1531. It was not manifestly clear, however, which printed version was the most authentic. While most princes could accept the quarto edition, Frederick had severe reservations about this version as well, because the version of *The Apology* that was published with it seemed to approach the doctrine of transubstantiation in its explanation of article 10. The princes

von Naumburg," *Archiv für Reformationsgeschichte* (1911): 181-214; Walter Henss, *Der Heidelberger Katechismus im konfessionspolitischen Kräftespiel seiner Frühzeit* (Zürich: Theolgischer Verlag, 1983), 46; Chadwick, "The Making of a Reforming Prince," 66-67. This discussion largely follows the analysis of Kluckhohn. The Frankfurt Recess of 18 March 1558 was a precursor to the Naumburg princes' conference. Here Ottheinrich and the other Lutheran princes agreed to a formula that accepted the real presence of Christ in the Lord's Supper and condemned the errors of the Catholics and the Zwinglians. This agreement was not successful in restoring unity between the Philippists and Gnesio-Lutherans.

97. This is a simplification of the textual history of the Augsburg Confession, whose complications will become more apparent in the subsequent section.

98. Kluckhohn, "Wie ist Kurfürst Friedrich III," 50-51; idem, *Friedrich der Fromme*, 85-88. The Latin version of the *Invariata* was less problematic for Frederick than the German text. Philip of Hesse shared Frederick's reservations about the original German text.

thus accepted the octavo edition (which was actually the second printed edition) as the basis of their discussions at Naumburg. Frederick still argued for the acceptance of the 1540 *Variata*. The best compromise he could arrange was that the princes recognized the *Invariata* as the official version of the Augsburg Confession, but that they accepted the *Variata* as a permissible interpretation of the Augsburg Confession. This concession was included in a preface to their agreement that was composed by Frederick and Elector August of Saxony. The preface caused some controversy at the conference, but Frederick was able to win the support of the majority of the princes for accepting it with an impassioned speech.

Frederick had done his cause a great service at the Naumburg princes' conference but had not won a decisive victory. At Naumburg, the future developments within German Protestantism were visible in an embryonic form. The hard-line Lutheran unwillingness to accept anything less than the full Eucharistic teaching of the unaltered Augsburg Confession would develop into the movement that led to the *Formula of Concord* (1577). We also see the opening for the future Palatine strategy of arguing that a Reformed understanding of the Lord's Supper was not in violation of the Augsburg Confession as seen through the lens of the *Variata*.[99] Frederick's success at Naumburg in 1561 opened the door for the HC and, perhaps, more importantly, made his defense of the HC at the Augsburg Diet of 1566 plausible.[100]

The Palatine Church and University on the Eve of the HC

Rapidly changing conditions on the ground made a more decisive movement into the Reformed camp seem inevitable. Erasmus von Minckwitz and Erasmus von Venningen, the most committed Lutherans among Frederick's top advisors, left the Palatinate. An influential power bloc of Reformed councilors, including Count Eberhard von Erbach, Christoph Ehem, and Christoph Prob, coalesced around the elector.[101] In the wake of the Lord's Supper controversies, the elector released numerous rigorous Lutheran pastors who could not abide by the terms of Melanchthon's *Judgment*. Their departure naturally opened the door to more individuals with either Philippist or outright Reformed persuasions and helped tip the confessional balance even further toward the Reformed camp. Other changes

99. In fact, John Calvin himself had accepted the *Variata* in 1541.

100. See Walter Hollweg, *Der Augsburger Reichstag von 1566 und seine Bedeutung für die Entstehung der Reformierten Kirche und ihres Bekenntnisses*, Beiträge zur Geschichte und Lehre der Reformierten Kirche, 17 (Neuenkirchen-Vluyn: Neukirchener Verlag, 1964); and Andreas Edel, *Der Kaiser und Kurpfalz. Eine Studie zu den Grundelementen politischen Handelns bei Maximilian II. (1564-1576)*, Schriftenreihe der Historischen Kommission bei der Bayerischen Akademie der Wissenschaften, 58 (Göttingen: Vandenhoek & Ruprecht, 1995).

101. Press, *Calvinismus und Territorialstaat*, 224-33.

in the parishes included the introduction of the Reformed practice of the "breaking of the bread" (*fractio panis*) in the Lord's Supper, perhaps as early as 1561.[102]

The church council at this point had a clear majority of Reformed activists.[103] The medical professor Erastus and the budding theologian and church superintendent Olevianus played the most prominent part in this transition period.[104] Erastus had been a member of the church council since the time of Ottheinrich and had played a critical role behind the scenes in reorienting Palatine church policy and disarming the Gnesio-Lutherans. Erastus published a tract titled *Fundamental Account, Regarding How the Words of Christ, "This is my body, etc.," Should be Understood*, which built both on Melanchthon's *Judgment* and on the Boquin-Klebitz Eucharistic theses.[105] The view of the Lord's Supper presented in this tract represented something of a melding of the Philippist and late-Zwinglian positions, as would later be seen in the HC. While Olevianus did not first attract attention as a theological talent, as a regional superintendent and as a member of the church council, he quickly became the chief organizer of the Palatine church.[106] Olevianus also briefly stepped into the third chair of theology at the University of Heidelberg. Like Erastus, he enjoyed close connections with the Heidelberg court, and he was the territory's prime link to the Genevan Reformers.

The new orientation in religious policy was also reflected in staffing changes at the University of Heidelberg in 1560-61. While there were still Philippist Lutherans present, the new appointments tended to have more manifest Reformed commitments. The departure of the Lutheran theologians Heshusius and Paul Einhorn opened two posts on the theology faculty. Boquin assumed the position of the first chair of theology. Although the Heidelbergers sought to win Peter Martyr Vermigli for the faculty, the elderly Italian exile turned them down but suggested his countryman Immanuel Tremellius. Tremellius, who was a convert from Judaism, was an impeccable Hebraist, and his appointment strengthened the university's academic reputation.[107] The theological faculty still

102. Wesel-Roth, *Erastus*, 131; See Bodo Nischan, "The 'Fractio Panis': A Reformed Communion Practice in Late Reformation Germany," *Church History* 53 (1984): 18.

103. Press, *Calvinismus und Territorialstaat*, 239-40. At the beginning of this period, the council consisted of Erastus, Boquin, Christoph Ehem, Stephan Cirler, and Michael Diller. Later, Olevianus and the strong Calvinist activist Wenzel Zuleger joined.

104. Sturm, *Der junge Zacharias Ursin*, 233.

105. [Thomas Erastus] *Gründtlicher bericht/ wie die wort Christi/ Das ist mein leib/ etc. zuverstehen seien* (Heidelberg: Ludwig Lück, 1562). The tract was published anonymously, though there is no doubt about its authorship. Gunnoe, "Erastus in Heidelberg," 96-117.

106. For Olevianus's life and impact, see J. F. Gerhard Goeters, "Caspar Olevianus als Theologe," *Monatshefte für Evangelische Kirchengeshichte des Rheinlandes* 37-38 (1988-1989): 287-319; Caspar Olevianus, *Der Gnadenbund Gottes 1590: Faksimilie-Edition mit einem Kommentar*, ed. Gunther Franz, J. F. Gerhard Goeters, and Wilhelm Holtmann (Cologne: Rheinland-Verlag, 1994); and Lyle Bierma, *German Calvinism in the Confessional Age: The Covenant Theology of Caspar Olevianus* (Grand Rapids: Baker, 1996).

107. Erastus's letter to Bullinger, Oct. 8, [1560], succinctly sums up the recruitment process. "Caremus adhuc professore in Schola, et in ecclesia concionatore. Unicornum princeps arbitror

lacked a native-German speaker of a high standing to enunciate and defend the emerging Palatine theology. Since the mid-1540s, the Palatinate had sought to acquire a theologian with a substantial reputation but had always been turned down. The university finally secured the long-sought-after theological talent when Zacharias Ursinus accepted their call in the summer of 1561.[108]

Conclusion

When surveying the period between the Heidelberg Disputation of 1518 and the release of the Heidelberg Catechism, it is possible to discern a large measure of continuity in the development of the Palatine Reformation, though the road took detours along the way—most notably in the period of the Interim. Certainly each ruler had distinct religious policies, but, as always, the seeds of the next era's religious orientation had been sown in the prior regime. During Ludwig's reign, despite his nominal allegiance to the Catholic Church, Protestantism put down extensive roots in Palatine territories and the Catholic ecclesiastical structure was critically weakened. By Ludwig's later years, Protestantism was approaching a de facto legal position in the Palatinate.

Building on this wild growth of Protestantism during Ludwig's era, the chameleon-like Frederick II offered the Protestant faith the official status for which preachers such as Strauss and Stoll had long labored. There is little doubt that the reforms of 1546 would have endured had it not been for the devastating Protestant defeat in the Schmalkaldic War. The general inclination toward Protestantism by the ruling elites was not seriously threatened by the Interim.

Ottheinrich sought to give order and official sanction to the largely Protestant territory that he inherited from Frederick II. He returned to the even older tradition of Palatine humanism and drew on the assistance of Wittenberg, Strasbourg, and Württemberg to nourish his church. In a true upper German

dimittet. Iam cum Emanuele Tremelio, qui D. Martyri notus est, agitur. Spero eum nobiscum futurum, quofacto .2. habebimus. Deest tertius, si nos iuvare poteris, rogo te plurimum, ut iuvare velis. Bouquino dabimus primum locum. Emanueli secundum, et Tertium ei, quem nobis Deus offeret. Concionatore bono et pio valde indigemus. Cupimus in hac quoque parte à te consilium et auxilium. D. Martyrem plurimum cupio, meis verbis saluteri. Voluimus Zanchium nuper ad nos vocare, sed nimium bene aiunt ei cum Marpachio conveni//re iam, De doctrina coeæ non puto eos consentire." Staatsarchiv des Kantons Zürich, E II 361, f. 8: [from the postscript]. Regarding the various machinations, see Sturm, *Der junge Zacharias Ursin*, 232-33.

108. Sturm, *Der junge Zacharias Ursin*, 237. For Ursinus's background and theological predilections see chap. 2 of this volume, pp. 18-25. In hindsight, it appears that such a theological talent was already present in the person of Olevianus. His contemporaries apparently were not impressed in 1560, and the university had even preferred Adam Neuser—the future Antitrinitarian—over Olevianus. Nevertheless, with the elector's insistence, Olevianus did briefly join the theological faculty only to move to a post at the *Heiliggeistkirche* to make room for Ursinus. While Olevianus has been frequently faulted for his sometimes harsh and unbending disposition, he seems to have born this transfer from the university to the *Heiliggeistkirche* with remarkable equanimity. See Christopher J. Burchill, *The Heidelberg Antitrinitarians*, Bibliotheca Dissidentium XI, ed. Andre Seguenny (Baden-Baden: Editions Valentin Koerner, 1989), 107-11; J. F. Gerhard Goeters, "Caspar Olevianus als Theologe," 295.

fashion, he sought to create a church in which the Lutheran gospel not only flourished but was cleansed of the vestiges of late-medieval "idolatry." Most importantly, the personnel that Ottheinrich recruited were responsible for engineering the shift from a Philippist/Gnesio-Lutheran theological axis to a Philippist/Reformed theological axis in the Palatinate early in the reign of Frederick III—a shift in which the Heidelberg Catechism would come to play a significant role.[109]

109. This particular reading of the Palatine Reformation is heavily indebted to the research of Volker Press, the past century's greatest historian of the sixteenth-century Palatinate. One of the chief labors of Press was to demonstrate a large degree of continuity between the upper German Reformation of the first half of the sixteenth century and the Palatine Reformation of the 1550s and 1560s. Press developed this interpretation in *Calvinismus und Territorialstaat* and numerous articles; this standpoint is succinctly expressed in "Die 'Zweite Reformation' in der Kurpfalz."

2

The Purpose and Authorship of the Heidelberg Catechism

Lyle D. Bierma

Early in 1562, Elector Frederick III ordered the preparation of a new catechism for his realm, a major step in the transformation of the Palatinate into a Melanchthonian-Reformed territory. Perhaps one should not make too much of this decision, because in sixteenth-century Europe it was common for cities and territories to produce their own catechisms. During the early years of the Reformation, numerous confessions and catechisms appeared, totaling hundreds of pages in modern collections of these works.[1] Even in the Palatinate itself several Lutheran and Reformed catechisms were in use at the time the Heidelberg Catechism was commissioned. What is surprising, therefore, is not so much that the Palatinate created its own catechism but that it had not done so earlier.

Nonetheless, a number of questions remain. Why did Frederick think that such a catechism was needed? How did he go about commissioning it? Who were the authors? How was the document prepared? What other catechisms were consulted in its preparation? Were minutes kept of the process? Most of these questions are difficult, if not impossible, to answer satisfactorily. In all likelihood, the Heidelberg Catechism (hereafter HC) was prepared in 1562 by a committee of churchmen who employed a variety of sources and met periodically throughout the year to discuss their work. However, no records of this process have survived—none, at least, of which we are aware. If such documents ever existed, they might have been moved, lost, or destroyed in the reversion of the Palatinate to Lutheran control after Frederick's death (1576) and in the expulsion of Reformed personnel from the Palatinate that followed. They might also have disappeared in the destruction and plunder of Heidelberg during the Thirty Years' War (1618-1648), in the takeover by a Roman Catholic branch of the dynastic

---

1. See, e.g., Ferdinand Cohrs, ed., *Die evangelische Katechismusversuche vor Luthers Enchiridion*, 5 vols. (Berlin: Hofmann, 1900-1907); Johann Michael Reu, ed., *Quellen zur Geschichte des kirchlichen Unterrichts in der evangelischen Kirche Deutschlands zwischen 1530 und 1600*, 2 vols. (1904-35; reprint, Hildesheim: Olms, 1976).

family in 1685, and/or in the occupation of the area by French armies in 1689 and 1692. At any rate, original sources for this period are hard to come by.[2]

There is one surviving source, however, that does address some of these questions—Frederick III's preface to the HC, which he attached to the catechism when he sent it to the publisher on January 19, 1563. His reflections there on the need for a new catechism and his mention of the persons involved in its production can serve as a starting point, at least, for an examination of the purpose and authorship of the HC.

Purpose

Frederick's preface offers several insights into his motives for commissioning a new catechism for the Palatinate.[3] He begins by acknowledging his God-given duty not only to promote quiet and peaceable living in the realm and to support the Christian life of his subjects, "but also and above all, constantly to admonish and lead them to devout knowledge and fear of the Almighty and His holy word of salvation, as the only foundation of all virtue and obedience." In other words, both the "temporal and eternal welfare" of his subjects are his responsibility.[4] Recognizing that his cousins and predecessors, the counts and electors of the Palatinate, have taken various measures "for the furtherance of the glory of God and the upholding of civil discipline and order," he believes nevertheless that "this purpose was not in every respect prosecuted with the appropriate zeal, and the expected and desired fruit did not accrue therefrom." Thus, he feels compelled "not only to renew the same, but also, as the exigencies of the times demand, to improve, reform, and further to establish them."[5]

Having outlined the state of affairs in the Palatinate in general terms, Frederick then proceeds to identify the problem more specifically. Alluding to the findings of a committee that had recently conducted a general visitation of the Palatine churches, he states:

> Therefore we also have ascertained that by no means the least defect of our system is found in the fact, that our blooming [developing] youth is disposed to be careless in respect to Christian doctrine, both in the schools and churches of our principality—some, indeed, being entirely without Christian instruction, others being unsystematically taught,

2. J. F. Goeters, "Entstehung und Frühgeschichte des Katechismus," in *Handbuch zum Heidelberger Katechismus*, ed. Lothar Coenen (Neukirchen-Vluyn: Neukirchener Verlag, 1963), 4.

3. This subsection on the purpose of the HC is adapted from Fred H. Klooster, *The Heidelberg Catechism: Origin and History* (Grand Rapids: Calvin Theological Seminary, 1982), 153-56.

4. George W. Richards, *The Heidelberg Catechism: Historical and Doctrinal Studies* (Philadelphia: Publication and Sunday School Board of the Reformed Church in the United States, 1913), 185, 187. On pp. 182-99 Richards provides a facsimile of the German text of the preface and an English translation on the facing pages. The German text can also be found in August Lang, *Der Heidelberger Katechismus und vier verwandte Katechismen* (Leipzig: Deichert, 1907), 2-4.

5. Richards, *Heidelberg Catechism*, 187, 189.

without any established, certain, and clear catechism, but merely according to individual plan or judgment; from which, among other great defects, the consequence has ensued, that they have, in too many instances, grown up without the fear of God and the knowledge of His word, having enjoyed no profitable instruction, or otherwise have been perplexed with irrelevant and needless questions, and at times have been burdened with unsound doctrines.[6]

A few lines later, he emphasizes again that "it is essential that our youth be trained in early life, and above all, in the pure and consistent doctrine of the holy Gospel, and be well exercised in the proper and true knowledge of God."[7] Therefore, he concludes, "to do away with this defect . . . we have secured the preparation of a summary course of instruction or catechism of our Christian Religion, according to the word of God."[8]

Frederick wanted this new catechism first of all, then, for the instruction of the children in sound doctrine. However, it is not only that the youth may be trained in piety, it is "also that the Pastors and Schoolmasters themselves may be provided with a fixed form and model, by which to regulate the instruction of youth, and not, at their option, adopt daily changes, or introduce erroneous doctrine."[9] All such instructors should thankfully accept this catechism, diligently explain it to the youth in the schools and the common people in the pews, and act and live in accordance with it; for if youth in early life are instructed aright in the word of God, one can have the assured hope that "it will please Almighty God also to grant reformation of public and private morals, and temporal and eternal welfare."[10]

The preface suggests, therefore, that Elector Frederick had at least three objectives for his new catechism: that it serve as a *catechetical tool* for teaching the children, as a *preaching guide* for instructing the common people in the churches, and as a *form for confessional unity* among the several Protestant factions in the Palatinate. To be sure, this last objective is not as clearly stated in the preface as the other two. Nonetheless, such phrases as "consistent doctrine of the holy Gospel," "a fixed form and model," "not, at their option, adopt daily changes," and "that you teach, and act, and live in accordance with [the catechism]"[11]

---

6. Ibid., 189, 191.

7. Ibid., 193.

8. Ibid., 193-95.

9. Ibid., 195-97. In a letter to his son-in-law, John Frederick of Saxony, on March 30, 1563, Frederick indicates again that this was a major goal in commissioning the Heidelberg Catechism: "It is not without good reason that I have called together all my superintendents, foremost Church officers (ministers) and theologians, . . . who agreed upon a uniform catechism, which is adapted to the youth, as well as to the Church officers (ministers) themselves, since I have found in my electorate a great lack of uniformity and many irregularities in the catechetical work, and in many places no catechism at all." August Kluckhohn, ed., *Briefe Friedrich des Frommen, Kurfürsten von der Pfalz* (Brunswick: Schwetschke, 1868-72), 1:390 (English translation in Otto Thelemann, *An Aid to the Heidelberg Catechism,* trans. M. Peters [Reading, Pa.: Good, 1896], 454 n. *).

10. Richards, *Heidelberg Catechism,* 197-99.

11. Ibid., 193, 195, 197.

certainly suggest the doctrinal unity, if not uniformity, that Frederick was seeking to achieve.

Moreover, from the beginning of his political life, Frederick had eschewed theological labels and had sought to ground his doctrine in the simple teachings of Scripture. That is also the case here. There is no evidence in the preface to the HC that he wanted a distinctly Reformed or Philippist catechism. Never once does he mention Melanchthon, Calvin, Beza, or Bullinger. Instead, he speaks in broad terms of "Christian doctrine," "Christian instruction," "the pure and consistent doctrine of the holy Gospel," and a "catechism of our Christian religion, according to the Word of God."[12] When one takes into account the existence of several Protestant parties in Heidelberg, the diversity of catechisms in use in the Palatinate in the early 1560s, Frederick III's doctrinal conflicts with the Gnesio-Lutherans, differences in the understanding of the Lord's Supper reflected at the "Wedding Debates," the recent confessional status of the ubiquity doctrine, and the disunity among the Protestant princes at the Naumburg Colloquy,[13] it is hardly surprising that Frederick would commission a new catechism as a standard preaching and teaching guide around which the major Protestant factions in his realm could unite.

Authorship

The father of the Heidelberg Catechism was Elector Frederick III. It was he who commissioned the HC, directed its production, secured its approval by a Heidelberg synod in January 1563, and defended it before the imperial diet three years later. Except for a few changes that he might have made in the final text, Frederick did not write the catechism. That distinction, according to a venerable tradition dating back to the seventeenth century, belonged to Zacharias Ursinus and Caspar Olevianus. By the late nineteenth century, it was widely held that Ursinus was responsible for the doctrinal substance of the catechism in an alleged first draft in Latin and Olevianus for the devotional and personal style of the final German version. This cooperation between professor and preacher accounted for the blend of theological depth and pastoral warmth for which the HC became so well known.

This old tradition, however, has not held up under the scrutiny of more recent scholarship. During the twentieth century, a consensus developed (1) that the HC was in some sense a team project; (2) that the role of Olevianus on this team was not as great as has been alleged in the past; and (3) that if any member of the team did serve as the primary author of the catechism, it was most likely Zacharias Ursinus. We shall examine each of these conclusions in turn.

12. Ibid., 189, 193, 195.
13. For details on these events leading up to the HC, see chapter 1.

A Team Project

The earliest and most reliable evidence for the involvement of a team or committee in the preparation of the HC is once again Frederick III's preface to the catechism. There he refers to "the advice and cooperation of our entire theological faculty in this place, and of all superintendents and distinguished servants of the Church, [through whom] we have secured the preparation of a summary course of instruction or catechism of our Christian Religion."[14] The team, therefore, comprised three groups of personnel: the theological faculty of Heidelberg University, the superintendents, and the "distinguished servants" or chief ministers (*Kirchendienern*) of the Palatine church. This statement also suggests that the committee participated not merely in synodical review and approval of the catechism but in the actual process of its preparation. The text literally reads that Frederick "had [the catechism] composed and made available" (*verfassen und stellen lassen*) with the advice and cooperation (or assistance) of these men.[15]

Several times during the next ten months, the elector echoed the comments he had made in the preface. In March 1563, he reported in a letter to John Frederick of Saxony that he had "called together all my superintendents, foremost Church officers (ministers) and theologians . . . who agreed upon a uniform catechism."[16] On April 10, he informed Count Albrecht of Prussia that after a period of great doctrinal unrest and the expulsion of some of the instigators, the Palatine theologians had reached "a good Christian concord" with respect to doctrine and ceremonies, as the copy of the HC accompanying his letter would show.[17] In a new preface in November for the Palatine Church Order, which included the text of the HC, Frederick again listed the "chief theologians, superintendents, church officers, and other godly, learned men and advisers" as those who had contributed to the study, review, and publication of the document.[18]

Frederick's testimony in these prefaces and letters was corroborated by other witnesses close to the project. Just eleven days after the official approval of the catechism, Thomas Erastus, professor of medicine at the university, the elector's

---

14. Richards, *Heidelberg Catechism*, 193, 195.

15. Ibid., 194. The suggestion that the committee was involved throughout the process is supported by Reuter's statement in the preface to his 1612 edition of Ursinus's *Opera theologica*: "Both [the Larger and Smaller] catechisms of Ursinus were submitted to those who had been appointed. Both were approved, but only from the Smaller Catechism was the larger part taken over into the New Catechism, published by the authorities in 1563" (pp. 10-11; English translation in Richards, *Heidelberg Catechism*, 51).

16. See n. 9 above.

17. Kluckhohn, *Briefe*, 2:1036-37.

18. "So haben wir ein kurtze kirchenordnung . . . durch unsere fürnemen theologen, superintendenten, kirchendiener und andere gottselige, gelehrte menner und räthe begreifen, besichtegen und endtlich in truck ausgehen lassen." Emil Sehling, *Die evangelischen Kirchenordnungen des 16. Jahrhunderts*, vol. 14, *Kurpfalz* (Tübingen: Mohr, 1969), 335.

personal physician, and an accomplished lay theologian, sent a letter to Heinrich Bullinger in which he declared:

> We have composed a catechism, in which several heads of doctrine, particularly the sacraments, are explained clearly and in detail according to the intent of the work. . . . No one will say, I think, that we are hiding anything. I have been involved in it for a long time already. For I always wanted the doctrine to become public.[19]

This comment is intriguing not only because of the first-person testimony it provides to Erastus's own role in the production of the HC but also because Erastus seems to identify himself as part of a group of authors. To be sure, the verb "we have composed" (*composuimus*) could be taken in an impersonal collective sense to refer to the Heidelberg community in general, but Erastus's personal references at the end of the quotation strongly suggest otherwise.[20]

Caspar Olevianus also implies plural authorship in a letter to Calvin (April 3, 1563) that accompanied two copies of the Latin translation of the HC he was sending to Calvin and Beza in Geneva. "If the catechism meets with your approval," he writes, "those who have collected the thoughts expressed in it will be most satisfied."[21] He goes on to refer to the difficulty that those in Heidelberg had experienced in "reconciling *many* heads" in the composition of the catechism.[22] Eleven days later (April 14, 1563), he sent copies of the German and Latin versions of the HC to Zurich and, in the cover letter to Bullinger, alludes several times to multiple authorship. He informs Bullinger that he is sending him "*our* Latin and German catechisms" and that "if there is any clarity in them, *we* owe it in good measure to you and to the sheer brilliance of the Swiss." The pious thoughts in the catechism "have been gathered not from one person but from many." After apologizing for not sending the catechisms earlier, Olevianus explains that he did not want to upstage his "most esteemed colleagues, especially Erastus" (who had sent Bullinger a copy of the catechism in February). He signs off with the words, "I send these booklets to you in the name of us all."[23]

19. Letter from Erastus to Bullinger (January 30, 1563), reprinted in Ruth Wesel-Roth, *Thomas Erastus: Ein Beitrag zur Geschichte der reformierten Kirche und zur Lehre von der Staatssouveränität* (Lahr: Schauenburg, 1954), 35.

20. For a detailed interpretation of this quotation, see Charles D. Gunnoe Jr., "Thomas Erastus in Heidelberg: A Renaissance Physician during the Second Reformation, 1558-1580" (Ph.D. diss., University of Virginia, 1998), 135-37.

21. "Si catechismus tuo iudicio probabitur, abunde iis erit satisfactum qui cogitationes suas contulerant." *Calvini opera*, 19:685.

22. "Tanta est difficultas in conciliandis *multis capitibus* et redigendis in unum." Ibid (italics added).

23. "et remitto Catechismos nostros latinos et Germanicos. Certe si qua in iis est perspicuitas, eius bonam partem tibi et candidis ingeniis Helvetiorum debemus. . . . Non unius sed multorum sunt collatae piae cogitationes. Certe factum est negligenter, quod citius ad te non est missus, sed ego nolui festinatione et praepropera liberalitate mea laudibus praeripere carissimis Collegis meis, Erasto praecipue. Sed utut sit, communi nostro nomine hosce libellos ad te mitto." The letter is reprinted in Karl Sudhoff, *C. Olevianus und Z. Ursinus: Leben und ausgewählte Schriften* (Elberfeld: Friderichs, 1857), 482-83 (italics added). Hendrikus Berkhof ("The

A final witness, Zacharias Ursinus, recalls in a published defense of the HC in 1564 that the responsibility for writing the catechism had been given "to certain devout scholars famous for their erudition in Christian doctrine."[24] Here, as in all but one of the other references above, not a single name is given. In fact, Ursinus seems to exclude himself from the group of scholars assigned to the task. That may be the mark of his characteristic modesty, but, as with the other sources, it is more likely an indication of the anonymity that seemed politically prudent at the time. As we have seen, one of the primary goals Frederick III was seeking to achieve through the HC was confessional unity among the various theological factions in Heidelberg. Because the committee very likely included representatives of these different theological viewpoints, public emphasis on collective authorship would serve to stress the unity of the elector's reformation and help to eliminate criticism of the HC as distinctively Calvinist, Zwinglian, or Philippist. Thus, even if one or two people had major responsibility for drafting the catechism, it was important that he or they remain anonymous.[25]

Nevertheless, we are able to reconstruct much of the membership of this committee from other sources. The makeup of two of the three groups that Frederick identifies as part of the team, namely, "our entire theological faculty in this place" and the "chief ministers of the church [*fürnemsten Kirchendienern*]," is spelled out in Heidelberg's letter of support for the *Confessio Vesaliensis* on December 12, 1562, just a month before the HC was published. The names listed there include the three theological professors at the university—Zacharias Ursinus (Dogmatics), Immanuel Tremmelius (Old Testament), and Petrus Boquinus (New Testament);[26] ministers Caspar Olevianus, Adam Neuser, Petrus Macheropoeus, Tilemann Mumius, and Johannes Brunner; the court preacher Michael Diller; and Konrad Marius, professor at the Sapience College.[27] Boquinus, Olevianus, and Diller were also part of the *Kirchenrat* (church council or consistory), which consisted of three ministers and three laymen and had responsibility for regulating Palatine ecclesiastical affairs. If, in fact, the entire council was involved in the preparation of the HC, the other three members would have been laymen Wenzelaus Zuleger, president of the council and the elector's political adviser; Stephanus Cirler, council secretary and Frederick's

Catechism in Historical Context," in *Essays on the Heidelberg Catechism* [Philadelphia: United Church, 1963], 79) incorrectly attributes the last quotation above to a letter from Olevianus to Beza.

24. Zacharinas Ursinus, "Apologia chatechismi ecclesiarum et scholarum electoralis palatitus," in *D. Zachariae Ursini . . . Opera theologica*, ed. Quirinus Reuter (Heidelberg: Lancellot, 1612), 2: preface [iii].

25. See Derk Visser, *Zacharias Ursinus: The Reluctant Reformer—His Life and Times* (New York: United Church, 1983), 116-19, 132.

26. On the possible influence of Boquinus on the HC, see G. P. Hartvelt, "Petrus Boquinus," *Gereformeerd Theologische Tijdschrift* 62 (1962): 76-77.

27. Goeters, "Caspar Olevianus als Theologe," *Monatshefte für Evangelische Kirchengeschichte des Rheinlandes* 37-38 (1988-89): 303.

private secretary; and physician-theologian Thomas Erastus, who, as we have already seen, identified himself as a member of the team.[28]

The third group mentioned by Frederick, the superintendents, consisted of nine men who functioned much like the former bishops of the Roman Catholic Church. They ordained pastors into their offices, made biannual visits to the congregations in their districts, and conducted worship services when a regular pastor could not be present. This group probably participated only in the final review and approval of the catechism in a five-day conference in January 1563.[29] The superintendents from this time whose names we know are Olevianus, Joannes Velvanus, Johannes Willing, Johannes Sylvanus, and Johannes Eisenmenger,[30] although, according to one report, an unnamed superintendent from Oppenheim registered a dissenting vote against the HC.[31]

Others who have been suggested as possible members of the team of authors include Petrus Dathenus, leader of the Dutch refugee congregation at Frankenthal and future preacher at Frederick's court, and Christoph Ehem, a lawyer and Frederick's counselor in foreign affairs.[32] In addition, one should not overlook Elector Frederick himself. According to one source, "several times [Frederick] had diligently read over [the catechism], reflected on it, and evaluated it by the rule and norm of God's word."[33] In defending the catechism before the Diet of Augsburg in 1566 against the Gnesio-Lutheran charge that it had been written in Zurich by Bullinger, Frederick even asserted that he could demonstrate from his own handwriting that he had "improved it in several places."[34] Indeed, he was so personally involved in the production of the HC that upon the urging of Olevianus, he added an entirely new question and answer on

---

28. An extended argument for Erastus as an author of the HC is found in Gunnoe, "Erastus in Heidelberg," 133-45. Pointing to evidence in letters from Olevianus to Bullinger, Erastus to Bullinger, and Olevianus to Calvin, Gunnoe makes a strong circumstantial case for Erastus's involvement in the production of the HC. Less convincing, however, is his appeal to Erastian influence on the HC's doctrine of the Lord's Supper. The eucharistic teaching of the HC cannot, in my judgment, be labeled "late-Zwinglian" (139), and the linguistic parallels Gunnoe finds between the HC and Erastus can also be found in Bullinger and Calvin. See Lyle Bierma, *The Doctrine of the Sacraments in the Heidelberg Catechism: Melanchthonian, Calvinist, or Zwinglian?*, Studies in Reformed Theology and History, New Series, no. 4. (Princeton: Princeton Theological Seminary, 1999), 9-20.

29. Goeters, "Olevianus als Theologe," 302-3.

30. Gerrit den Hartogh, *Voorzienigheid in donker licht: Herkomst en gebruik van het begrip 'Providentia Dei' in de reformatorische theologie, in het bijzonder bij Zacharias Ursinus* (Heerenveen: Groen, 1999), 31.

31. Goeters, "Olevianus als Theologe," 303 n. 93.

32. Gunnoe, "Erastus in Heidelberg," 130-32.

33. Letter of Philipp von Gemmingen and Hieronymus Gerhard to Wolfgang and Christof (October 21, 1563), in Kluckhohn, *Briefe*, 1:465.

34. Ibid., 726. One of the places he might have had in mind here is HC 78, whose original wording was altered out of concern that the answer might sound too Zwinglian. Arguments for and against this possibility are discussed in Maurits A. Gooszen, "Inleiding," in De *Heidelbergsche Catechismus: Textus Receptus met Toelichtende Teksten* (Leiden: Brill, 1890), 98-99, esp. n. 1.

the Roman Catholic mass (HC 80) after the first edition had already been published.[35]

The HC, therefore, was certainly produced through the combined efforts of many people, not least Elector Frederick III himself. Most committees, however, operate by delegating preliminary work to one or more of their members. Was that true in the case of the HC team? More specifically, is there any truth in the old tradition that the chief authors of the catechism were Olevianus and Ursinus?

The Role of Olevianus

Life. Caspar Olevianus was born on August 10, 1536, in the ancient Mosel River city of Trier.[36] His father Gerhard, a baker, guild master, city councilman, and treasurer, hailed from the nearby village of Olewig, from which the family derived its surname. Following the premature death of his father, Olevianus was reared in the home of his maternal grandfather and attended local schools until he was thirteen. Years later, he would recall that it was the instruction of an aged priest at the St. German Collegium in Trier that awakened in him an interest in the message of Scripture.[37]

In 1549, his grandfather sent him off to France with funds to study arts in Paris and then law in Orléans and Bourges. Sometime during his years as a law student, Olevianus joined the underground Protestant movement in France and, following a brush with death in 1556, became a zealous supporter of his newfound faith. While in Bourges, he had developed a friendship with the son of the future Elector Frederick III of the Palatinate. As the two were strolling along the riverbank one day, a group of drunken students invited them on a boat trip to the other shore. The prince joined the party; Olevianus refused. Partway across the river, the rowdy bunch accidentally overturned the boat, fell into the water, and drowned. Olevianus dived into the water in an attempt to save the prince but soon found himself in danger of going under. In desperation, he promised God that should his life be spared, he would devote himself to the preaching of the

---

35. In his letter to Calvin on April 3, 1563 (*Calvini opera*, 19:684), Olevianus states, "Admonitus a me Princeps voluit in secunda editione germanica et prima editione latina addi." Walter Hollweg also noted several striking parallels between Frederick's language in a letter to his son-in-law on June 10, 1562 (Kluckhohn, *Briefe*, 1:307-13) and that of HC 1, 52, 57. *Der Augsburger Reichstag von 1566 und seine Bedeutung für die Entstehung der Reformierten Kirche und ihre Bekenntnisses* (Neukirchen-Vluyn: Neukirchener Verlag, 1964), 29 n. 84.

36. For biographical information on Olevianus, see Johannes Piscator, *Kurtzer Bericht vom Leben und Sterben D. Gasparis Oleviani*, which was published separately in 1587 and later as part of Olevianus's *Der Gnadenbund Gottes* (Herborn: Rab, 1590); Melchior Adam, *Vitae Germanorum theologorum* (Frankfurt, 1653), 596-603; Sudhoff, *Olevianus und Ursinus*; G. Bouwmeester, *Caspar Olevianus en zijn Reformatorische arbeid* (The Hague: Willem de Zwijgerstichting, 1954); Goeters, "Olevianus als Theologe," 287-319; and *Theologische Realenzyklopädie*, s.v. "Olevian, Kaspar." A bibliography of Olevianus's writings is appended to Goeters, "Olevianus als Theologe," 320-35. The following biographical sketch is adapted from Lyle Bierma, *German Calvinism in the Confessional Age: The Covenant Theology of Caspar Olevianus* (Grand Rapids: Baker, 1996), 12-20.

37. See Olevianus's preface to the youth in his *Expositio symboli apostolici* (Frankfurt: Wechel, 1576), 16.

gospel in his homeland. Moments later, a servant of one of the drowned students pulled him to safety.

Following his dramatic rescue, Olevianus began an intensive personal study of the Bible and writings of the reformers, particularly Calvin. After graduating with a doctorate in civil law in 1557 and practicing law in Trier for several months, he spent a year in Switzerland (1558-59) studying with Calvin in Geneva and Vermigli in Zurich. During this time, he also made the acquaintance of the reformers Bullinger, Farel, Viret, and Beza. When word reached Geneva in 1559 that a growing band of Protestants in Trier was in need of a minister, Calvin and others urged Olevianus to return to his birthplace.

Upon his arrival in Trier in June 1559, Olevianus applied to the city council for a teaching position and was offered a post as a gymnasium lecturer in logic and philosophy. For a basic textbook, he selected Melanchthon's *Dialectices* (1547), and its frequent biblical and doctrinal references provided ample opportunity for Protestant comment. For two months, he was able to teach freely, but after a public sermon in August in which he attacked the Roman Catholic Church and proclaimed the Protestant doctrine of justification, Catholic opposition began to mount. Over the next five months, as the number of Protestants continued to increase, the Bishop-Elector of Trier engineered a successful suppression of the movement, arresting Olevianus and other ringleaders and banning all Protestants from the city. Olevianus won release only through the intervention of several German Protestant princes, one of whom, Frederick III of the Palatinate, invited him to Heidelberg in January 1560.

Olevianus took up duties in Heidelberg first as an administrator and instructor at the Sapience College, a pastoral training school, and then in March 1561 as professor of dogmatics at the university. In July of the same year, the university awarded him his doctorate in theology. A year later he relinquished his teaching responsibilities to Zacharias Ursinus and became pastor of Heidelberg's St. Peter's Church (and later of the Holy Spirit Church) and one of five members of the *Kirchenrat* (church council), the highest ecclesiastical body in the realm. His uncertain role in the composition of the HC in 1562 will be discussed below, but we do know that by October 1563 he had completed a catechism of his own with striking similarities to parts of the HC: *Vester Grundt, das ist, Die Artickel des alten, waren, ungezweiffelten Christlichen Glaubens.*[38] During these years in Heidelberg, he also designed a new Palatine church order (1563) and a Genevan form of church discipline and became involved in various eucharistic disputes with the Lutherans of southern Germany.[39]

The Lutherans returned to power in Heidelberg in 1576, the same year that Olevianus published his second major theological work, *Expositio symbolici*

---

38. *Vester Grundt* was not actually published until 1567. For bibliographical data on this work, see Goeters' "Bibliographia Oleviana," entry 3 ("Olevianus als Theologe," 323).

39. For some of Olevianus's polemical sermons and tracts on the sacraments, see Caspar Olevian, *Der Gnadenbund Gottes 1590: Faksimile-Edition mit einem Kommentar*, ed. Gunther Franz, J. F. Gerhard Goeters, and Wilhelm Holtmann (Cologne: Rheinland-Verlag, 1994), 225-423, 427-33.

apostoloci.[40] Olevianus was dismissed from office, placed under house arrest, and eventually expelled from the city, but, in early 1577, he accepted an invitation from Count Ludwig von Wittgenstein to come to Berleburg as a tutor for his sons. During this time, Olevianus directed a reorganization of the church in Wittgenstein and the neighboring Wetterau districts and published commentaries on Paul's epistles to the Galatians, Romans, Philippians, and Colossians.[41]

In 1584, he answered the call of Count John VI of Nassau to become court chaplain and chief preacher of the city of Herborn and to assist in the founding of a Reformed ministerial training school. The Herborn Academy opened in July 1584 with Olevianus as its first professor of dogmatics. While in Herborn, he also published his major treatise on the covenant, *De substanitia foederis* (1585)[42] and a compendium of Calvins's *Institutes*.[43] Early in 1587, his health began to decline, and he died in Herborn on March 15 at the age of fifty.[44]

Authorship of the Catechism. Olevianus's name has long been associated with the composition of the HC in 1562. The historiography of the last 350 years has identified him with at least two phases of the preparation of the catechism: the writing of one of the rough drafts assigned by Frederick III, and the conversion of Ursinus's Latin Smaller Catechism (hereafter SC) into the final German version. The oldest accounts of Olevianus's role are contained in the works of the German Reformed theologian Heinrich Alting (1583-1644) who was the first ever to identify the authors of the HC by name. Alting was born in Emden; studied in Groningen, Heidelberg (1601-1602), and Herborn; and served as professor of dogmatics at the universities of Heidelberg (1613-1622) and Groningen. His father Menso had come to Heidelberg as a student just two years after the HC was published and had formed a friendship with Olevianus.[45]

Between 1619 and 1622, Alting delivered a series of lectures at Heidelberg on the HC, which were published by his son two years after his death. In that work, Alting makes reference to "the authors [of the HC], especially Dr. Ursinus and Olevianus, who, . . . after joint consultation and labors, completed the catechism."[46] Later, after fleeing into exile in the Netherlands during the Thirty Years' War, Alting expanded on this statement in his history of the Palatine Church (1644):

---

40. See Goeters' "Bibliographia Oleviana," entry 6 ("Olevianus als Theologe," 325-27).

41. Ibid., entries 7-9 (327-29).

42. Ibid., entry 12 (329-30).

43. Ibid., entry 13 (330-31).

44. For Olevianus's many posthumous publications, see ibid., entries 15-25 (331-37).

45. At least according to F. W. Cuno, who bases this claim on an autograph of a letter from Olevianus to Menso Alting to which he had access but about which he gives no further information. "Können Wir Olevianus mit Recht als Mitfasser des Heidelberger Katechismus neben Ursinus stellen?" *Reformierte Kirchen-Zeitung* 25 (1902): 213.

46. Heinrich Alting, *Scriptorum theologicorum Heidelbergensium tomus tertius, continens Explicationem Catecheseos Palatinae* (Amsterdam, 1646), 5. The Latin text is quoted in Sudhoff, *Olevianus und Ursinus*, 108 (note). What appears to be a rather free German translation can be found in Goeters, "Olevianus als Theologe," 299.

This task [of preparing the HC] was assigned in 1562 to two theologians, Olevianus and Dr. Ursinus, both of them Germans and accomplished in writing the German language. Each of them prepared his own draft: Olevianus, a popular exposition of the covenant of grace; Ursinus, a twofold catechism—a larger one for those more advanced, and a smaller one for the youth. From these two works the Palatine Catechism was composed.[47]

In both of these accounts, Alting is vague about the roles of Ursinus and Olevianus apart from their preparation of the rough drafts. In the one, he states that the authors, particularly Ursinus and Olevianus, "completed the catechism [*confecissent Catechesin*]"; in the other, only that from their drafts the Palatine Catechism "was composed [*contracta est*]." In subsequent centuries, however, other scholars would define these roles more precisely. Wundt, for example, argued in the late 1700s that Olevianus gave the catechism its "Idee" and Ursinus worked it out in its final form.[48] The dominant view in the nineteenth and early twentieth centuries, however, was that Olevianus was responsible for converting the heavily theological language of Ursinus's Latin SC, or a draft based on it, into the warm and personal style of the final German text.[49]

This view was not without its critics. The first dissent appeared in an early nineteenth-century history of the Dutch Reformed Church by Ypeij and Dermout, who were convinced that the evidence for Olevianus's participation was so weak that he could not be considered a coauthor: "Ursinus . . . alone was the author of the Heidelberg Catechism."[50] Cuno was prompted in 1902 to respond to questions about Olevianus's contribution that were surfacing particularly among theologians in the German Reformed Church in North

47. Heinrich Alting, "Historia ecclesiae Palatinae," in Ludwig Christian Mieg, *Monumenta pietatis et litteraria virorum in re publica et litteraria illustrium selecta* (Frankfurt, 1701), 189 (Latin text in Gooszen, "Inleiding," in *Heidelbergsche Catechismus*, 1 n. 1).

48. D. L. Wundt, *Magazin für die Kirchen- und Gelehrten- geschichte der Pfalz* (Heidelberg, 1790), 57; idem, *Grundriss der Pfälzischen Kirchengeschichte* (Heidelberg, 1796), 47, cited in Cuno, "Können Wir Olevianus," 221.

49. Sudhoff, *Olevianus und Ursinus*, 167-68; Kluckhohn, *Friedrich der Fromme* (Nördlingen: Beck, 1879), 131; Gooszen, "Inleiding," in *Heidelbergsche Catechismus*, 97, 111-12; M. Lauterburg, *Realencyklopädie für protestantische Theologie und Kirche*, 3d ed. (1901), s.v. "Katechismus, Heidelberger"; Cuno, "Können Wir Olevianus," 221; Lang, *Heidelberger Katechismus*, LXXXVII; Hollweg, *Evangelische Kirchenlexicon* (1958), s.v. "Heidelberger Catechismus"; Heinrich Graffmann, *Die Religion in Geschichte und Gegenwart*, 3d ed. (1959), s.v. "Heidelberger Katechismus." Even the preface to a new English translation of the HC published by the World Alliance of Reformed Churches on the 400th anniversary of the HC's birth states that "to Olevianus was given the responsibility for a final revision and translation into German." *The Heidelberg Catechism* (New York: Reformed Church in America, 1962), 5. Cuno actually insists that Olevianus did more than just translate and revise an earlier draft of the HC; he actually composed some of the questions and answers himself. "Können Wir Olevianus," 221.

50. "Die bewijzen echter, nader bij het licht beschouwd, zijn zoo zwak, dat zij den oordeelkundigen onderzoeker an Olevianus niet kunnen doen denken, als medearbeider in het opstellen van den katechismus. . . . Ursinus . . . alleen is de schrijver geweest van den Heidelbergschen katechismus." Anne Ypeij and Isaac J. Dermout, *Geschiedenis der Nederlandsche Hervormde Kerk* (Breda: van Bergen, 1819-27), 1:456, 457.

America.[51] In 1913, on the basis of a letter about Olevianus from Dathenus to Beza in 1570, van Schelven publicly expressed a change of mind about Olevianus's role as the final redactor of the catechism.[52] Bauer, too, concluded in an encyclopedia entry on the HC in 1928 that "Olevianus's share in the work cannot be proven."[53]

By the 1960s, however, the weight of opinion began to shift toward this minority view—largely the result of a rigorous critique of Olevianus's part in the catechism by Walter Hollweg in 1961.[54] Objections to the traditional position focused on two issues: the reliability of Alting's account of dual authorship and the claim that Olevianus served as translator and final redactor of the German text. Critics expressed several reservations about Alting's accounts. First, Alting was writing many decades after the publication of the HC and the deaths of its alleged authors, and he provided no supporting evidence, not even Frederick's preface to the HC.[55] Second, the two rough drafts by Ursinus that Alting mentions have long been thought to be a reference to Ursinus's SC and Larger Catechism (hereafter LC). The problem is that whereas the SC was indeed created as a draft for the HC, the LC was quite possibly composed after the SC and for a different purpose—as a textbook for theological instruction at the university.[56]

The most serious difficulty with Alting's report, however, has to do with his reference to "a popular exposition of the covenant of grace" that supposedly served as Olevianus's rough draft of the HC. Scholars have long speculated about the identity of this document, but the most likely candidate is Olevianus's book, *Der Gnadenbund Gottes* (God's Covenant of Grace).[57] This work, however, was

51. "Können Wir Olevianus," 212.

52. A. A. Van Schelven, "De Heidelbergsche Catechismus (1563 – Januari – 1913)," *Nederlandsch Archief voor Kerkgeschiedenis*, n.s., 10 (1913): 1-6.

53. Johannes Bauer, *Die Religion in Geschichte und Gegenwart*, 2d ed. (1928), s.v. "Heidelberger Katechismus."

54. Walter Hollweg, "Bearbeitete Caspar Olevianus den deutschen Text zum Heidelberger Katechismus?" in *Neue Untersuchungen zur Geschichte des Heidelberger Katechismus* (Neukirchen: Neukirchener Verlag, 1961), 124-52.

55. Fred H. Klooster, "The Priority of Ursinus in the Composition of the Heidelberg Catechism," in *Controversy and Conciliation: The Reformation and the Palatinate 1559-83*, ed. Derk Visser (Allison Park, PA: Pickwick, 1986), 74. One of the primary objections to Olevianus's co-authorship that Cuno was addressing in 1902 was that "Alting . . . hat sechzig Jahre nach der Abfassung des Katechismus erst seine Geschichte geschrieben, er stand nicht mehr im Kontakte mit dem oder den Verfassern desselben, seine Quellen, aus denen er geschöpft, flossen nicht mehr rein." "Können Wir Olevianus," 213.

56. Erdmann Sturm, *Der junge Zacharias Ursinus: Sein Weg vom Philippismus zum Calvinismus* (Neukirchen: Neukirchener Verlag, 1972), 239-41, 246-48, 253.

57. Sudhoff (*Olevianus und Ursinus*, 88) speaks of a "katechetischen Entwurf" by Olevianus but does not name this document or explain its ultimate fate. H. E. Vinke (*Libri Symbolici Ecclesiae Reformatae Nederlandicae* [Utrecht: Van Terveen, 1846], liv) and Cuno ("Können Wir Olevianus," 221) identify the document as *Der Gnadenbund Gottes*. Lauterburg, *Realencyklopädie*, s.v. "Katechismus, Heidelberger" describes the document as belonging "ins Reich des Mythos." I myself suggested the possibility of a draft prepared by Olevianus that has not survived, in "Olevianus and the Authorship of the Heidelberg Catechism: Another Look," *The Sixteenth*

actually a *collection* of some of Olevianus's German writings and was not published until three years after his death.[58] The fact that this collection included an exposition of the Apostles' Creed in which the covenant of grace figured prominently (*Vester Grundt* [*A Firm Foundation*]), that this exposition was indeed a popular treatise in its day, and, above all, that it exhibited striking linguistic similarities to the HC all suggest that this is the document Alting had in mind.[59] Nevertheless, *A Firm Foundation* (hereafter FF) could not have functioned as a preliminary draft for the HC, because it was written sometime *after* the HC and was first published in 1567.[60] In fact, as Hollweg points out, Olevianus's entire theological corpus appeared (and was most likely composed) subsequent to the catechism itself.[61]

Hollweg was even more skeptical of the second tradition that had developed around Olevianus, namely, that Olevianus had functioned as the translator and editor of the final German redaction of the HC. Hollweg's critique of this thesis can be summarized in five main points:

First, he questioned Olevianus's catechetical gifts, arguing that a letter from Ursinus to Crato in 1563 that is often cited as testimony to Olevianus's abilities as

---

Century Journal 13, no. 4 (1982): 26-27. For a critique of my hypothesis see Klooster, "Priority of Ursinus," 84-87; Goeters, "Olevianus als Theologe," 306; and Gunnoe, "Erastus in Heidelberg," 126-27. I have since modified my view in Lyle Bierma, "*Vester Grundt* and the Origins of the Heidelberg Catechism," in *Later Calvinism: International Perspectives*, ed. W. Fred Graham, Sixteenth Century Essays & Studies, ed. Charles G. Nauert Jr., vol. 22 (Kirksville, Mo.: Sixteenth Century Journal, 1994), 307-8.

58. Caspar Olevianus, *Der Gnadenbund Gottes/Erkläret in den Artickeln unsers allgemeynen/ungezweiffelten Christlichen Glaubens . . .* (Herborn: Rab, 1590). For a recent edition of this work, see Olevian, *Der Gnadenbund Gottes 1590: Faksimile-Edition*, ed. Franz, Goeters, and Holtmann.

59. Caspar Olevianus, *Vester Grundt, das ist, Die Artikel des alten, waren, ungegezweifelten Christlichen Glaubens* was first published in Heidelberg in 1567 and reprinted there in 1570. A revised and expanded edition appeared in Heidelberg in 1573, in Neustadt in 1582, 1585, 1590, and 1591, and in Herborn in 1590, 1593, and 1602 (the latter three as part of *Der Gnadenbund Gottes*). See Goeters' "Bibliographia Oleviana," entry 3 ("Olevianus als Theologe," 323). For an English translation and identification of the many parallels to the HC, see Caspar Olevianus, *A Firm Foundation: An Aid to Interpreting the Heidelberg Catechism*, trans. and ed. Lyle D. Bierma (Grand Rapids: Baker, 1995).

60. Nine months after the appearance of the first edition of the HC, Olevianus wrote Bullinger that he had in hand a "more detailed catechism" in which he had "observed the same method found in the smaller one [HC]" in treating the doctrinal core of the Christian faith (letter of October 25, 1563, reprinted in Sudhoff, *Olevianus und Ursinus*, 485). None of Olevianus's extant works fits the description of this more detailed catechism better than *A Firm Foundation*, and Olevianus's words above certainly imply that the HC was composed first. See Gooszen, "Inleiding," in *Heidelbergsche Catechismus*, 13-14.

61. Hollweg, "Bearbeitete Caspar Olevianus," 141. Hollweg goes on to ask rhetorically, "Weist denn etwa vorhandene Übereinstimmung in Wortlaut und Stil oder in der theologischen Formulierung auf eine Abhängigkeit des Katechismus von Olevian oder hat nicht umgekehrt der Katechismus . . . auf die Schriften Olevians abgefärbt?" (141-42).

a catechete is usually mistranslated and, in fact, says nothing at all about such talents.[62]

Second, he attacked the image of Olevianus as a popular and pious preacher. Citing several of Olevianus's contemporaries, he contended that Olevianus had a reputation for being obstinate and vengeful and that on at least one occasion he had abused his pulpit authority to settle a personal score. Could a person with such a character, he asked, ever have written a document such as the HC, recognized the world over for its warm and pious tone?[63]

Third, Hollweg maintained that no one has really documented the claim that there are similarities of vocabulary and style between the HC and Olevianus's other writings. Even if such affinities can be shown, the lines of influence must run from the catechism to these other writings, not vice versa, because no part of Olevianus's extant theological corpus was published before the HC.[64]

Fourth, Hollweg questioned whether Olevianus had the literary-poetic gifts to compose such a masterpiece as the HC. As an example, he referred to Olevianus's description of Ursinus as "[one] who surpasses me in the ability to give particular ideas their proper shape and form," thereby expressing reservations about his own literary talents.[65]

Finally, Hollweg pointed out that as late as 1570 Olevianus still had objections to the wording of HC 36, which Olevianus apparently felt too narrowly confined the work of Christ to his conception and birth and overlooked the significance of the Cross. If Olevianus had been responsible for the German redaction of the catechism, it would have been a simple matter to change or clarify this answer to his satisfaction.[66] On the basis of a comparison of the SC with the HC, Hollweg was certain that there was a single redactor of the German text of the HC, but he was just as certain that it was not Olevianus. Who it actually was is still a mystery.[67]

Despite the affirmation that Hollweg's critique has received in some quarters,[68] his arguments are not wholly persuasive. First of all, to call into question Olevianus's catechetical abilities largely by challenging one alleged letter of testimony thereto is hardly convincing. Hollweg does note that Olevianus's later *Bauernkatechismus* gives no indication of any special catechetical ability, but

62. Ibid., 136-38.
63. Ibid., 138-41.
64. See n. 60 above.
65. Hollweg, "Bearbeitete Caspar Olevianus," 142, 144.
66. Ibid., 146-51.
67. Ibid., 126-35, 151-52.
68. Goeters states that "erst 1961 hat dann Walter Hollweg die bis dahin immer wieder nachgeschriebene Hypothese von des Olevianus' Verantwortlichkeit für die deutsche Endredaktion des Katechismus mit starken Gründen erschüttert." "Olevianus als Theologe," 301. Cf. also Wilhelm H. Neuser, "Die Väter des Heidelberger Katechismus," *Theologische Zeitschrift* 35 (1979): 177: "Im Jahre 1961 hat Walter Hollweg Sudhoff und seine Nachfolger widerlegt. Die Frage nach der Verfasserschaft des Heidelberger Katechismus war wieder offen. Ein hervorragender Beitrag Olevians ist auszuschliessen."

he provides neither the criteria nor the documentation for this judgment.[69] He also makes no mention of Olevianus's other catechetical work—FF (1567), which was an expansion of the second section of the HC, and *Expositio symboli apostolici* (1576), a commentary on the Apostles' Creed based on Olevianus's catechetical sermons. FF especially is the work of an accomplished catechete, whose originality can be seen not only in the many new questions and answers he composes but also in the skillful way he weaves selected strands of Scripture and of at least six other catechisms and confessions into the fabric of the commentary.[70]

Hollweg's attack on the traditional picture of Olevianus as a preacher of great power and piety is also open to question. First of all, to call upon an individual's opponents as character witnesses is, as Hollweg himself admits, not the most direct route to the truth. Nevertheless, he relies heavily upon the testimony of Thomas Erastus from a time when Erastus and Olevianus were on opposite sides of a controversy over church discipline in the Palatinate. Hollweg is on firmer ground when he notes that even Beza, a friend of Olevianus, was concerned about the latter's intransigence. What he does not mention is that Beza also thought highly enough of Olevianus's preaching to edit three commentaries based on Olevianus's sermons on Galatians, Romans, and Philippians-Colossians.[71] Finally, even a cursory reading of Olevianus's theological works will show that they are suffused with the same warmth and piety as the HC. Whatever personal shortcomings he may have had, they rarely surfaced in his formal writing.

Hollweg's concern about the lack of documentation for alleged similarities between the HC and Olevianus's other writings has also been addressed. Already in the mid-nineteenth century, Vinke had documented twenty examples of parallels between FF and the HC that could not be found in either of Ursinus's earlier catechisms.[72] Furthermore, my own comparison of the HC with FF has shown that of the fifty-three questions and answers that HC Lord's Days 5-24 comprise, all or parts of forty-five are found verbatim in FF, and of the remaining

---

69. Hollweg, "Bearbeitete Caspar Olevianus," 138. The Bauernkatechismus was a simple exposition of the Apostles' Creed, sacraments, Law, and Lord's Prayer, designed, as Olevianus states in the introduction, for "dem gemeynen mann . . . sonderlich dem armen Bawersvolck." For the text of the catechism and a more complimentary assessment of it than Hollweg gives, see Olevian, *Der Gnadenbund Gottes 1590: Faksimile-Edition*, ed. Franz, Goeters, and Holtmann, 204-23, 491-94. Holtmann suggests that "Olevian könnte den Katechismus während seiner Berleburger Zeit [1577-84] verfaßt haben" (491).

70. See the introduction to Olevianus, *Firm Foundation*, ed. Bierma, xix-xxv.

71. Theodore Beza, *In Epistolam D. Pauli apost. ad Galatas notae, ex concionibus Gasparis Oleviani excerptae, et a Theodore Beza editae cum praefatione eiusdem Bezae* (Geneva: Vignon, 1578); Theodore Beza, *In epistolam D. Pauli Apostoli ad Romanos notae, ex Gasparis Oleviani concionibus excerptae et a Theodoro Beza editae, cum praefatione eiusdem Bezae* (Geneva: Vignon, 1579); Theodore Beza, *In Epistolas D. Pauli Apostoli ad Philippenses et Colossenses notae, ex Gasparis Oleviani concionibus excerptae et a Theodore Beza editae, cum praefatione eiusdem Bezae* (Geneva: Vignon, 1580). See also n. 41 above.

72. Vinke, *Libri Symbolici*, liv-lx.

eight, six appear there in paraphrase.[73] Even though FF appeared after the HC, the fact that it was finished just nine months later may indicate that Olevianus was able to draw upon earlier work that he had done on the HC committee in 1562.[74]

Hollweg argues against Olevianus's literary talents on the basis of the latter's description of Ursinus as one "qui me facultate linguae superat," which Hollweg translates as "who surpasses me in the ability to give particular ideas their proper shape and form." As Gunnoe has noted, however, this clause is more of a positive statement about Ursinus than a negative one about Olevianus.[75] Moreover, in the letter to Calvin in which this clause appears, Olevianus is talking primarily about his abilities as a translator, not as a literary stylist. Whatever modesty or self-doubt might lie behind this phrase, it did not prevent him from producing translations of several French texts into German.[76]

Finally, Olevianus's longstanding displeasure with HC 36 could be interpreted not as an argument against his authorship of the catechism, as Hollweg does, but as an argument for the collaborative nature of the project. If Olevianus was part of a team of writers and if decisions about the finished form of the document were not in the hands of just one individual, it is hardly surprising that a member of the team might be unhappy with some of the final wording.

Ironically, Hollweg's case against Olevianus in 1961 was mitigated by some of his own later research. In the same volume in which he published the article challenging Olevianus's role as final redactor of the HC, he included another essay on the influence on the HC of two confessions by Theodore Beza, the *Confessio christianae fidei* (1559) and a shorter version of the confession, the *Altera brevis fidei confessio* (1559). In a 1968 response to critics of this essay, Hollweg added some fascinating new details to the story of Beza's two confessions and the HC—all involving Olevianus.[77] Hollweg had learned in a letter from Olevianus to Beza on April 10, 1561, that during Olevianus's imprisonment in Trier in 1559, he had been greatly consoled by Beza's "French confession" (presumably the shorter one). The letter also revealed that Olevianus very much wanted this

---

73. See the introduction to Olevianus, *Firm Foundation*, ed. Bierma, xviii-xxii, xxiv-xxv, and marginal notations in the text. Cf. also Goeters' comparison of the two catechisms in his commentary "Olevian's *Fester Grund*: Entstehung, Geschichte, Inhalt," in Olevian, *Der Gnadenbund Gottes 1590: Faksimile-Edition*, ed. Franz, Goeters, and Holtmann, 467-90, esp. 468, 470.

74. See Olevianus, *Firm Foundation*, ed. Bierma, xxvii-xxviii.

75. Gunnoe, "Erastus in Heidelberg," 123 n. 13.

76. "Catechismus tuus germanice prodit hisce nundinis bene conversus a Zacharia Ursino, qui me facultate linguae superat. . . . Omnia fideliter sunt reddita" (*Calvini opera*, 19:684). As we shall see below, Hollweg himself concluded that Olevianus was most likely the translator of the French version of Beza's *Altera brevis fidei confessio* in 1562. "Zur Quellenfrage des Heidelberger Katechismus," in *Neue Untersuchungen*, vol. 2 (1968), 38-47. Olevianus also translated a number of Calvin's sermons into German: *Vier Predigten* . . . (Herborn: Rab, 1586), and *Predigten H. Johannis Calvini über das buch Job*, 4 vols. (Herborn: Rab, 1587-88). See Goeters' "Bibliographia Oleviana," entries 15, 16 ("Olevianus als Theologe," 331).

77. Hollweg, "Zur Quellenfrage," 38-47.

confession translated into German but felt that such a project required "a better translator than I." Nevertheless, he committed himself to producing such a translation within the next eighteen months.[78] In 1562, less than a year after this letter to Beza, a German translation of the short confession was published in Heidelberg. Hollweg concluded that there could be little doubt that Olevianus was the translator. Moreover,

> this publication appeared at the very time that the people in Heidelberg were hard at work on the edition of the Heidelberg Catechism. It was done by the same Olevianus who was also busily working on the edition of the Heidelberg Catechism. Is it not obvious, then, that the man who was involved in both projects simultaneously was responsible for the insertion of key ideas from the confession into the catechism? Olevianus's great love for Beza's confession made it a source for the Heidelberg Catechism.[79]

There is yet another link, however, between Beza's confessions and Olevianus that Hollweg never mentioned, namely, the influence of these documents on Olevianus's own catechism, *A Firm Foundation*. In a number of places in FF, the echoes of either the *Confessio christianae fidei* (hereafter C) or the *Altera brevis fidei confessio* (hereafter Cb) can be clearly heard; for example, in the questions and answers on the mediator (FF 1, Cb 6; FF 6, C.III.20), the history of salvation (FF 2, Cb 12), the differences between law and gospel (FF 10, C.IV.22), the definition of faith (FF 12, Cb 19), the sufficiency of Christ as Savior (FF 157, C.IV.6), good works (FF 170, C.IV.19), and the two temptations of Satan (FF 165-77, C.IV.10-13).[80]

What bearing does all this have on the question of Olevianus's coauthorship? We have before us the following data: (1) At least one of Beza's confessions had made a deep impression on Olevianus during a personal crisis in Trier in 1559. (2) Olevianus was almost certainly the translator of the German edition of Cb in 1562. (3) As one of the church superintendents in Heidelberg, Olevianus was a member of the HC drafting committee in 1562. (4) Both C and Cb exerted a discernible influence on the HC.[81] (5) The influence of C and Cb on Olevianus's catechetical commentary on the HC is beyond question. Running through all these data are two common threads: a literary relationship among C/Cb, the HC, and FF and a personal connection between Olevianus and each one of these three documents. When these two threads are spliced, they suggest at the very least that Olevianus played a more significant role in the composition of the HC

---

78. Ibid., 39-41.

79. Ibid., 41.

80. For the citations from FF, see Olevianus, *A Firm Foundation*, ed. Bierma. For the citations from C, see the Latin text adopted (with minor alterations) by the Hungarian Reformed Church in 1562 and reprinted in E. F. K. Müller, *Die Bekenntnisschriften der reformierten Kirchen* (Leipzig: Deichert, 1903), 376-449. The German translation of Cb is found in Hollweg, "Die beiden Konfessionen Theodor von Bezas: Zwei bisher unbeachtete Quellen zum Heidelberger Katechismus," in *Neue Untersuchungen*, 111-23.

81. For evidence of this, see Hollweg, "Beiden Konfessionen," 86-110. We will take a closer look at this evidence in chapter 3.

than most recent scholarship has recognized. If he greatly admired the Bezan confessions, translated one of them into German around the very time that the HC team was at work, and blended some of their themes into his own catechetical commentary on the HC, is it not reasonable to suppose that, as a member of the HC committee and the one most familiar with the Bezan sources, it was also he who wove some of that Bezan material into the text of the HC itself? Hollweg, for one, certainly seems to think so.

In summary, there is indeed no solid evidence for the longstanding claims that Olevianus was one of two main authors of the HC or that he was responsible for the final German redaction. In that respect, Hollweg and others are correct. However, the critics have not presented convincing arguments that Olevianus could *not* have been the final redactor or could not have played a major part in the production of the HC. In fact, the many parallels among the HC, earlier confessions, and FF as well as the completion of FF no later than October 1563, point—circumstantially at least—to more than a minor role for Olevianus on the committee that drafted the HC.

The Role of Ursinus

Life. Zacharias Ursinus was born on July 18, 1534, in the Silesian city of Breslau, a commercial center on the Oder River in what today is Poland but at that time was part of Austria.[82] His father, Caspar Bär (Ursinus),[83] hailed from Neustadt, Austria, and after studying at the University of Vienna, eventually moved to Breslau as a tutor for the sons of a local patrician. He also served as a deacon of the St. Elizabeth Church, sometimes even substituting for one of the preachers, Ambrosius Moibanus, a moderate Melanchthonian who had helped to introduce the Protestant Reformation to Breslau in the 1520s. By the time Ursinus was born, therefore, the Reformation had made considerable progress in Breslau, and the Bär family was already Lutheran.

Young Ursinus attended the St. Elizabeth Gymnasium in Breslau, where he was a good student and completed his studies at the age of fifteen. While still in Breslau, he was probably catechized by Moibanus who, in 1533, had composed his own catechism for instruction of the youth. This catechism emphasized the comfort of the gospel, a thematic seed that probably came to flower in Ursinus's own Smaller Catechism and the Heidelberg Catechism many years later.[84]

---

82. This subsection on Ursinus's life is adapted from Klooster, *Heidelberg Catechism*, 119-28. Detailed biographical data on Ursinus can be found in Melchior Adam, *Vitae germanorum theologorum . . .* (Frankfurt: Rosae, 1653); Sudhoff, *Olevianus und Ursinus*; James I. Good, *The Heidelberg Catechism in Its Newest Light* (Philadelphia: Publication and Sunday School Board of the Reformed Church in the United States, 1914); G. Bouwmeester, *Zacharias Ursinus en de Heidelbergse Catechismus* (The Hague: Willem de Zwijgerstichting, 1954); Sturm, *Zacharias Ursinus*; Derk Visser, *Reluctant Reformer*; and den Hartogh, *Voorzienigheid in donker licht*, 8-23.

83. "Ursinus" is the Latinized form of the German family name Bär or Beer (bear).

84. For a review and analysis of the scholarly discussion of Moibanus's theological influence on Ursinus, see Good, *Heidelberg Catechism*, 80-101, and Visser, *Reluctant Reformer*, 35-38.

On April 30, 1550, fifteen-year-old Ursinus enrolled at Wittenberg University. Luther had died four years earlier, and Melanchthon, just past fifty, was now the leading spirit of the university. Part of the cost of Ursinus's education was covered by a grant from the Breslau City Council, which had stipulated that he return to the city as a teacher upon completion of his studies.

Although Ursinus did not take advantage of the opportunity to live at Melanchthon's house, he and his mentor did become friends and theological allies. When the Gnesio-Lutherans began to charge in the 1550s that Melanchthon was abandoning Luther's teaching and moving closer to Calvin, Ursinus, who fully shared his mentor's views,[85] wrote to his friend Crato:

> I am of the opinion that Dr. Philip teaches what is right, and has been fortunate enough to teach us in a holy and pure way, the real substance of the holy sacrament. Dr. Philip never swerves, but sticks to what is true, secure, important and necessary, never losing sight of what is sublime and divine. Personally, I do not hesitate to confess that I have benefited and learned more from his impressive method of teaching than from the vague commentaries of his opponents.[86]

After completing his studies in Wittenberg in 1557, Ursinus, now twenty-three, embarked on a study tour of the major centers of the Reformation to become acquainted with some of the leaders of the evangelical movement. His first stop was Worms in August 1557, where Melanchthon had asked Ursinus to join him at the religious colloquy to be held there. During the month of September, Ursinus listened to discussions between the Roman Catholic and Protestant participants in this historic city where Luther had made his courageous stand before the emperor in 1521. In October, Ursinus began an extended journey up the Rhine to Strasbourg and Basel, and then on to Zurich, Bern, Lausanne, and Geneva[87] where he met John Calvin and received a set of the reformer's works as a personal gift. From there, he made his way through France, stopping in Lyons, Orléans, and finally Paris, where he spent about four months to improve his French and attend lectures on the Hebrew language.

In April 1558, eight months after leaving Wittenberg, Ursinus began the return trip by way of Geneva, Zurich, and southern Germany. In Zurich, he became better acquainted with several prominent Swiss Reformed theologians, among them Heinrich Bullinger and the Italian Calvinist Peter Martyr Vermigli, who seems to have made the greatest theological impact on Ursinus. He took up

---

85. He once wrote that "when Philip [Melanchthon] has spoken, I cannot and dare not think otherwise." Letter to Crato (February 27, 1557), in Wilhelm Becker, "Zacharias Ursins Briefe an Crato von Crafftheim," *Theologische Arbeiten aus dem rheinischen wissenschaftlichen Prediger-Verein* 12 (1892): 58.

86. Letter to Crato (January 10, 1557), cited in Good, *Heidelberg Catechism*, 246. The original text of the entire letter is in Becker, "Ursins Briefe," 46-50.

87. For a reconstruction of this itinerary from various sources, see Sturm, *Zacharias Ursinus*, 105-10.

his studies once again in Wittenberg until September 1558, when the Breslau City Council called him to return as a professor at his alma mater, the St. Elizabeth School.

Ursinus was twenty-four when he began his professional career at the Breslau gymnasium. Assigned to teach classical languages and Christian doctrine, he delivered an inaugural lecture in September 1558 entitled "An Exhortation to the Study of Sacred Theology and Catechetical Doctrine,"[88] in which he urged the serious study of theology and emphasized the importance of catechizing:

> Neither is a catechism anything else than a summary declaration of such sentences of Scripture. Now this little book [Melanchthon's *Examination of Ordinands*[89]] we intend to propose to you is such, and its author has faithfully and with great dexterity comprehended the chief grounds of Christianity in proper and plain language. And it seems that it would be beneficial that in other churches there should be a like form of catechism extant. Prepare yourselves to learn it speedily.[90]

However, Ursinus's enthusiasm about Melanchthon's catechism, his use of it as a textbook in the gymnasium, and his relationships with several leading Reformed theologians soon brought him under suspicion.[91] Breslau had been predominantly Melanchthonian during Ursinus's study in Wittenberg, but by 1558 there were several Gnesio-Lutheran ministers in the city. These ministers soon charged that Ursinus was not a genuine Lutheran but a "sacramentarian," especially because he supported Melanchthon's rejection of Christ's bodily presence in the Eucharistic elements. To explain more fully his position on the sacraments and to defend himself against the charges of the Gnesio-Lutherans, Ursinus prepared "123 Theses . . . on the Sacraments" in 1559—fifty-one propositions on the sacraments in general, twelve on baptism, and sixty on the Lord's Supper.[92] Much of the content had been derived from Melanchthon, but the arrangement and form of the theses so impressed Melanchthon that he informed a friend of Ursinus's that he had "never seen anything so brilliant as in this work."[93]

88. Latin title: "Paranesis ad S. Theologiae, Catecheticaeque doctrinae studium," in Ursinus, *Opera theologica*, 1:3-9.

89. *Examen ordinandorum*, a catechetical textbook composed by Melanchthon in 1552 for instructing ministerial candidates.

90. "Paranesis," in Ursinus, *Opera theologica*, 1:9; English translation (which I have revised slightly) in Good, *Heidelberg Catechism*, 249.

91. This account of Ursinus's experiences in Breslau from 1558 until his departure in 1560 follows the interpretation developed by Adam, Sudhoff, Gillet, Sturm et al. See Visser (*Reluctant Reformer*, 62-98) for a review of this line of argument and for an alternative view that "no evidence exists that Ursinus openly took sides in the controversies on the Eucharist" (Visser, *Reluctant Reformer*, 72).

92. Zacharias Ursinus, "Theses complectentes breviter et perspicue summam verae Doctrinae de Sacramentis," in *Zacharias Ursini . . . volumen tractationum theologicarum* (Neustadt: n.p., 1584), 1:339-82; also in Ursinus, *Opera theologica*, 1:766-802.

93. According to Sudhoff (*Olevianus und Ursinus*, 5), this reaction by Melanchthon is reported in a letter Ursinus received from his friend Ferinarius.

Tensions between the two Lutheran parties in Breslau and ongoing controversy over what constituted adiaphora in the Mass[94] finally led Ursinus on April 26, 1560, to seek a leave of absence from his post so as to further his studies. The city council agreed on the condition that he return when they called him back to service. But where would he go? Melanchthon had died just a week earlier, depriving Wittenberg of much of its attraction. Moreover, in many of the German cities Melanchthon's enemies held sway. Ursinus decided upon Zurich. After a brief stop in Wittenberg, where friends urged him to stay and join the university faculty, he made his way to Zurich, where he arrived on October 3 to take up studies with Peter Martyr Vermigli. He never returned to Breslau.

Ursinus spent a fruitful year in Zurich studying with the "pious, great, and learned men" he had referred to earlier, especially Vermigli. Back in Germany, meanwhile, Frederick III was inviting Melanchthonian and Reformed personnel to assist him with his reformation of the Palatinate. Friends had recommended Ursinus to the Heidelberg authorities, and, by July 1561, Ursinus had accepted an invitation to go to Heidelberg. He did have some misgivings about the decision; in words reminiscent of Calvin's reluctance to leave Basel for Geneva, he wrote, "Oh, that I could remain hidden in a corner. I would give anything for shelter in some quiet village."[95] Nevertheless, he made the journey north and arrived in Heidelberg on September 9, 1561.

His initial responsibilities in Heidelberg included preaching and serving as rector and teacher at the Sapience College, a former monastery and university preparatory school that Frederick III had converted into a pastoral training school. Ursinus was not yet married, and he lived in the college with the approximately one hundred student boarders under his charge. On October 13, 1561, he also matriculated as a doctoral student in the university.

Upon receiving his doctorate in theology the next year, he was promoted to professor of dogmatics at the university on August 25, replacing Caspar Olevianus, who became minister of St. Peter's Church (and later of the Holy Spirit Church) in Heidelberg and a church administrator for the Palatinate. Sometime after September 1, 1562, Ursinus began a course of lectures on dogmatics at the university that lasted until he relinquished his teaching post there to Jerome Zanchius in 1568.[96] In addition, he devoted time to the writing of several catechisms: first, the Smaller Catechism (*Catechesis minor*) in 1562, likely intended for children and the laity;[97] then the Larger Catechism, the so-called

---

94. For a detailed discussion of this controversy, see Visser, *Reluctant Reformer*, 82-95.

95. Letter to Crato (July 27, 1561), in Becker, "Ursins Briefe," 79-86.

96. This incomplete set of loci lectures was published as "Summa religionis christianae" in Ursinus, *Tractationum theologicarum*, 1:1-338.

97. Zacharias Ursinus, "Catechesis, hoc est, rudimenta religionis christianae," in Ursinus, *Tractationum theologicarum*, 1:620-51; also published as "Catechesis minor, perspicua brevitate christianam fidem complectens," in Ursinus, *Opera theologica*, 1:34-39, and in Lang, *Heidelberger Katechismus*, 200-18.

Catechesis maior,[98] also composed in 1562 probably as a guide for his teaching at the university.[99] The most significant single contribution he made during his Heidelberg days, however, was to the Heidelberg Catechism. As we shall see in the next section, much of the work on the HC apparently fell to Ursinus, and much of the rest of his life would be linked with this document.

Authorship of the Catechism. The most compelling case against Caspar Olevianus as the final redactor of the HC has been made not with arguments *against* Olevianus, as Hollweg tried to do, but with arguments *for* Ursinus in that role. Hollweg concluded that one person must have been responsible for crafting the final text of the HC, but he was not able to say who it was. The scholarly consensus since then is that that person was in all likelihood Zacharias Ursinus.[100] Because we lack firsthand evidence, this, too, is a circumstantial case, but it is a stronger one than can be made for Olevianus. It can be summarized in six points.[101]

In the first place, Ursinus, unlike anyone else on the HC committee, was involved with catechesis throughout his entire academic career. As we saw in the preceding section, in his inaugural lecture in Breslau in 1558, entitled "An Exhortation to the Study of Sacred Theology and Catechetical Doctrine," he emphasized the importance of catechizing and commended the catechism he was about to use in his own classroom, Melanchthon's *Examination of Ordinands*. In his early teaching in Heidelberg, he made use of the Strasbourg Catechism at the Sapience College,[102] and of his own LC at the Sapience College and the university. Once the HC was published in 1563, he became its chief interpreter, lecturing on it regularly in both Heidelberg and Neustadt until his death twenty years later. Numerous versions and editions of these lectures were published

98. Zacharinas Ursinus, "Catechesis, Summa Theologiae, per quaestiones et responsiones exposita: sive capita religionis Christianae continens," in Ursinus, *Opera theologica*, 1:10-33; also in Lang, *Heidelberger Katechismus*, 152-99.

99. Sturm, *Zacharias Ursinus*, 238-41, 253; C. Graafland, *Van Calvijn tot Comrie: Oorsprong en ontwikkeling van de leer van het verbond in het Gereformeerd Protestantisme* (Zoetermeer: Boekencentrum, 1994), 2:13-14.

100. Goeters, "Entstehung," 15, 17; Joachim Staedtke, "Entstehung und Bedeutung des Heidelberger Katechismus," in *Warum Wirst Du Ein Christ Genannt?*, ed. W. Herrenbruck and U. Smidt (Neukirchen-Vluyn: Neukirchener Verlag, 1965), 130; Otto Weber, "Analytische Theologie," ibid., 130; Wulf Metz, *Necessitas satisfactionis? Eine systematische Studie zu den Fragen 12-18 des Heidelberger Katechismus und zur Theologie des Zacharias Ursinus* (Zurich: Zwingli-Verlag, 1970), 63-69; Gustav A. Benrath, "Zacharias Ursinus als Mensch, Christ und Theologe," *Reformierte Kirchenzeitung* 124 (1983): 155; Walter Henss, *Der Heidelberger Katechismus im konfessionspolitischen Kräftespiel seiner Frühzeit* (Zurich: Theologischer Verlag, 1983), 27-28, 44; Klooster, "Priority of Ursinus," 76, 97.

101. For these and several additional arguments, see Klooster, "Priority of Ursinus," 89-97.

102. Sehling, *Die evangelischen Kirchenordnungen*, 14:40.

throughout Europe after his death.[103] From the beginning to the end of his academic life, therefore, Ursinus employed catechisms in his doctrinal instruction of students.

Second, Ursinus composed two catechisms of his own, at least one of which served as a major source for the HC. His Larger Catechism (*Summa theologiae*, or *Catechesis maior*), consisting of 323 questions and answers, was long thought to be composed before the SC as a preliminary draft of the HC. As Sturm has pointed out, however, Ursinus's comments in his inaugural lecture at Heidelberg University in September 1562 suggest that he wrote the LC after the SC and as an instructional text for his students at the Sapience College and the university.[104] Nevertheless, parts of it are found or reflected in the HC. The Smaller Catechism (*Catechesis minor*) of 1562 brings us into the immediate vicinity of the HC, since around 90 of the HC's 129 questions and answers are based on it. Lang and Neuser maintained that the SC itself was a team project, but Sturm has made a more compelling case for Ursinus as sole author.[105]

Third, Ursinus was involved in more than the teaching and writing of catechisms; he also translated Calvin's Genevan Catechism (1541) from French into German around the very time the HC was being composed. In his letter to Calvin on April 3, 1563, Olevianus reported that "on this market day your catechism is coming out in German, well translated by Zacharias Ursinus."[106] Because of the considerable influence of the Genevan Catechism on Ursinus's LC[107] and the relationship between the LC and the HC, Ursinus's translating of Calvin's work may point to his unique role in the production of the HC as well.

A fourth consideration is the fact that in August 1563 Ursinus replaced Olevianus in preaching the catechism sermon on Sunday afternoons. As pastor of the Holy Spirit Church, Olevianus had been responsible for these sermons after the HC was published in January 1563, but seven months later the task was turned over to Ursinus. Why? Ursinus already had plenty to do, having earlier replaced Olevianus as head of the Sapience College and professor of dogmatics at

103. Zacharias Ursinus, *Doctrinae christianae compendium* (Geneva, Leiden, 1584; Cambridge, 1585; London, 1586; Neustadt, 1587); and Zacharias Ursinus, *Explicationum catecheticarum* (Neustadt, 1585; Cambridge, 1587) were early versions of Ursinus's commentary on the HC based on student lecture notes. David Pareus (1548-1622), Ursinus's former student, spent a lifetime revising and publishing a number of editions of Ursinus's HC commentary under three different titles: *Explicationum catecheticarum*, which appeared in at least seven editions from 1591-1608 and was also included as *Explicationes catecheseos* in the first volume of Reuter's *Ursini . . . opera theologica* (Heidelberg, 1612); *Corpus doctrinae orthodoxae* (1612, 1616); and *Corpus doctrinae Christianae* (1621, 1623, 1634, 1651). According to T. D. Smid, the editions of 1634 and 1651 are without a doubt the most reliable. "Bibliographische Opmerkingen over de *Explicationes catecheticae* van Zacharias Ursinus," *Gereformeerd Theologisch Tijdschrift* 41 (1940): 241. The best English translation is G. W. Williard, *The Commentary of Dr. Zacharias Ursinus on the Heidelberg Catechism* (Cincinnati: Bucher, 1851; reprint, Grand Rapids: Eerdmans, 1954).

104. Sturm, *Zacharias Ursinus*, 239-41; den Hartogh, *Voorzienigheid in donker licht*, 37.

105. Lang, *Heidelberger Katechismus*, LXXVIII; Neuser, "Die Erwählungslehre im Heidelberger Katechismus," *Zeitschrift für Kirchengeschichte* 75 (1964): 311; Sturm, *Zacharias Ursinus*, 246-48.

106. See n. 76 above.

107. Lang, *Heidelberger Katechismus* LXVI.

the university. In a letter to Crato near the end of August 1563, he complained about an intolerable workload. Previously, he had had to prepare and deliver four lectures per week, which he found difficult to do; now he not only had an additional lecture but also at three o'clock every Sunday afternoon had to preach on the Heidelberg Catechism.[108] Was the catechism preaching transferred to Ursinus because Olevianus was too busy working on the new church order? Or could it have been because Ursinus had a more intimate role in composing the catechism and was therefore better equipped to explain it in the Sunday afternoon service? The latter is certainly plausible.

Ursinus became not only the chief expositor of the HC but also, in the fifth place, its chief apologist. It was to him primarily, though not exclusively, that Frederick III entrusted the task of officially defending the catechism against its Roman Catholic and Lutheran critics—especially Brenz, Andreae, Illyricus, and Hesshus. During 1564, Ursinus published three tracts in defense of the HC: (1) *Antwort auff etlicher Theologen Censur uber die am rand dess Heydelbergischen Catechismi auss heiliger Schrifft angezogene zeugnusse*, a refutation of attacks on the HC by the Württemberg theologians; (2) *Gründtlicher Bericht vom heiligen Abendmahl . . .* , which dealt primarily with the Lord's Supper; and most important of all, (3) *Verantwortung wider die ungegründten aufflagen unnd verkerungen, mit welchen der Catechismus Christlicher lere . . . von etlichen unbillicher weise beschweret ist.* The latter two he actually composed on behalf of the entire theological faculty, under whose name they were published.[109]

Ursinus's involvement in the teaching, translating, and writing of related catechisms before the HC and in the exposition and defense of the HC after its appearance all point, albeit circumstantially, to his priority in its composition. A final consideration, however, has to do with the HC not as an instructional and homiletical guide but as a confessional document. If, as we have noted, Frederick III commissioned the HC in part to achieve a doctrinal consensus among the major Protestant parties in Heidelberg, then he could hardly have found a more suitable author than Ursinus. Not only was Ursinus of the same irenic temperament as the elector, but also his theological pilgrimage had exposed him to the very theological traditions he was now being called upon to reconcile. Ideologically, as well as geographically, he had made his way to Heidelberg via Wittenberg, Zurich, and Geneva. At each stop, he had studied with some of the leading lights of the day: Melanchthon in Wittenberg, Bullinger and Martyr in Zurich, and Calvin and Beza in Geneva—most of whom left their mark on his thinking.[110] No one among the theology professors and major churchmen of

108. Kluckhohn, *Briefe*, 1:443.

109. Henss, *Heidelberger Katechismus*, 44-45.

110. For the influences on Ursinus's early theology, see Sturm, *Zacharias Ursinus*, 1-3, passim; Lang, *Heidelberger Katechismus*, LXIVff.; Benrath, "Die Eigenart der Pfälzischen Reformation und die Vorgeschichte des Heidelberger Katechismus," *Heidelberger Jahrbücher* 7 (1963): 24-26; and Neuser, "Väter des Heidelberger Katechismus," 181ff. Regarding Ursinus's mature theology, Richard A. Muller concludes that "in the years between 1563 and 1577 Ursinus . . . produced a synthesis of Reformed theology with the established scholastic method, related in its central motifs

Heidelberg had had this firsthand exposure to the range of theological views now represented in the Palatinate. Would not someone whose own theology had been shaped in the major centers of Philippist, Zwinglian, and Calvinist thought be in the best position to prepare a consensus formula that would bridge these three traditions in Heidelberg? From Frederick's point of view, one would think, Ursinus was the most logical choice to serve as the primary author of the HC.

In conclusion, then, it seems clear that the HC was in some sense a team project involving the leading theologians and church officials of the Palatinate and, in no small way, Elector Frederick III himself. Nevertheless, one person very likely had primary responsibility for the final draft. The organization of the traditional elements of catechesis—creed, law, prayer, and sacraments—under a central theme, and the careful linking of each question to the ones that precede and follow it point to a single literary craftsman of considerable skill. Little evidence exists to suggest that this person was Olevianus, although his role on the committee was probably not as minimal as many today would have us believe. The preponderance of circumstantial evidence points toward one person in that role—Zacharias Ursinus.

not only to the thought of Calvin but also to the theology of Bullinger, Vermigli, [and] Musculus, and to that of Luther, Melanchthon, and Bucer." *Christ and the Decree: Christology and Predestination in Reformed Theology from Calvin to Perkins* (Durham, N. C., 1986), 124.

3

The Sources and Theological Orientation of the Heidelberg Catechism

Lyle D. Bierma

It has long been recognized that the authors of the HC used a variety of earlier catechisms and other sources in the preparation of their new confessional standard. Little agreement has been reached, however, about the identity of those earlier works or about the influence they had on the general theological orientation of the catechism. So far as textual dependence is concerned, scholars as far back as Reuter and Alting in the seventeenth century noted that the most direct source of the HC was Ursinus's own Smaller Catechism (SC), and to a lesser extent his Larger Catechism (LC).[1] Parts or all of some 90 of the HC's 129 questions and answers can be traced to the text of the SC, and there are linguistic parallels to the LC as well.[2]

However, when it comes to the sources that underlie the SC, the LC, and those sections of the HC not dependent on Ursinus's earlier catechisms, several hypotheses have been proposed. In the late nineteenth century, Gooszen suggested a connection between the HC and *nine* other catechisms by laying the text of the HC next to parallel questions and answers from not only the SC and LC but also two catechisms by Leo Jud, one by Bullinger, Calvin's Genevan Catechism, and three of the London-Emden catechisms by à Lasco and Micronius.[3] Building on Gooszen's research, August Lang, nearly twenty years later, broadened the scope of the investigation to include yet another catechism by à Lasco as well as the Strasbourg catechisms of Bucer and Zell. He then highlighted in painstaking detail the linguistic similarities between the HC and numerous other works.[4] More recently, it has been suggested that we also take into account catechisms by Brenz (Bard Thompson), Beza (Walter Hollweg),

---

1. See in this volume chapter 2, nn. 15, 47.
2. For a detailed textual comparison of the HC with Ursinus's Smaller and Larger Catechisms, see the introduction by August Lang, *Der Heidelberger Katechismus und vier verwandte Katechismen* (Leipzig: Deichert, 1907), LXXXVII-XCVI. Cf. also the cross-references in the notes to the translation of the Smaller and Larger Catechisms in chapter 6 of this volume.
3. Gooszen, "Catechismus," in *Heidelbergsche Catechismus*, 1-241.
4. Lang, *Heidelberger Katechismus*, I-CIV, esp. LXXXVII-XCVI.

Melanchthon (Hollweg), and Luther (Wilhelm Neuser).[5] None of these scholars apportioned the influence of the older catechisms in quite the same way, but, as Thompson's conclusion illustrates, they detected a multiplicity of sources beneath the text of the HC:

> Of 129 questions in the *Heidelberg Catechism*, considerably more than half were taken from existing catechetical works. Of that number, 35 at very least must be attributed to à Lasco's catechisms. Perhaps ten can be traced directly to Calvin; five to Brenz's *Landescatechismus*. More significant, the catechisms of à Lasco contributed the formative questions—on comfort (1, 21, 26, 31, 53, 54), faith (21), atonement (37), church (54), Creed, Commandments and Lord's Prayer. And the four questions which teach election as a source of comfort (1, 31, 53, 54) were all taken from à Lasco's works.[6]

No less debated has been the general theological slant or orientation of the HC. That discussion was triggered in the second half of the nineteenth century by three figures in particular: Heinrich Heppe, who identified the catechism as uniquely "deutsch-evangelisch," or Melanchthonian; Karl Sudhoff, who considered it Calvinist in origin and expression; and Maurits Gooszen, who traced the primary influence on the catechism to neither Melanchthon nor Calvin but to what he called the "original Reformed Protestantism" of Zwingli and Bullinger in Zurich.[7]

Since then little consensus has emerged. Some have continued to apply a single theological label to the catechism. Dahlmann, for example, found an irenic spirit in the HC but at the same time "a clear, definite and popular statement of Reformed doctrine over against Lutheranism."[8] Lang, who, as we have seen, recognized multiple influences on the HC, maintained that "in its characteristic features, the Heidelberg Catechism is not Lutheran, nor Melanchthonian, nor Zwinglian, nor Bullingerian, nor Bucerian, but Calvinistic."[9] Klooster, too, could

---

5. Bard Thompson, "The Palatinate Church Order of 1563," *Church History* 23, no. 4 (December 1954): 339-54; Hollweg, "Beiden Konfessionen," 111-23; idem, "Zur Quellenfrage," 42-47; Neuser, "Väter des Heidelberger Katechismus," 181-82.

6. Thompson, "Palatinate Church Order," 347.

7. Heinrich Heppe, *Geschichte des deutschen Protestantismus in den Jahren 1555-1581* (Marburg: Elwert, 1852), 1:446 n. 2; Sudhoff, *Olevianus und Ursinus*, 113-18; Gooszen, "Inleiding," in *Heidelbergsche Catechismus*, 10, 149-50, 155-56; idem, *De Heidelbergsche Catechismus en Het Boekje van de Breking des Broods, in het Jaar 1563-1564 Bestreden en Verdedigd* (Leiden: Brill, 1892), 276, 331-32, 401, 406, 408-9, 411.

8. A. E. Dahlmann, "The Theology of the Heidelberg Catechism," *The Reformed Church Review*, 4th ser., 17 (April 1913): 176.

9. Lang, "The Religious and Theological Character of the Heidelberg Catechism," *The Reformed Church Review*, 4th ser., 18 (October 1914): 462.

describe the HC as an "original tapestry marvelously woven"[10] from a variety of catechetical threads, but in its general disposition and many of its features it was "thoroughly Calvinistic."[11]

Others, however, have found in the HC a juxtaposition of two or more Reformation traditions. According to Neuser, one can pick up in the text the distinct voices of at least four "fathers" of the HC: Luther, Melanchthon, Calvin, and Zwingli and his followers, with Calvin's voice by far the strongest.[12] In Schnucker's view, the HC "espouses Reformed theology as dictated by Frederick III, but Lutheran ideas were not slighted."[13] Verboom concluded that although the HC can be considered "authentically Reformed," one finds within it a combination of some of the characteristic views of several major reformers, such as Melanchthon (on law), Bullinger (on covenant), and Calvin (on creation).[14]

Finally, there are those who refrain from attaching traditional theological labels to the HC because they see the catechism either as a unique alloy of different Protestant traditions or as an "ecumenical" statement of theological consensus. Goeters, for example, understood the HC in its broadest terms as an amalgamation (*Verschmelzung*) of Melanchthonianism and Calvinism into a third theological type that he termed "German Reformed."[15] McCord, Lekkerkerker, and Hageman all traced the theology of the HC to a variety of influences but in the end regarded it as essentially an ecumenical confession, not favoring any one of the traditions that gave it nurture. The genius of Ursinus, says Hageman, was that in a fresh and original way he incorporated into the HC the theological essentials that bridged several Protestant traditions while omitting most of the issues that divided them. Ursinus's work was not broadly ecumenical in the contemporary understanding of the term, but it was Reformation ecumenism at its best.[16]

Perhaps the best way to evaluate these divergent views of the sources and theology of the HC is to start not with the text of the HC, as so many in the past have done, but with a brief review of the historical context. As we saw in earlier chapters, Elector Frederick commissioned the HC in 1562 as a confession for the

10. Klooster, *Heidelberg Catechism*, 177.

11. Klooster, *Our Only Comfort: A Comprehensive Commentary on the Heidelberg Catechism*, 2 vols. (Grand Rapids: Faith Alive, 2001), 1:46. Cf. also idem, *A Mighty Comfort: The Christian Faith according to the Heidelberg Catechism* (Grand Rapids: CRC Publications, 1990), 35-37.

12. Neuser, "Väter des Heidelberger Katechismus," 177-99.

13. Robert V. Schnucker, *Evangelical Dictionary of Theology*, s.v. "Heidelberg Catechism."

14. Willem Verboom, *De Theologie van de Heidelbergse Catechismus* (Zoetermeer: Boekencentrum, 1996), 24-25. Jan Rohls, too, finds in the HC an "integration of very diverse doctrines." *Reformed Confessions: Theology from Zurich to Barmen*, trans. John Hoffmeyer, Columbia Series in Reformed Theology (Louisville: Westminster John Knox, 1997), 20.

15. J. F. Goeters, "Christologie und Rechtfertigung nach dem Heidelberger Katechismus," in *Das Kreuz Jesu Christi als Grund des Heils*, ed. Ernst Bizer (Gütersloh: Mohn, 1967), 34.

16. James I. McCord, "The Heidelberg Catechism: An Ecumenical Confession," *The Princeton Seminary Bulletin* 56, no. 2 (February 1963): 13-14; A. F. N. Lekkerkerker, *Gespreken over de Heidelberger* (Wageningen: Zomer & Keunings, 1964), 24-26; Howard Hageman, "The Lasting Significance of Ursinus," in *Controversy and Conciliation: The Reformation and the Palatinate 1559-1583*, ed. Derk Visser (Allison Park, Pa.: Pickwick, 1986), 229-30.

Palatinate, a territory that already in the 1540s had begun to shift its official religion from Roman Catholicism to Lutheranism. According to the Peace of Augsburg (1555), all non-Catholic princes and territories of the German Empire were required to adhere to Lutheranism as defined by the Augsburg Confession; no other varieties of Protestantism were permitted. In designing a new catechism for the Palatinate, therefore, Frederick III found himself in a delicate position. How could he as a Lutheran elector confessionally repudiate certain Gnesio-Lutheran doctrines that he found objectionable and unify the Melanchthonian-Lutheran, Calvinist, and Zwinglian factions in his realm without straying outside the bounds of the Augsburg Confession and thus violating the terms of the Peace of Augsburg? His answer was the HC.

Given the context in which the catechism was written, therefore, we should not be surprised if we do not find in the text either an apology for a distinctive brand of sixteenth-century Protestantism or a broad ecumenical consensus in the modern sense of the term. What we should expect to find, and do indeed find, is a more limited theological consensus that fits within the framework of the Augsburg Confession. In other words, what we find in the HC is doctrinal outer boundaries, on the one hand, and common ground and key silences within those boundaries, on the other.

Outer Boundaries

The HC may indeed have been "the most irenic and catholic expression of the Christian faith to come out of the Reformation,"[17] but it is not free from polemics altogether. First of all, there is a decidedly anti-Roman Catholic tone throughout the document, expressed most explicitly in HC 80:

Q. How does the Lord's Supper differ from the Roman Catholic Mass?

A. The Lord's Supper declares to us that our sins have been completely forgiven through the one sacrifice of Jesus Christ which he himself finished on the cross once for all. It also declares to us that the Holy Spirit grafts us into Christ, who with his very body is now in heaven at the right hand of the Father where he wants us to worship him.

But the Mass teaches that the living and the dead do not have their sins forgiven through the suffering of Christ unless Christ is still offered for them daily by the priest. It also teaches that Christ is bodily present in the form of bread and wine where Christ is therefore to be worshiped.

Thus the Mass is basically nothing but a denial of the one sacrifice and suffering of Jesus Christ and a condemnable idolatry.[18]

17. I. John Hesselink, "The Dramatic Story of the Heidelberg Catechism," in *Later Calvinism: International Perspectives*, ed. W. Fred Graham (Kirksville, Mo.: Sixteenth Century Journal Publishers, 1994), 288.
18. All quotations from the HC in this chapter follow the 1975 English translation by the Christian Reformed Church in North America in *Ecumenical Creeds and Reformed Confessions*

HC 80 did not appear in the first edition of the HC but was added at the elector's behest to the second and (in slightly expanded form) third German editions of 1563, quite possibly in response to the strong anti-Protestant statement on the Mass adopted by the Council of Trent in late 1562.[19]

Nowhere else does the HC mention Roman Catholics by name, but the repudiation of such things as trust in saints (HC 30, 94), justification by good works (62-64), baptismal regeneration (72), transubstantiation (78), and worship of images (97, 98) clearly has Roman Catholic doctrine and practice in mind. In fact, the questions posed at the beginning of HC 63, 64, and 98 really function as objections to Protestant teaching that might be raised by theological opponents, opponents whom Ursinus later identifies in his commentary as "Papists."[20] In addition, there are less explicit anti-Catholic elements in HC 1, 8, 13, 18, 29, 34, 40, 44, 60, 61, 66-68, 83-85, 91, 102, 110, 126, and perhaps others. Like so many confessional documents of the Reformation era, including the Augsburg Confession, the HC defines Protestant teaching in part by the way in which it is not Catholic.

An unnamed target of the HC on the other side of the theological spectrum is the Anabaptist tradition. This is most obvious at the end of the HC's treatment of baptism (HC 69-74), where the addition of a separate question on the legitimacy of paedobaptism and a defense of it in the answer (HC 74) would hardly have been necessary had it not been for the challenge posed by sixteenth-century Anabaptists. Anabaptist teaching is almost certainly in view also in the HC's exposition of the third commandment, which includes a separate question and answer on the permissibility of oath-swearing (HC 101), and in several references to the legitimate authority of the civil government and the Christian's duty of submission to it (HC 101, 104, 105).

Apart from HC 80, however, some of the most polemical material in the catechism is reserved for the Gnesio-Lutheran doctrine of the ubiquity or omnipresence of Christ's human nature. This doctrine, which Luther had employed already in the 1520s to support his belief in the real presence of Christ's humanity in the Lord's Supper, was elevated to confessional status in Brenz's Stuttgart Confession in Württemberg in 1559, thus driving an even deeper wedge

(Grand Rapids: CRC Publications, 1988), 13-77. In some cases, I have slightly altered the translation to conform more closely to the original German text, which can be found in Lang, *Heidelberger Katechismus*, 2-52.

19. In a letter from Olevianus to Calvin on April 3, 1563, Olevianus writes that "in the first German edition . . . the question on the difference between the Lord's Supper and the papal Mass was omitted" but that "after some urging on my part [*admonitus a me*], the elector decided that it should be added to the second German and first Latin editions" (*Calvini Opera*, 19:684). It is not clear from this letter why HC 80 was omitted from the first edition. Nor is it clear who exactly was responsible for the wording. The fact that it was Olevianus who urged the elector to add this material may indicate that Olevianus was himself the composer.

20. Zacharas Ursinus, *The Commentary of Dr. Zacharias Ursinus on the Heidelberg Catechism*, trans. G. W. Williard (1852; reprint, Grand Rapids: Eerdmans, 1954), 334, 336, 530.

between the Gnesio-Lutherans, on the one hand, and Philippist (Melanchthonian) Lutherans, Calvinists, and Zwinglians, on the other. [21]

Given Frederick III's growing disillusionment with Gnesio-Lutheranism during the course of his reign, it is not surprising that on the issue of ubiquity the HC sides with the Melanchthonians and the Reformed. After just a single question on the resurrection of Christ (45), the catechism devotes no fewer than four questions (46-49) to his ascension, a doctrine that focuses on the status and whereabouts of Christ's human nature. According to HC 46, when we recite the clause in the Apostles' Creed "He ascended to heaven," we mean that Christ "was lifted up from the earth to heaven and will be there for our good until he comes again to judge the living and the dead." But if Christ is "there" in heaven, how can he fulfill his promise to be here with us until the end of the world (Q 47)? At this point, the catechism explicitly rejects the ubiquity doctrine by stating that "in his human nature Christ is not now on earth"; he is present with us only by his "divinity, majesty, grace, and Spirit" (A 47). Question 48 then anticipates the charge that this is tantamount to the ancient Nestorian heresy, which tended to divide the two natures of Christ: "If his humanity is not present wherever his divinity is, then aren't the two natures of Christ separated from each other?" Answer 48 responds with the so-called *extra Calvinisticum* teaching: "Christ's divinity is surely beyond the bounds [Latin: *extra*] of the humanity he has taken on" but that "at the same time his divinity is in and remains personally united to his humanity." This does not present a barrier to our eating and drinking the body and blood of Christ at the Lord's Supper, for "although he is in heaven and we are on the earth," at the Supper "we are united more and more to Christ's blessed body" through the Holy Spirit (HC 76). [22]

That still leaves the question of whether such an anti-Lutheran stance falls outside the bounds of the Augsburg Confession. As Winter has noted, however, the Augsburger says no more than that the two natures of Christ are "inseparably joined together in unity of person" (Art. 3). To be sure, underneath that text lie unstated suppositions of Luther's Christology that are at odds with the HC's *extra Calvinisticum*, but the affirmation in HC 48 that "his divinity is in and remains personally united to his humanity" is, on the surface at least, in full compliance with the wording of Augsburg Confession Art. 3. [23] Indeed, when Frederick III had to defend his allegiance to the HC before the emperor at the Diet of Augsburg in 1566, Elector August of Saxony supported him by arguing that on this point the

21. For a comprehensive treatment of the historical background to this doctrine and of the HC's treatment of it, see Klooster, *Our Only Comfort*, 1:592-623.

22. Note the similar language in A 80, which some have understood as an attack on the Lutheran as well as Roman Catholic doctrine of the Eucharist. See, e.g., Ulrich Asendorf, "Luther's Small Catechism and the Heidelberg Catechism," in *Luther's Catechisms—450 Years: Essays Commemorating the Small and Large Catechisms of Dr. Martin Luther*, ed. David P. Scaer and Robert D. Preus (Fort Wayne: Concordia Theological Seminary, 1979), 6.

23. Friedrich Winter, *Confessio Augustana und Heidelberger Katechismus in vergleichender Betrachtung* (Berlin: Evangelische Verlagsanstalt, 1954), 70-71. For the text of Art. 3, see "The Augsburg Confession," in *The Creeds of Christendom: With a History and Critical Notes*, ed. Philip Schaff, vol. 3, *The Evangelical Protestant Creeds* (1931; reprint, Grand Rapids: Baker, 1990), 9.

HC had no more strayed beyond the Augsburg Confession than had Brenz's Gnesio-Lutheran Stuttgart Confession in 1559.[24] Both could be regarded as different interpretations of the same confessional text.

Common Ground

Between the boundaries formed by various Roman Catholic and Gnesio-Lutheran teachings on one side of the spectrum and several Anabaptist tenets on the other, the HC forges a remarkable consensus by highlighting common theological ground among the followers of Zwingli and Bullinger, Calvin, and Melanchthon. This can be illustrated in a number of places in the HC, but we shall limit ourselves to four—the threefold structure of the catechism, the theme of gratitude in part 3, the uses of the law in parts 1 and 3, and the doctrine of the sacraments in part 2—all of which have been appealed to as evidence of the HC's espousal of a particular branch of Protestantism:

Threefold Structure

One of the best-known distinguishing features of the HC is its threefold structure, outlined in HC 2:

Q. How many things must you know to live and die happily in this comfort?

A. Three things: first, how great my sin and misery are; second, how I am delivered from all my sin and misery; and third, how I am to be thankful to God for such deliverance.

The most likely source of this question and answer is, of course, not difficult to identify. It follows closely the wording of the so-called *Catechesis minor*, or Smaller Catechism, probably composed by Zacharias Ursinus as a preparatory document for the HC sometime in 1562. SC 3 reads as follows:

Q. What does God's word teach?

A. First, it shows us our misery; second, how we are delivered from it; and third, what thanks must be given to God for this deliverance.[25]

Like HC 2, this answer serves to introduce the major divisions of the catechism to follow.

What, then, were the roots of the SC's tripartite structure? Gooszen was the first to propose an answer when he suggested that we look to Philip Melanchthon, who had long exercised an influence on the Palatinate and on Ursinus, his former student in Wittenberg. Noting a similarity in structure between the SC and Melanchthon's first edition of the *Loci communes theologici* of 1521, Gooszen traced the ultimate source of this design to Paul's Epistle to the

---

24. Klooster, *Heidelberg Catechism*, 97.
25. For the Latin text of the SC, see Lang, *Heidelberger Katechismus*, 200-218. For the English translation, see ch. 6 of this work.

Romans, whose main themes had provided the inspiration for Melanchthon's *Loci* in the first place. Romans proceeds from a treatment of human sin (chs. 1:18-3:20) to the great drama of redemption (3:21-11:36) to the thankful life of the Christian (12:1-16:27), and it was the Melanchthonian adaptation of this Pauline arrangement, Gooszen argued, that had the most direct influence on the structure of the SC and, subsequently, on the structure of the HC itself.[26]

Gooszen's thesis found its supporters well into the twentieth century,[27] but it underwent an important adjustment in 1904 at the hands of Johann Reu. Reu drew attention to an anonymous summary of Christian doctrine published in Regensburg in 1547 and reprinted in Heidelberg in 1558. The treatise included a forward by the Gnesio-Lutheran Nicholas Gallus, a former student of Melanchthon's who had later become a strong critic of his teacher's theology. What is so remarkable about this document is not only its threefold structure but also the content of each of the three divisions. Part 1 is entitled "The Law, the Origin of Sin, and Repentance," part 2 "The Gospel and Faith," and part 3 "Good Works." Even more striking is the terminology in each section that would later appear in both the SC and the HC. It is through the law that we come to know our frailty and "misery" (*elend*), through Christ that God has "delivered" (*erlöste*) us from such misery, and through the keeping of the commandments that we show ourselves "thankful" (*danckbarlich*) to God for what he has done on our behalf. Reu concluded that if the structure of Melanchthon's *Loci* and the book of Romans exerted any influence on Ursinus at all, it could only have been through the more developed form of this structure in the Regensburg "Summa." One of the HC's most noteworthy features, therefore, its three-part systematic arrangement, had its origins in a Lutheran catechism.[28]

This claim of a Lutheran, even Melanchthonian, provenance to the structure of the HC met two significant challenges in the next sixty years by scholars who argued for a more Calvinist, or at least generally Reformed, influence on this structure. First, in his massive introduction to the HC in 1907, August Lang maintained that the first two divisions of the SC and HC had their roots in

26. Gooszen, "Inleiding," in *Heidelbergsche Catechismus*, 75. On the influence of Romans on Melanchthon's *Loci*, see Timothy J. Wengert, "Philip Melanchthon's 1522 Annotations on Romans and the Lutheran Origins of Rhetorical Criticism," in *Biblical Interpretation in the Era of the Reformation: Essays Presented to David C. Steinmetz in Honor of His Sixtieth Birthday*, ed. Richard A. Muller and John L. Thompson (Grand Rapids: Eerdmans, 1996), 131.

27. Thompson, "Palatinate Church Order," 347; Sturm, *Zacharias Ursinus*, 250; Rohls, *Reformed Confessions*, 20.

28. Johann Reu, ed., *Quellen zur Geschichte des kirchlichen Unterrichts in der evangelischen Kirche Deutschlands zwischen 1530 und 1600*, pt. 1, *Quellen zur Geschichte des Katechismus-Unterrichts*, vol. 1, *Süddeutsche Katechismen* (1904; reprint, Hildesheim: Olms, 1976), 198-99, 201-3. The Gallus treatise, "Ein Kurtze Ordenliche summa der rechten Waren Lehre unsers heyligen Christlichen Glaubens," is found in Reu, *Quellen zur Geschichte*, 720-34. Verboom (*Theologie van de Heidelbergse Catechismus*, 21) points to a similar threefold division in a 1557 catechism by Johann Meckhart, "Kurtze christenliche bakantnusz für junge kinder und einfeltige menschen." Unlike Gallus, however, Meckhart does not use the actual terminology of misery, deliverance, and gratitude to distinguish the three parts of his catechism.

neither Melanchthon nor the Regensburg "Summa" but in Luther himself, more particularly in the widely used arrangement of catechetical material that Luther had introduced in his "Eyn kurcz form der zeehen gepott . . ." of 1520. The similarity in structure between the HC and the first edition of Melanchthon's *Loci* could more easily be explained by a common dependence on Luther than by a direct dependence of Ursinus on Melanchthon. If the "Summa" played any role at all in the construction of the SC and HC, it was only as an external reinforcement of a structure that arose out of an "inner necessity" from Ursinus's earlier *Catechesis maior*, or Larger Catechism. What was unique about the structure of the SC and the HC was the combination of the Lutheran emphases on misery and deliverance in parts 1 and 2 with the Reformed theme of gratitude in part 3. In the most distinctive feature of these catechisms, the treatment of the Ten Commandments in the section on gratitude, Ursinus clearly owed a debt to John Calvin. Melanchthon's influence on the HC could be detected only in the definitions of faith and conversion and in two places in the exposition of the law.[29]

In the 1960s, Walter Hollweg turned this discussion in a new direction. While granting that some of Melanchthon's formulations could be found in the HC, Hollweg contended that the two confessions by Theodore Beza, the *Confessio fidei christianae* and *Altera brevis fidei confessio* (both 1559), significantly influenced the structure, content, and even some of the phraseology of the HC.[30] Hollweg pointed out a striking structural parallel between the threefold division of the HC and the threefold work of the Holy Spirit in articles 17-21 of the *Altera confessio*: first, the Spirit makes us aware of our sinfulness through the law; second, he comforts us with the message of salvation in the gospel; and third, he sanctifies us by mortifying the old nature and creating a new one. Hollweg admitted the difference between the third element here (sanctification) and the third heading of the HC ("Gratitude") but maintained that the substructure of the HC required that sanctification be treated in part 2 under the exposition of the Apostles' Creed (cf. HC 24: "God the Holy Spirit and our Sanctification").[31] Nevertheless, even the themes of gratitude, good works, and prayer in part 3 had their roots in these Bezan confessions and not in the Lutheran "Summa" of Regensburg. Any connection between the HC and the "Summa" was purely formal, because Calvinistic authors of the HC understood gratitude as a motivation for doing good aroused by the Holy Spirit, and not, like the "Summa," as the content of an objective obligation.[32]

---

29. Lang, *Heidelberger Katechismus*, LXXIX-LXXX, LXXXI-LXXXII, CI-CII.

30. Hollweg, "Beiden Konfessionen," 86-123; idem, "Zur Quellenfrage," 38-47.

31. Hollweg, "Beiden Konfessionen," 98-105. The text of the 1562 German translation of the *Altera confessio* is appended to Hollweg's article on pp. 111-23 (Arts. 17-21, pp. 116-18).

32. Ibid., 105 n. 32. For these different approaches to gratitude in the HC and the "Summa," Hollweg cites Otto Ritschl, *Dogmengeschichte des Protestantismus*, vol. 3, *Orthodoxie und Synkretismus in der altprotestantischen Theologie* (Göttingen: Vandenhoeck & Ruprecht, 1926), 265 n. 142.

Has the case been made, then, for a Calvinist rather than a Lutheran or Melanchthonian influence on the framework of the HC? Hollweg's claim that the threefold division is rooted in Beza's Calvinistic confessions of 1559 is certainly attractive. Beza had developed close ties with members of the Heidelberg community in the late 1550s and likely published his *Confessio christianae fidei* in 1560 in response to a request from the Palatinate's Elector Frederick III. The shorter confession, the *Altera brevis fidei confessio*, was also well known in Heidelberg, especially after its translation into German in 1562, probably by Caspar Olevianus, one the contributors to the HC.[33] Therefore, we should not be surprised at some of the linguistic parallels that Hollweg points out between these confessions and the HC.[34]

Nevertheless, this proposal can be questioned on several grounds. For one thing, the threefold work of the Holy Spirit in Beza's *Altera confessio* comprises a section of just five articles out of a total of thirty-three and does not determine the structure of his document as a whole. Furthermore, unlike the HC, the smaller confession never uses the term *gratitude*, and in the one place in the larger confession where it does appear (IV.16), it is connected only indirectly to good works: Prayer is the noblest of good works, and giving thanks is one kind of prayer.[35] Finally, Hollweg does not make clear why this is the only possible explanation for the threefold organization of the HC. By appealing first to an author's personal connections to Heidelberg and then to similarities between his confessional writings and the HC, one could make just as strong a case, it would seem, for the influence of Melanchthon.

Melanchthon, too, had significant connections to the Heidelberg community.[36] Ever since the Palatinate had first granted official status to Lutheranism in the 1540s, he had provided political, educational, and theological advice to the Palatine electors. Elector Otto Henry had incorporated Melanchthon's catechism, the *Examen ordinandorum* (1552), into the Palatinate church order of 1556 and had sought his assistance during the reorganization of Heidelberg University in 1558. Otto Henry's successor, Frederick III, had been a signatory to a Melanchthonian confessional consensus in Frankfurt in 1558 and throughout his reign supported Melanchthon's "altered" version of the Augsburg Confession. Some historians have characterized the entire phase of the territorial reformation led by these two electors as "Melanchthonian" or "Philippist."[37]

33. Hollweg, "Beiden Konfessionen," 87-94; "Zur Quellenfrage," 38-42.

34. Hollweg, "Beiden Konfessionen," 106-10.

35. E. F. K. Müller, *Die Bekenntnisschriften der reformierten Kirchen* (Leipzig: Deichert, 1903), 376-449.

36. For a summary of these connections see Lyle D. Bierma, "What Hath Wittenberg to Do with Heidelberg? Philip Melanchthon and the Heidelberg Catechism," in *Melanchthon in Europe: His Work and Influence Beyond Wittenberg*, ed. Karin Maag, Texts & Studies in Reformation and Post-Reformation Thought, ed. Richard A. Muller (Grand Rapids: Baker; Carlisle, UK: Paternoster, 1999), 105-8, and the sources noted there.

37. E.g., James I. Good, *The Origin of the Reformed Church in Germany* (Reading, Pa.: Daniel Miller, 1887), 128, 134; idem, *Heidelberg Catechism*, 133; Klooster, *Heidelberg Catechism*, 83, 104; Henss, *Heidelberger Katechismus*, 1; Christopher J. Burchill, "On the Consolation of a Christian

The flagship of this reformation was, of course, the HC, around which Frederick III hoped to build a theological consensus within the bounds of his subscription to Melanchthon's Augsburg Confession (Altered). As we saw in the previous chapter, the probable chief author of the HC, Zacharias Ursinus, had studied with Melanchthon in Wittenberg for seven years, had used his mentor's *Examen ordinandorum* in his own teaching in Breslau, and had even composed a treatise in 1559 defending Melanchthon's doctrine of the sacraments. We would not be surprised, therefore, if Melanchthon's influence on Frederick III and Ursinus was reflected in some way in the text of the HC.

Indeed the parallels are there. As Gooszen observed over a century ago, the triadic structure of the HC is foreshadowed already in the outline of Melanchthon's 1521 *Loci*, which proceeds, generally speaking, from the topics of law and sin, to the gospel and justification, and finally to the life of Christian love. This triad, however, is also found in later works by Melanchthon—his Visitation Articles of 1528, for example, of which sorrow for sin, faith, and good works form the basic structure.[38] Moreover, the triple work of the Holy Spirit, which caught Hollweg's attention in the shorter confession of Theodore Beza, was adumbrated in Melanchthon's Augsburg Confession almost thirty years earlier. According to Article 20 (*Editio princeps*), the Holy Spirit produces knowledge of sin, faith, and the virtues that God requires of us in the Ten Commandments.[39] This is echoed in his Apology of the Augsburg Confession when he asserts that repentance consists of two parts, contrition and faith, and that he will not object if one adds a third part, namely, the fruits worthy of repentance. Hence, "the sum of the preaching of the gospel is to condemn sin and to offer the forgiveness of sins . . . and eternal life, so that having been reborn we might do good."[40]

One could make a fairly strong circumstantial case, therefore, for Melanchthon's influence on the structure of the HC. To conclude, however, from these personal connections and linguistic parallels that Melanchthon's *Loci* or his other works provided the direct inspiration for the threefold division of the HC is more than the available evidence will allow. The same is true of Beza's confessions. There is no more reason to believe that the Bezan documents stood in the background of the threefold organization of the HC than that Melanchthon's writings did—or, for that matter, Luther's works, or the Regensburg "Summa," or Calvin's first catechism, or the book of Romans itself.[41]

Scholar: Zacharias Ursinus (1534-83) and the Reformation in Heidelberg," *Journal of Ecclesiastical History* 37, no. 4 (1986): 569.

38. Timothy J. Wengert, *Law and Gospel: Philip Melanchthon's Debate with John Agricola of Eisleben over Poenitentia*, Texts and Studies in Reformation and Post-Reformation Thought, ed. Richard A. Muller (Grand Rapids: Baker; Carlisle, UK: Paternoster, 1997), 144-45.

39. *Die Bekenntnisschriften der evangelisch-lutherischen Kirche*, 4th ed. (Göttingen: Vandenhoeck & Ruprecht, 1959), 83 (hereafter BSELK).

40. Ibid., 257. English translation: *The Book of Concord: The Confessions of the Evangelical Lutheran Church*, ed. Robert Kolb and Timothy J. Wengert, trans. Charles Arand et al. (Minneapolis: Fortress, 2000), 191-92.

41. In his first catechism (French, 1537; Latin, 1538), Calvin moves, generally speaking, from knowledge of sin through the law, to the gospel of salvation through faith in Christ, to a life

By the mid-sixteenth century, the triad of law-gospel-good works or sin-faith-love had become so much a part of the common stock of Protestant theology that the threefold division of the HC cannot be traced with any certainty to a particular source or author.[42] The Pauline triad found its earliest Reformation form in Luther and especially in Melanchthon, but it could have made its way to Heidelberg in the 1560s by any number of paths.[43]

Gratitude

As we have seen, August Lang identified the theme of gratitude in part 3 as the one feature of the SC and HC that was characteristically Reformed. Hollweg, too, was convinced that this theme, especially HC 86 on gratitude and good works, had its roots in the Reformed tradition, more particularly in the two confessions by Beza. Others have since made similar claims.[44] Once again, however, such claims cannot be justified, for this, too, is an emphasis that one finds already earlier in the Lutheran tradition, especially in Melanchthon. As far back as the 1521 *Loci*, Melanchthon had stated that "when we have tasted the mercy of God through faith and have come to know the divine goodness through the word of the gospel . . . , the mind cannot help loving God in return; it exults and witnesses to its own thankfulness for such great mercy by some form of reciprocated service."[45] Luther himself taught in his Small Catechism of 1529 that one is "duty bound to thank, praise, serve, and obey" God for all that he has done for us.[46] A year later in the Augsburg Confession, Melanchthon listed thanks to God as one of the virtues required in the Ten Commandments that is reawakened in the regenerate by the Holy Spirit.[47] Just a year after that, he explicitly stated in the Apology of the Augsburg Confession that "good works ought to follow faith as thanksgiving to God" and that thanksgiving is one of the good fruits of repentance that are taught us in the Commandments.[48] This theme would appear

---

of obedience and prayer. See I. John Hesselink, *Calvin's First Catechism: A Commentary*, Columbia Series in Reformed Theology (Louisville: Westminster John Knox, 1997), 8-33.

42. Cf. Heinrich Graffmann, *Unterricht im Heidelberger Katechismus* (Neukirchen: Buchhandlung des Erziehungsvereins, 1951), 3:656: "Abschliessend wird man sagen müssen, dass die Einteilung des Heidelberger Catechismus nicht spezifisch reformiert ist, wenigstens was die Überschriften der einzelnen Teile betrifft."

43. For a fuller critique of Hollweg's thesis, see Sturm, *Zacharias Ursinus*, 251-53.

44. Graffmann, *Unterricht*, 3:656; Schnucker, *Evangelical Dictionary of Theology*, s. v. "Heidelberg Catechism"; Shirley C. Guthrie, *Encyclopedia of the Reformed Faith*, s. v. "Heidelberg Catechism."

45. Philip Melanchthon, "Loci communes (1521)," in *Corpus Reformatorum: Philippi Melanchthonis opera quae supersunt omnia* (hereafter CR), ed. Karl Bretschneider and Heinrich Bindseil (Halle: A. Schwetschke and Sons, 1834-60), 21:181. English translation: *The Library of Christian Classics*, vol. 19, *Melanchthon and Bucer*, ed. Wilhelm Pauck (Philadelphia: Westminster, 1969), 109.

46. BESLK, 511. English translation: *Creeds of Christendom*, ed. Schaff, 3:78. For this citation, the citations in nn. 47 and 48, and the reference to Rhegius in note 49, I am indebted to Sturm, *Zacharias Ursinus*, 249-50.

47. BESLK, 83.

48. Ibid., 197 (English translation: *Book of Concord*, 150), 290.

again in Melanchthon's Scholia of 1534, in a doctrinal handbook by the Lutheran Urbanus Rhegius in 1536, and, of course, in the Lutheran Regensburg "Summa" of 1547.[49] Perhaps most striking, however, in its linguistic similarities to HC 86 was a question and answer in a catechism by the Lutheran Johannes Brenz from 1535:

Q. Why ought we to do good works?

A. Not because we pay for sin and earn eternal life with our deeds—for Christ alone has paid for sin and earned eternal life—but rather because we ought to bear witness to our faith with good works and be thankful to our Lord God for his good deeds.[50]

By the 1540s and 1550s, this theme had made its appearance also in Reformed catechisms by Leo Jud and Johannes à Lasco, in the larger confession of Theodore Beza, and in Calvin' *Institutes*.[51] Where Ursinus first encountered it is impossible to say, but there are no grounds for maintaining that this aspect of the structure of the HC is distinctively Reformed or necessarily dependent on Reformed sources. As with the entire triadic arrangement of the HC, the connection between gratitude and good works in part 3 made its first appearance in Lutheran works, especially those by Melanchthon, but by the 1560s had become so widely dispersed throughout Protestant theology that its literary path to the HC can no longer be traced.

What then of Hollweg's contention (following Otto Ritschl) that the authors of the HC, trained at the feet of Calvin, understood gratitude as a subjective motivation for doing good aroused in the believer by the Holy Spirit, whereas the Lutheran "Summa" treated gratitude as the content of an objective obligation?[52] In my judgment, Hollweg and Ritschl have presented us here with a false dichotomy. To be sure, the HC portrays a subjective side of gratitude. As HC 86 declares, "Christ by his Spirit is also renewing us in his image in order that in all our living we may show ourselves thankful to God." Or as HC 64 puts it earlier, "it is impossible for those grafted into Christ by true faith not to produce fruits of gratitude." Gratitude seems to be one of the products of our incorporation into Christ and the renewing work of the Spirit. Nevertheless, HC 86 makes clear that

49. For Melanchthon's Scholia, see Wengert, *Law and Gospel*, 188-89. For Rhegius, see Urbanus Rhegius, *Wie man fürsichtiglich und ohne Ärgernis reden soll von den fürnemesten Artikeln Christlicher Lehre*, ed. A. Uckeley, Quellenschriften zur Geschichte des Protestantismus, vol. 6 (Leipzig: Deichert, 1908), 47. For the "Summa," see Reu, *Süddeutsche Katechismen*, 731.

50. Johannes Brenz, "Fragstücke des christlichen Glaubens," in Christoph Weismann, *Eine Kleine Biblia: Die Katechismen von Luther und Brenz* (Stuttgart: Calver, 1985), 114.

51. See, for example, Leo Jud, "*Ein kürtze Christenliche underweysung . . .*" (1541), in Lang, *Heidelberger Katechismus*, 79: "Güte werck . . . als ein dancksagung die wir Gott thünd" (Q/A 86), and Johnnes à Lasco, "*De Catechismus, oft Kinder leere, diemen te Londen in de Duytsche ghemeynte, is ghebruyckende* (1551)," in *Joannis a Lasco opera*, ed. Abraham Kuyper (Amsterdam: F. Müller, 1866; Hague: M. Nijhoff, 1866), 2:397, 399, where the keeping of the law is described as a "danckseegginghe" to God for redeeming us (Q/A 97). For Calvin's 1559 *Institutes* see, e.g., 2.16.2 and 3.4.37.

52. See n. 32 above.

it is the believer's obligation to demonstrate this thankfulness in a particular way, namely, by doing good works: "Why ought we [*warumb sollen wir*] to do good works? We ought to do good works [*darumb*]. . . in order that . . . we may show ourselves thankful to God." Heidelberg Catechism 91 defines the good deeds by which we are obligated to show our thankfulness as those that conform to God's law. Finally, the law should be pointedly preached to believers so that while "asking God for the grace of the Holy Spirit, they never stop striving to be renewed more and more after the image of God" (HC 115). That the law should be preached so that we never stop striving to conform to it suggests a divine expectation of obedience on the part of those whom the Spirit is renewing. According to part 3 of the HC, therefore, gratitude is indeed a motivation kindled in the believer by the Spirit, but it can only properly be demonstrated by meeting one's obligation to fulfill the law. The internal motivation of gratitude and the external way of expressing it go hand in hand.[53]

This same correlation of objective duty and subjective motivation is found in the Regensburg "Summa." Because of God's redemptive work on our behalf, we ought thankfully (*sollen . . . danckbarlich*) to show ourselves as his obedient children by keeping his commandments.[54] This sounds as if thankfulness is a part of our duty, or at least as if our keeping of the commandments, which we ought to do, is itself a form of thankfulness. However, the context suggests that thankfulness here should also be understood as the motivation for obedience, because the author goes on to say that the Holy Spirit kindles a *love* for God in our hearts that helps us observe the commandments in some measure. Indeed, not to love God in this way is characteristic of "*ungrateful* children."[55]

These similar approaches in the Summa and HC to Spirit-motivated obedience to the law should not lead us to conclude that on this point the latter document was dependent on the former. This correlation appears also in earlier sources in Reformation theology. Melanchthon, for example, who speaks in the 1521 *Loci* of the spontaneity of thanks and in the Augsburg Confession of thanks to God as one of the virtues effected by the Holy Spirit, also refers in the Apology of the Augsburg Confession to good works as expressions of thanks that ought to (*sollen*) follow faith and that one ought to (*soll*) and must (*muss*) do.[56] He perhaps best articulates this combination of motivation and duty in his *Annotations on Romans* of 1522, where he identifies multiple grounds for good works, including both an "impulsive cause" (the creational obligation to obedience) and an "efficient cause" (the Holy Spirit).[57] This correlation, however, can also be found

53. This represents a modification of my position in "What Hath Wittenberg to Do with Heidelberg?" 115-17, where I acknowledged only the subjective side of this correlation in the HC.

54. In Reu, *Süddeutsche Katechismen*, 731.

55. Ibid., 732 (italics added).

56. BESLK, 197. For the references to Melanchthon's *Loci* and the Augsburg Confession, see nn. 46 and 48 above.

57. CR 15:926.

in Leo Jud's shorter catechism and in Calvin's Genevan Catechism, to name just a couple of representatives.[58] Once again, whatever literary trail there might have been to the HC is beyond recovery.

Uses of the Law

It is commonly alleged that the HC reveals its Calvinist ancestry most clearly in its treatment of the law in part 3 as the norm for a life of gratitude, the so-called third use of the law.[59] Neuser did find this third use of the law also in Melanchthon but maintained that by placing its commentary on the Decalogue in the section on thanksgiving, the HC followed Calvin in making this the principal use. For Melanchthon, the first use, the law as a teacher of sin, remained primary. Neuser also detected a Calvinistic stamp on the HC's portrayal of the law in part 1 as a mirror for our misery. The fact that HC 4 answers the question, "What does God's law require of us?" with the words, "*Christ* teaches us this in summary in Matthew 22" (italics added) suggests a Calvinistic understanding of the law— one in which law and gospel are not polar opposites but different expressions of the gracious righteousness of God. This represented a significant revision of the first part of the SC, where we encounter a sharp Melanchthonian contrast between law and gospel. Therefore, Neuser concluded, whoever was the final redactor of the HC was certainly a Calvinist.[60]

Let us examine the latter claim first. The case for a shift from a Melanchthonian approach to the law in SC 4-7 to a Calvinist approach in HC 3-4 is less than convincing. The differences between the two texts are actually rather minor. Neuser is correct that HC part 1 refers only to the summary of "the law" as a teacher of sin and no longer (in what he regards as a more typically Lutheran fashion) to "the Decalogue" and "the summary of the Decalogue" (SC 4). Direct reference to the Decalogue is indeed reserved in the HC for the emphasis on the third use of the law in part 3. What Neuser fails to take into account, however, is that the law is explicitly defined as the Decalogue in part 3 (HC 92) and, as we shall see below, that one of the functions of the Ten Commandments in part 3 is to expose the sin of the regenerate (HC 115). The Decalogue as such, therefore, clearly has a pedagogical or exposure function also in the HC.

Furthermore, the quotation in HC 4 of Christ's double command of love as the requirement of the law does not mitigate the contrast between law and gospel that we find in the SC. The SC, too, quotes Christ's summary of the law (SC 7) in

---

58. Jud, "Kürtze Christenliche underweysung," in Lang, *Heidelberger Katechismus*, 78-79 (Q/A 85, 86); Calvin, "Genevan Catechism," in *Joannis Calvini Opera Selecta* [OS], ed. Peter Barth and Wilhelm Niesel (Munich: Kaiser, 1952), 2:94, 95-96, 111, 112 (Q/A 121, 122, 128-32, 225, 229). Of the two, however, only Jud's catechism links the correlation specifically to gratitude.

59. See, for example, Lang, *Heidelberger Katechismus*, CI; Klooster, *Mighty Comfort*, 37; Berard, Marthaler, *The Catechism Today and Yesterday: The Evolution of a Genre* (Collegeville, Mn: Liturgical Press, 1995), 30; and Rohls, *Reformed Confessions*, 20.

60. Neuser, "Väter des Heidelberger Katechismus," 188-90. The point that HC 4 suggests a Calvinistic approach to law and gospel had been made earlier by Graffmann, *Unterricht*, 3:657.

relation to the knowledge of human misery (SC 4, 8ff.).[61] The fact that it is the words of Christ that are cited here seems less an indication that the law is an expression of divine grace than that nowhere else in Scripture do we find such a succinct summary of the law. Indeed, just six answers later, the HC clarifies this role of the law in words rooted in the Old Testament: "Cursed is everyone who does not continue to do everything written in the Book of the Law" (HC 10, Galatians 3:10, Deuteronomy 27:26). The fact remains that in both the SC and the HC, the law as a teacher of sin is first introduced in the section on sin and misery, not grace and deliverance.[62] If this approach to law and gospel ought not to be characterized as distinctively Calvinistic, there is also nothing to suggest that it is distinctively Melanchthonian either; structurally and substantively it can be found also in Luther's catechisms of 1529 and in Calvin's first catechisms in the late 1530s.[63]

If the first use of the law in part 1 of the HC is neither distinctly Calvinistic nor Melanchthonian, what then about the third use in part 3 where the law is introduced as a rule of gratitude? The closest the HC comes to an explanation of the functions of the law is in its treatment in HC 115 of the purpose of preaching the law:

> Q. No one in this life can obey the Ten Commandments perfectly: why then does God want them preached so pointedly?
>
> A. First, so that the longer we live the more we may come to know our sin-fullness and the more eagerly look to Christ for forgiveness of sins and righteousness.
>
> Second, so that, while praying to God for the grace of the Holy Spirit, we may never stop striving to be renewed more and more after God's image, until after this life we reach our goal: perfection.

This second reason for preaching the law, namely, so that believers will persevere in their striving to be renewed in God's image, has a distinctly Calvinian ring to it. Similar language can be found in Calvin's *Institutes* and Genevan Catechism, the latter of which likely served as a source for the HC.[64]

The first reason for preaching the law—so that believers may increasingly come to know their sinfulness and look to Christ for forgiveness—is missing in Calvin, at least as part of the third use of the law. Where it appears in Calvin is only in reference to unbelievers or to believers prior to conversion (the first use of

---

61. In Lang, *Heidelberger Katechismus*, 200-201.

62. Goeters points out that the contrast and relationship between law and gospel is evident even at the beginning of the HC's section on deliverance, which opens with the assertion in HC 12 that the claims of God's justice must be satisfied either by us (law) or another (gospel) and then elaborates on this point in HC 13-19. "Christologie und Rechtfertigung," 38-39.

63. For the movement from law to gospel in Luther's Larger and Shorter Catechisms, see BESLK, 501ff., 545ff. For Calvin's catechisms of 1537-38, see Hesselink, *Calvin's First Catechism*, 10-19.

64. Calvin, *Institutes* 2.7.12; Genevan Catechism 229, in OS 2:112. Cf. Ursinus's LC 150, in Lang, *Heidelberger Katechismus*, 174.

the law)—and not, as in the HC, in reference to the redeemed after conversion.[65] What previous scholarship has overlooked, however, is that this is identified also as a third use of the law by Philip Melanchthon, who actually introduced the concept of a third use into Protestant theology in 1534.[66] In his 1543 edition of the *Loci*, Melanchthon distinguishes two aspects to this third role of the law. First, the law reveals the remnants of sin in the believer's life so that he or she may grow in both knowledge of sin and repentance. Second, it teaches the particular works by which God wants us to exercise obedience.[67] This second, or didactic, dimension to the third use of the law is found also in Calvin.[68] The first, or pedagogical, dimension to the third use is not; it is a uniquely Melanchthonian formulation.

Was it this Melanchthonian formulation, then, that eventually found its way into the HC? That is a strong possibility but, once again, not the only one. What Melanchthon describes here as a dimension of the third use of the law, Luther had characterized as an application of the second use (Calvin's first use) to believers.[69] Because the HC never actually numbers the functions of the law, it is difficult to say whether 115a is a closer parallel to Luther or to Melanchthon. In any case, to identify the use of the law in part 3 as strictly Calvinistic is hardly correct. In point of fact, the HC combines a Lutheran emphasis on the exposure of residual sin in the life of the believer with a Calvinistic emphasis on the exhortation to good works.

Sacraments

A final issue long disputed among HC scholars is the theological slant of the catechism's doctrine of the sacraments. Is it Melanchthonian, Calvinist, Zwinglian, Bullingerian, or some combination of these traditions?[70] Once again, however, that is to pose the wrong question, for what has been claimed as evidence in the HC of a distinctive theological perspective on the sacraments is often the common property of two or more Reformation traditions. Numerous examples of this could be cited, but because we have developed this point at length in another monograph,[71] we shall limit ourselves here to a summary of the debate surrounding just two questions and answers, HC 66 and 79.

HC 66, the second of four introductory questions on the sacraments in general, furnishes this definition:

---

65. Calvin, *Institutes* 2.7.6-9; Genevan Catechism 228, in OS 2:111-12. Cf. Ursinus's LC 149, in Lang, *Heidelberger Katechismus*, 173.

66. Wengert, "The Origins of the Third Use of the Law: Philip Melanchthon's Commentary on Colossians (1534)" (paper presented at the annual Sixteenth Century Studies Conference, San Francisco, October 1995).

67. CR 21:719.

68. See n. 64 above.

69. See Paul Althaus, *The Theology of Martin Luther*, trans. Robert C. Schultz (Philadelphia: Fortress, 1966), 269-70, and the references to Luther cited there.

70. For an overview of this debate, see Bierma, *Sacraments in the Heidelberg Catechism*, 1-7.

71. Ibid., 9-20.

Q. What are sacraments?

A. They are visible holy signs and seals, instituted by God, so that by our use of them he might make us understand the promise of the gospel more clearly and seal it. This promise of the gospel is that by grace he will grant us forgiveness of sins and eternal life because of Christ's one sacrifice finished on the cross.

Gooszen and Neuser suggested the Melanchthonian origin of this answer by noting similarities in structure and language between HC 66 and Ursinus's LC 275, and, in turn, between LC 275 and Melanchthon's definition of sacraments in the *Examen ordinandorum*.[72] Sturm, however, argued that the definition is essentially Zwinglian because the sacraments are connected here, and again in HC 67, to the sacrificial work of Christ in the past, not to the presence of Christ in the sacraments at the time they are celebrated.[73] Additionally, Bavinck, Richards, and Hesse all picked up a "Calvinist" accent in HC 66ff. on the primary role of God, not the congregation, in the sacramental action.[74]

None of these features of HC 66, however, belongs exclusively to the tradition with which it has been identified. The common structure of the definition of sacraments in HC 66, LC 275, and Melanchthon's *Examen* can also be found in Bullinger, and elements of the text itself have their parallels not only or not always in Melanchthon but also in catechisms by Bullinger, Calvin, Jud, à Lasco, and Micronius.[75] The allegedly Zwinglian approach to the sacraments in HC 66 and 67 as reminders of the sacrifice of Christ in the past appears also in Calvin[76] and, moreover, cannot be interpreted apart from the HC's own emphasis elsewhere on the present action of Christ in the sacraments (e.g., HC 75-78). Finally, the Calvinist primary stress in HC 66ff. on divine, not human, activity in the sacrament has antecedents in Bullinger and Melanchthon as well.[77]

Similar differences have arisen in the interpretation of HC 79 on the Lord's Supper:

Q. Why then does Christ call the bread his body and the cup his blood?

72. Gooszen, "Inleiding," in *Heidelbergsche Catechismus*, 65-66; Neuser, "Erwählungslehre im Heidelberger Katechismus," 311.

73. Sturm, *Zacharias Ursinus*, 294.

74. Jan Bavinck, *De Heidelbergsche Catechismus in 60 leerredenen verklaard* (Kampen: Kok, 1913-14), 2:523-24; Richards, *Heidelberg Catechism*, 90; Hermann Hesse, "Zur Sakramentslehre des Heidelberger Katechismus nach den Fragen 65-68," in *Theologische Aufsätze: Karl Barth zum 50. Geburtstag*, ed. E. Wolf (Munich: Kaiser, 1936), 473-74, 478, 484.

75. For the details of these parallels and the primary source citations, see Bierma, *Sacraments in the Heidelberg Catechism*, 11-13.

76. See, e.g., Q/A 347-49 of "The Catechism of the Church of Geneva" (1545), in *Calvin: Theological Treatises*, ed. J. K. S. Reid (Philadelphia: Westminster, 1954), 136-37 (OS 2:139).

77. Bullinger, *The Decades of Henry Bullinger*, ed. Thomas Harding (1849-52; reprint, New York: Johnson Reprint, 1968), 4:240, 316-17, 327, 403, 443; Melanchthon, *Examen ordinandorum*, in CR 23:39-40.

A. Christ . . . wishes to teach us that just as bread and wine sustain the temporal life, so his crucified body and shed blood are the true food and drink of our souls unto eternal life. But more important, he wants to assure us . . . that we, through the Holy Spirit's work, share in his true body and blood as surely as we receive these holy signs with the physical mouth. . . .

Two of the prominent features of this answer, and of several others in the HC's treatment of the sacraments, are, first, the parallelism between physical and spiritual action in the sacrament and, second, the role of the Holy Spirit in the spiritual action. The first of these features has been identified as typically Calvinist by some[78] and as more characteristic of Bullinger by others.[79] The second is almost always regarded as a distinctively Calvinist emphasis.[80]

In the first case, however, both Calvin and Bullinger make use of the language of sacramental parallelism.[81] In a question in the Genevan Catechism on the symbolism of the bread and wine of the Lord's Supper, Calvin states:

By this we are taught that the body of our Lord has the same virtue spiritually to nourish our souls as bread has in nourishing our bodies for the sustenance of this present life. As wine exhilarates the heart of men, refreshes their strength, and fortifies the whole body, so from the blood of our Lord the very same benefits are received by our souls.[82]

Bullinger makes much the same point in the Decades:

Now in the Lord's Supper bread and wine represent the very body and blood of Christ. . . . As bread nourisheth and strengtheneth man. . . . so the body of Christ, eaten by faith, feedeth and satisfieth the soul of man. . . . As wine is drink to the thirsty, . . . so the blood of our Lord Jesus, drunken by faith, doth quench the thirst of the burning conscience.[83]

When it comes to the second case, there is no question that the Holy Spirit's facilitation of the union between the believer and Christ is a key theme in Calvin's doctrine of the sacraments. It is even true that this theme cannot be found in this context in Melanchthon, although Melanchthon does highlight the

---

78. Hendrikus Berkhof, "The Catechism as an Expression of Our Faith," in *Essays on the Heidelberg Catechism*, ed. Bard Thompson et al. (Philadelphia: United Church, 1963), 113.

79. Brian A. Gerrish, "Sign and Reality: The Lord's Supper in the Reformed Confessions," in *The Old Protestantism and the New: Essays on the Reformation Heritage* (Chicago: University of Chicago Press, 1982), 124, 126; Paul Rorem, "The Consensus Tigurinus (1549): Did Calvin Compromise?" in *Calvinus Sacrae Scripturae Professor: Calvin as Confessor of Holy Scripture*, ed. Wilhelm H. Neuser (Grand Rapids: Eerdmans, 1994), 90.

80. Sudhoff, *Olevianus und Ursinus*, 116-17; Richards, *Heidelberg Catechism*, 90; Benrath, "Die Eigenart der Pfälzischen Reformation und die Vorgeschichte des Heidelberger Katechismus," *Heidelberger Jahrbücher* 7 (1963): 25; Berkhof, "Catechism as an Expression of Our Faith," 113; Gerrish, "Sign and Reality," 125; Sturm, *Zacharias Ursinus*, 302, 304, 305.

81. For a fuller treatment of this point, see Bierma, *Sacraments in the Heidelberg Catechism*, 14-16.

82. Q/A 341, in *Theological Treatises*, 135-36 (OS 2:137).

83. Bullinger, *Decades*, 4:329.

work of the Spirit in his treatment of the sacraments in general.[84] To claim that it is distinctively Calvinian is to overlook the presence of this theme also in the Zurich Consensus that Calvin reached with Bullinger in 1549[85] and in Bullinger's own later works. For Bullinger, too, the body and blood of Christ are "communicated to us spiritually by the Spirit of God" and received by us "not in a corporeal but in a spiritual mode, through the Holy Spirit."[86]

In short, all the aspects of the HC's doctrine of the sacraments that past scholarship has identified as uniquely Melanchthonian, Calvinist, or Zwinglian/Bullingerian can be located in one or both of the other traditions as well. They represent not a particular theological slant but a common platform on which all the major Protestant parties of Heidelberg could stand.

Key Silences

If a desire to build consensus among Palatine Protestants led the writers of the HC to emphasize common theological ground within the framework of the Augsburg Confession, it also seems to have led them to avoid issues with the potential for controversy. Their goal was, in Verboom's words, not just "maximal consensus" but also "minimal dissensus."[87] Three of the issues on which the HC apparently sought to minimize conflict are particularly worthy of note: predestination, covenant, and certain aspects of sacramental doctrine.

Predestination

It is often pointed out that the HC contains no doctrine of predestination.[88] The most that one can find is two passing references to election: When Christ returns to judge the living and the dead, he will "take me with all the elect

---

84. Ralph W. Quere, "Christ's Efficacious Presence in the Lord's Supper: Directions in the Development of Melanchthon's Theology after Augsburg," *The Lutheran Quarterly* 29 (1977): 22-23, 25.

85. The Latin text of the Zurich Consensus can be found in CR 7:733-48. An English translation by Ian Bunting was published in the *Journal of Presbyterian History* 44 (1966): 45-61. See esp. paragraphs 3, 5, 6, 8, 9, 12, 14, and 23.

86. Bullinger, "The Second Helvetic Confession [*Confessio Helvetica posterior*]" (1566) 21.6, 5, in *Creeds of Christendom*, ed. Schaff, 3:292, 293. See also Bierma, *Sacraments in the Heidelberg Catechism*, 17-20, and the references to Bullinger cited there.

87. "In de HC is getracht formuleringen te gebruiken waarin zoveel mogelijk protestanten zich zouden kunnen herkennen en zo weinig mogelijk onnodige aanstoot aan niet-gereformeerden zou worden gegeven. Men zocht een maximale consensus en een minimale dissensus." Verboom, *Theologie van de Heidelbergse Catechismus*, 215. Verboom's reference here is only to the HC's doctrine of the sacraments, but it could apply to the document as a whole.

88. Heppe noted already in the mid-nineteenth century that "regelmäßig wird bei allen Excursen über den Heidelberger Katechismus an demselben rühmend hervorgehoben, daß er—als reformiertes, Calvinisches Lehrbuch—doch die Lehre von der Prädestination nicht enthalte." *Geschichte des deutschen Protestantismus*, 1:446. Cf. also Lang, *Heidelberger Katechismus*, XCII; Dahlmann, "Theology of the Heidelberg Catechism," 176-77; Neuser, "Erwählungslehre im Heidelberger Katechismus," 313; Goeters, "Christologie und Rechtfertigung," 45-47; and Verboom, *Theologie van de Heidelbergse Catechismus*, 167.

[*auszerwehlten*] to himself in heavenly joy and glory" (HC 52), and the church is "a community elected [*auszerwelte*] to eternal life" (HC 54).

This is only true, however, if one is talking about explicit references to predestination. HC 26 speaks of an "eternal decree" [*ewigen raht*] and providence by which God the Father upholds and rules all that he has created. This can give believers confidence that nothing in all creation will separate them from his love (HC 28). Heidelberg Catechism 20 teaches that salvation is limited to those who are grafted into Christ by true faith—a faith that we learn in HC 65 is produced in believers by the Holy Spirit. If one thinks of perseverance of the saints (elect) as yet another fruit of predestination to salvation, one finds implicit references to election in several other places as well:[89]

HC 1:   "Christ by his Holy Spirit assures me of eternal life and makes me wholeheartedly willing and ready from now on to live for him."

HC 21:   "True faith is . . . a heartfelt trust . . . that . . . I too . . . have been granted by God eternal life and salvation."

HC 32:   "and afterward to reign with Christ over all creation for eternity."

HC 53:   "[The Holy Spirit] . . . will remain with me into eternity."

HC 56:   "I believe that God . . . will nevermore remember all my sins or sinful nature . . . I nevermore need to experience judgment."

HC 57:   "my soul will be taken immediately after this life to Christ its head. . . ."

HC 58:   "I now experience in my heart the beginning of eternal joy. . . ."

HC 59:   "That in Christ I am . . . an heir to eternal life."

Neuser even suggests that all the "I" references in the HC's twenty-eight questions and answers in the first person singular could really be read as "I as one of the elect."[90] Nevertheless, the fact remains that there are no questions in the HC devoted specifically to election and no mention whatsoever of double predestination, reprobation, or limited atonement.

How does one account for such a muted treatment of election and total silence on reprobation? One possibility is that the authors did not find the topic appropriate for the genre, purpose, and readers of the HC. Predestination is simply too abstract and difficult a subject to include in an instructional tool intended for a general audience of youth and lay adults. After all, Calvin, who wrote extensively about predestination in other works, did not devote a separate question or section to it in his popular Genevan Catechism either.[91]

This line of argument is not wholly convincing, however, for at least two reasons. First, as Dahlmann has pointed out, the HC does not shy away from

89. Neuser, "Erwählungslehre im Heidelberger Katechismus," 315.
90. Ibid., 316.
91. Klooster, *Mighty Comfort*, 36.

other challenging theological abstractions, such as the doctrine of the Trinity (HC 24-58) and the relationship between the two natures of Christ (HC 46-49).[92] Second, Ursinus's SC, on which so much of the HC is based and which was also intended for a lay audience, has three complete questions and answers on election, the first of which (Q 50) includes a reference also to reprobation:

> Q. Why is it that this gift comes to you instead of to so many others who are lost forever?

> A. Because God elected me in Christ for eternal life before the foundations of the world were laid, and he now regenerates me by the special grace of his Spirit. For unless this had happened, the corruption of my nature is such that I would have knowingly and willingly perished in my sins just like the many reprobate.

Neither these three questions nor other explicit references in the SC to the elect were carried over into the HC.[93]

A more likely possibility for the HC's near silence on predestination is that the authors intentionally steered clear of it for the sake of doctrinal harmony.[94] If Frederick III had had to deal with just the Calvinists in Heidelberg, the outcome might have been different. His consensus also involved followers of Melanchthon and Bullinger, neither of whom had wished to probe the doctrine of predestination as deeply as Calvin had. It was already a topic that "Melanchthon had, so to speak, declared off limits in the 1535 *Loci*,"[95] and Calvin himself admitted that Melanchthon did not want "to give curious folk a reason for inquiring too deeply into the secrets of God."[96] Bullinger, too, though not diverging substantially from Calvin's doctrine of predestination, seemed "uncomfortable with too speculative or thoroughgoing an analysis of the various aspects of the divine decree," including reprobation.[97] Therefore, given Frederick III's own Melanchthonian predilections and his desire to bridge the theological divisions in his realm, it would not be hard to imagine a refusal on his part to grant confessional status to an area of doctrine into which Melanchthon, Bullinger, and their adherents had feared to tread.

92. Dahlmann, "Theology of the Heidelberg Catechism," 176-77.

93. Cf., e.g., SC 12 and HC 21, SC 39 and HC 53, SC 43 and HC 57, where references to the elect in the SC have been dropped in the parallel answers in the HC. Neuser, "Erwählungslehre im Heidelberger Katechismus," 316.

94. "In een gebied als de Paltz, waar de verschillende confessionele stromingen op kwetsbare wijze de koers moesten volgen die de keurvorst Frederik III uitzette, was het belangrijk dat de leer van de predestinatie geen onnodige conflicten zou veroorzaken." Verboom, *Theologie van de Heidelbergse Catechismus*, 167.

95. Wengert, "'We Will Feast Together in Heaven Forever': The Epistolary Friendship of John Calvin and Philip Melanchthon," in *Melanchthon in Europe*, ed. Maag, 27.

96. Calvin, *Calvini Opera*, 11:381, cited in Wengert, "Epistolary Friendship," 31.

97. Cornelis P. Venema, *Heinrich Bullinger and the Doctrine of Predestination: Author of "the Other Reformed Tradition"?* Texts & Studies in Reformation and Post-Reformation Thought, ed. Richard A. Muller (Grand Rapids: Baker, 2002), 119. See also pp. 105-7.

Covenant

By the early 1560s, theological reflection on the biblical notion of covenant was becoming one of the distinguishing features of the Reformed branch of Protestantism. Zwingli, Oecolampadius, Bucer, Bullinger, Musculus, and Calvin had all paid it some attention.[98] It may seem odd, therefore, that the HC, which so many have considered Reformed in its orientation, employs the term *covenant* only five times in 129 questions and answers: twice in HC 74, which states that believers' children, too, are "in the covenant of God" and should receive baptism as "a sign of the covenant"; once each in HC 77 and 79, where Jesus' reference to a new covenant in his blood is quoted; and once in HC 82, which warns that "the covenant of God would be profaned" if ungodly persons were admitted to the Lord's Supper. Even more odd is the fact that Ursinus's LC contains 55 references to covenant in 38 of its questions and answers, whereas the SC has only three such references—two of them in parallel to HC 74 and 82 (SC 63, 71), and one in an introductory question on the sacraments (SC 55). How does one account for such a divergence among documents written so close together?

Gooszen surmised over a century ago that the numerous references to covenant in the LC were omitted in the SC and HC under pressure from Palatinate theologians who thought they sounded too "sacramentarian" or "Zwinglian." To Lutheran ears trained by the Augsburg Confession, references to sacraments as "signs" of the covenant might sound too much like "bare signs" or "mere signs."[99] Lang, too, viewed this abrupt change as a concession to (Lutheran?) critics of the LC, but he hypothesized that it was the concept of "the natural covenant" in the LC that became the stumbling block that led to the elimination of nearly all references to covenant in the catechisms that followed.[100]

As attractive as these suggestions might be, they are not without their difficulties. Both Gooszen and Lang assumed that the LC was composed before the SC and that Ursinus was under pressure from readers of the first document to keep the covenant idea out of the second. As Sturm has shown, however, it is more likely that the SC was written first;[101] hence Ursinus must have *added* covenant references to the LC, not *omitted* them from the SC under pressure. Furthermore, the argument that a Zwinglian ring to the phrase "signs of the covenant" prevented all but three appearances of *covenant* in the SC and five in the HC is not entirely convincing. Would all nonsacramental uses of the term need to be sacrificed just to avoid confusion about one sacramental use? Moreover, how do we explain the fact that "sign of the covenant" still appears in HC 74 or that the Palatinate Church Order of 1563 does not shy away from the terms *covenant* and *covenant signs* in its liturgical forms for baptism and the Lord's

98. See, among others, Peter A. Lillback, *The Binding of God: Calvin's Role in the Development of Covenant Theology*, Texts and Studies in Reformation and Post-Reformation Thought, ed. Richard A. Muller (Grand Rapids: Baker; Carlisle, UK: Paternoster, 2001). Part 1 of this work treats the early history of covenant theology and part 2, Calvin's contribution.

99. Gooszen, "Inleiding," in *Heidelbergsche Catechismus*, 74.

100. Lang, *Heidelberger Katechismus*, LXXVIII-LXXIX.

101. See ch. 2 n. 104.

Supper?[102] Finally, if Ursinus had to forego practically all mention of covenant in the SC and HC because he could not employ the offending term *natural covenant*, why does he return to the covenant theme in his later writings without ever again referring to a natural covenant?[103]

Another possibility for the disparate treatment of covenant in these catechisms is that the documents were prepared for different audiences and purposes. The HC and its earlier draft, the SC, were confessions written for a general audience, whereas the LC was a more technical work intended for theological instruction at the Sapience College and the university. A rather esoteric subject such as the covenant, therefore, might be appropriate study material for students of theology, but it was hardly fitting for a lay catechism.[104] This theory, however, both overestimates the complexity of the doctrine of the covenant in the LC and underestimates the presence of the covenant concept in the HC, even if the terminology itself is missing.[105]

Perhaps the best way to approach the question of the uneven usage of covenant language in Ursinus is to look at it as part of a process of theological maturation. The fact that the LC was never published in Ursinus's own lifetime, that it appeared in print posthumously against his earlier wishes, that covenant is given less prominence and a different accent in his later HC lectures, and that he never again referred to a natural covenant in his later works all suggest a measure of development in his thought on this point.[106] Because the LC represents only a first, provisional stage in this process, it would be quite understandable if Ursinus intentionally avoided in the SC and HC all but a few explicit references to a doctrine that he was only beginning to think through, especially if there was any danger that showcasing such a doctrine in a consensus catechism might provoke Lutheran criticism on both sides of the Palatinate border.

---

102. *Die evangelischen Kirchenordnungen des 16. Jahrhunderts*, ed. Emil Sehling, vol. 14, Kurpfalz (Tübingen: Mohr, 1957), 337, 339-41, 385, 390.

103. See, e.g., Ursinus's lectures on the HC, *Corpus doctrinae Christianae* (Hannover: Aubrius, 1634), 2-3, 96-100, 394-404, 418, 464; English translation: *Commentary of Dr. Zacharias Ursinus*, trans. Williard, 2-3, 96-100, 366-76, 387-88, 430.

104. Sturm, *Zacharias Ursinus*, 238-41, 253; C. Graafland, *Van Calvijn tot Comrie: Oorsprong en ontwikkeling van de leer van het verbond in het Gereformeerd Protestantisme* (Zoetermeer: Boekencentrum, 1994), 2:13-14.

105. Goeters, e.g., concludes concerning HC 19 that "auch wenn hier der Begriff des Gnadenbundes fehlt, so ist er der Sache nach hier augenfällig vorhanden." "Christologie und Rechtfertigung," 39. Verboom, too, notes that "hoewel de HC het woord verbond niet gebruikt, zou je ook kunnen zeggen dat de verbondsgedachte het cement van het bouwwerk in zondag 10 [HC 27-28] is." *Theologie van de Heidelbergse Catechismus*, 92. Cf. also Lothar Coenen, "Gottes Bund und Erwählung," in *Handbuch zum Heidelberger Katechismus*, ed. Lothar Coenen (Neukirchen-Vluyn: Neukirchener Verlag, 1963), 128-32.

106. For a fuller treatment of this point, see Bierma, "Law and Grace in Ursinus' Doctrine of the Natural Covenant: A Reappraisal," in *Protestant Scholasticism: Essays in Reassessment*, ed. Carl R. Trueman and R. Scott Clark (Carlisle, UK: Paternoster, 1999), 101-2.

Sacraments

One of the great ironies of the Reformation is that some of the very doctrinal issues that led to the Protestant break with Rome ended up dividing Protestants as well. Perhaps nowhere is this truer than with the doctrine of the sacraments. A significant part of what distinguished not only Protestants from Catholics but also Lutheran Protestants from Reformed Protestants, Gnesio-Lutherans from Philippist Lutherans, and Zwinglian Reformed from Calvinist Reformed was related to sacramental teaching, particularly the doctrine of the Lord's Supper. As we saw in chapter 1, when Frederick III became elector of the Palatinate and began his quest for religious unity, all of these Protestant parties were already present in his territory and engaged in fierce eucharistic debate. It is little wonder, then, that in his new territorial catechism he sought not only to distance himself from the Gnesio-Lutheran position and emphasize common ground among the other parties but also to avoid sacramental issues and language that might identify the HC too closely with a particular branch of Protestantism. We briefly note at least three possible instances of such intentional silence.

First, in the SC and LC, Ursinus had defined the sacraments not only as means by which God reminded and assured believers of the promises of the gospel but also as means by which believers, in turn, might "obligate themselves to faith and a holy life" (SC 54; cf. LC 275). Melanchthon, Calvin, and Bullinger had also included this human reciprocation in their definitions.[107] On this point, however, the HC is conspicuously silent, even though the rest of its definition of the sacraments follows the wording of Ursinus's earlier catechisms quite closely.[108] Could it not be the case, as several have suggested, that because of an early-Zwinglian *emphasis* on sacraments as signs of human obligation, the HC steered clear of such language to avoid any charges of Zwinglianism by Calvinists and Melanchthonians in the Palatinate and by Lutheran princes in other territories of the empire?[109]

Second, Melanchthon, Calvin, and Ursinus had all used "substance" language to describe the presence and communication of Christ in the Lord's Supper. In LC 300, for example, we read:

> Q. Does eating Christ mean only that we share in Christ's merit and in the Holy Spirit's gifts?

---

107. Melanchthon, "Loci Theologici" [1543 ed.], in CR 21:848; Calvin, *Institutes* 4.14.1; Bullinger, *Compendium Christianae Religionis* (Zurich: Froschouer, 1569), 112v.

108. Cf., e.g., HC 66 with SC 54 and LC 275; HC 69 with SC 57; and HC 75 with SC 64.

109. Gooszen, "Inleiding", in *Heidelbergsche Catechismus*, 105-7; Lang, *Heidelberger Katechismus*, XCIII; Hesse, "Sakramentslehre des Heidelberger Katechismus," 475-76; Walter Kreck, "Die Abendmahlslehre in den reformierten Bekenntnisschriften," in *Die Abendmahlslehre in den reformatorischen Bekenntnisschriften* (Munich: C. Kaiser, 1955), 43; Bierma, *Sacraments in the Heidelberg Catechism*, 22.

A. It is not only this but also a communication of the person and substance [*substantiae*] of Christ himself. For his divinity dwells in us, but his body is joined to our bodies in such a way that we are one with him.[110]

Bullinger, however, had rejected such language,[111] and it never surfaces in the SC, or the HC either. Its absence from these two catechisms might be explained by the fact that they sought to eschew technical theological vocabulary.[112] Once again, however, it is also possible that, for the sake of consensus, the authors of the HC were just as concerned about sounding too Lutheran or Calvinist on this point as they were about sounding too Zwinglian on the issue of the sacraments as signs of human responsibility.

Finally, the HC is silent on the most controversial sacramental question of the sixteenth century—how exactly the outward physical signs are connected to the spiritual blessings they signify.[113] With respect to the Lord's Supper, Paul Rorem has identified two views that have coexisted within the Reformed confessional tradition for centuries:

Does a given Reformed statement of faith consider the Lord's Supper as a testimony, an analogy, a parallel, even a simultaneous parallel to the internal workings of God's grace in granting communion with Christ? If so, the actual ancestor may be Heinrich Bullinger, Zwingli's successor in Zurich. Or does it explicitly identify the Supper as the very instrument or means through which God offers and confers the grace of full communion with Christ's body? The lineage would then go back to John Calvin (and to Martin Bucer).[114]

Where does the HC fit into this paradigm? Certainly it is not distinctively Calvinist here. Calvin could say, for example in his "Short Treatise on the Lord's Supper," that the bread and wine "are as *instruments by which* our Lord Jesus Christ distributes" his body and blood to us.[115] According to HC 75, however, the Lord's Supper reminds and assures the believer only that "as surely as I receive from the hand of the one who serves and taste with my mouth the bread and cup of the Lord, . . . so surely he nourishes and refreshes my soul for eternal life with his crucified body and poured-out blood." It is striking that nothing is said here about when or how exactly this happens. The believer can be confident that as certainly as the physical feeding takes place, so also does the spiritual feeding, but there is no reference here to the elements as "instruments" or "means" by which

110. See also Ursinus, "*Theses*," in *Tractationum theologicarum*, 1:359. For Melanchthon, see Quere, "Christ's Efficacious Presence," 31 n. 41. For Calvin, see Genevan Catechism 353, in OS 2:140.

111. Second Helvetic Confession 21.4, in *Creeds of Christendom*, ed. Schaff, 3:292. See also Neuser, "Erwählungslehre im Heidelberger Katechismus," 311 n. 12.

112. Sturm, *Zacharias Ursinus*, 303-4.

113. What follows is a condensation of my treatment of this question in Bierma, *Sacraments in the Heidelberg Catechism*, 23-30.

114. Rorem, "The *Consensus Tigurinus*," 90.

115. In Calvin, *Theological Treatises*, 147 (OS 1:508; italics added).

this spiritual feeding occurs, even though Ursinus did not hesitate to use such language in the SC and LC.[116]

Nor is the HC distinctively Zwinglian or neo-Zwinglian (Bullingerian) on the relationship between sign and signified. One finds a parallelism between inner and outer action in the sacrament (see HC 69, 73, 75, 79), but as we noted earlier, this parallelism is as characteristic of Calvin as it is of Bullinger. What separated the two reformers was not

> whether the sign and signified are parallel but . . . whether they are *merely* parallel. Are sacramental signs and actions only visual analogies to the grace that the Holy Spirit bestows apart from them (Bullinger), or are they more than analogies, namely, the very means or instruments through which that grace is communicated to believers (Calvin)? That is a question the HC does not address. It neither affirms nor denies one position or the other. The catechism extends as far as the two reformers might agree, but no further.[117]

That still leaves the question of whether this approach conforms to the Augsburg Confession. Melanchthon's original 1530 edition of the Augsburger had stated: "The body and blood of Christ are truly present and distributed to those that eat in the Lord's Supper." The German version was even more explicit: "The true body and blood of Christ are truly present under the form of the bread and wine and are distributed and received there."[118] Following a change of mind, however, Melanchthon restated his view in the altered edition of the Augsburg Confession of 1540: "With bread and wine are truly exhibited the body and blood of Christ to those that eat in the Lord's Supper."[119] To say that the body and blood of Christ are exhibited or offered with the bread and wine is much less precise than to say that they are present under the form of bread and wine. Melanchthon later echoed this position in his *Responsio* to Frederick III during the eucharistic controversies in the Palatinate when he advised the elector to be content simply with Paul's reference in 1 Corinthians 10:16 to the sacramental bread as "the communion of the body of Christ."[120] Far from being out of line with the (Altered) Augsburg Confession, therefore, the HC's silence on the relationship of sign and signified may well reflect Frederick's lifelong loyalty to the Lutheran confession and his heeding of Melanchthon's advice.

Conclusion

What then can we conclude from this brief study? At the very least, we have shown that when it comes to the sources and theological orientation of the HC,

116. SC 53; LC 266, 267.

117. Bierma, *Sacraments in the Heidelberg Catechism*, 27.

118. *Creeds of Christendom*, ed. Schaff, vol. 1, *The History of Creeds* (1931; reprint, Grand Rapids: Baker, 1990), 241.

119. Ibid.

120. CR 9:960-62. Cf. HC 77, where the authors quote from 1 Cor. 10:16 in answer to a question about where Christ promises to nourish and refresh believers with his body and blood.

we have to be careful how we use labels. For example, to apply the modern term *ecumenical* to a premodern document such as the HC can be misleading. As with so many confessions of its age, the HC is anything but ecumenical in those places where it defines its teaching over against Roman Catholicism, Anabaptism, and the brand of Lutheranism later embodied in the Formula of Concord. The modern term also has primarily ecclesiastical and theological connotations, which could lead one to overlook the political pressures that motivated so much of sixteenth-century ecumenism, including the production of the HC.

However, to go to the other extreme and identify the HC as Calvinist, Melanchthonian, Zwinglian, or Bullingerian is even less helpful. In the past, these labels have been used largely in one of two ways: either to suggest literary dependence of the HC on the works of a particular theologian or to suggest the presence in the HC of doctrinal distinctives from a particular theological tradition. In neither case, however, have these labels proven to be accurate. So far as literary dependence is concerned, we cannot say, for example, that the HC any more obviously derived its structure directly from Melanchthon's *Loci* than it did from the Lutheran "Summa" of Regensburg or the Reformed confessions of Theodore Beza. Furthermore, the theological slant of the theme of gratitude in HC part 3 or of the uses of the law in parts 1 and 3 is not distinctively Calvinistic, as has often been claimed. Nor does the sacramental teaching of the HC reflect a distinctive doctrinal viewpoint. Indeed, on theological issues where such angularities might most be expected to surface—predestination, covenant, the relationship between sign and signified in the sacraments—the HC is either muted or silent. The focus is nearly always on common theological ground among the followers of Melanchthon, Calvin, and Bullinger. In this limited respect, at least, we may speak of the ecumenical spirit of the HC.

This elusive theological ancestry should not really surprise us. By the time the HC was being composed in the early 1560s, the triadic structure and much of the doctrinal material that filled out that structure had become part of the common property of the Protestant world, and without records of the actual sources used in the preparation of the catechism, we are not in a position to establish precise literary paternity.[121] Even more important, however, is that the HC represented an attempt by Frederick III, who personally disliked theological labels, to forge a consensus among the Melanchthonians, Calvinists, and Zwinglians in his realm. Little wonder, then, that so few distinctives of these theological traditions can be detected in the structure or doctrinal content of the HC. If one still insists on using labels, the most that should be said is that the HC was a Melanchthonian-Reformed gloss on the altered Augsburg Confession—but a gloss that emphasized consensus among the Protestant parties of the Palatinate. To press these labels on the HC any harder is to do it an injustice, for the intent of the catechism was to overcome the very divisions that such labels represent.

121. Cf. Reu's comment that "wenn man aber weiss, wie gar manche Ausführungen in den katechetischen Schriften dieser Zeit Gemeingut der ganzen evangelischen Kirche waren, wird man sich nicht viel bemühen, solchen Anklängen nachzugehen, denn man könnte solche fast aus der ganzen damaligen Katechismusliteratur beibringen." *Süddeutsche Katechismen*, 201.

4

Early Editions and Translations of the Heidelberg Catechism

Karin Y. Maag

While other contributions in this volume examine the origins, authorship, and theological sources of the Heidelberg Catechism, this chapter provides an overview of the early editions and translations of the Heidelberg Catechism, covering the first hundred years from its original publication in 1563. Indeed, it is important to look at the printing history of the Catechism as it circulated across Europe in many different languages, for one of the best ways of gauging its effectiveness is to analyze how the Heidelberg Catechism spread and how it was received. The focus of this contribution will not only be the Catechism itself but also related works, such as commentaries and polemical texts, for or against the Catechism. The inclusion of these related works indicates how significant an impact the Catechism had beyond the standard use of the text as a tool to teach doctrine to the young. Indeed, the Heidelberg Catechism served as a rallying point in ongoing doctrinal controversies, especially between the Reformed and the Lutherans. Thus, this study of the early versions of the Catechism will open a window into the complex world of the Reformation, where a catechism designed to teach the Christian faith could also serve to delineate the borders between confessional groups.

The earliest editions of the Heidelberg Catechism were printed in Heidelberg in 1563. Heidelberg was the chief city of the Palatinate, one of the princely states of the Holy Roman Empire. The city served as the Palatine political and educational headquarters, especially given the presence of Heidelberg University, established in 1386.[1] From the late 1550s, under the leadership of the Elector Ottheinrich, the Palatinate had moved from Catholicism to Lutheranism. His successor, Elector Frederick III the Pious, brought the Palatinate from

---

1. For more on the history of Heidelberg University from the mid-sixteenth century to the start of the Thirty Years' War, see Karin Maag, *Seminary or University? The Genevan Academy and Reformed Higher Education, 1560-1620* (Ashgate: Scolar Press, 1995), 154-71.

Lutheranism to a more Reformed Protestant position.[2] In the process, the Elector and his advisors worked to create a series of texts that were designed to shape Reformed Protestantism in the Palatinate. In other words, the Palatine leaders strove to ensure consistency of belief and practice in the churches by providing key documents for use by the faithful. The Heidelberg Catechism was one such work. It clearly went through a process of revision even after it was published. Four different versions in German were all published during the course of 1563, between January and November, if one relies upon the dates of the prefaces.[3]

The first version, *Catechismus oder Christlicher Underricht, wie der in Kirchen und Schulen der Churfürstlichen Pfaltz getrieben wirdt*, had a preface dated January 19, 1563 and was put out in the name of the Palatine Elector Frederick III. In the preface, he noted that his aim was to help teachers and pastors throughout the Palatinate teach young people the bases of their faith in a consistent manner. The Elector especially singled out for criticism the range of catechisms used up to that point, and the teachers' tendency to "make daily changes at will" in the texts they used.[4] Thanks to this official Catechism, shaped by the advice of the theology faculty of Heidelberg University and by the superintendents and leading churchmen of the Palatinate, the Elector's intention was to ensure that the youth would be taught pure and consistent Scriptural doctrine.[5] Thus, the purpose of the Catechism was not only to teach good doctrine but also to replace the eclectic collection of homemade catechisms fashioned by pastors who had each made an attempt to present Reformed doctrines in an accessible question-and-answer format.[6]

Apart from a few minor textual revisions, the main difference between the first version and the second version of the Heidelberg Catechism was the insertion in the second edition of a question and answer on the difference between the Lord's Supper and the Mass.[7] The last folio of the Catechism (f. 96) stated that the added question and answer had been omitted from the first edition but now were inserted on the order of the Palatine elector.[8] The new section underlined the division between Protestants and Catholics over their

2. For an in-depth analysis of the historical background of the Palatinate, as it relates to the history of the Heidelberg Catechism, see Fred Klooster, *The Heidelberg Catechism: Origin and History* (Grand Rapids: Calvin Theological Seminary, 1981), 6-145.

3. J. I. Doedes, *De Heidelbergsche Catechismus in zijne eerste levensjaren, 1563-1567* (Utrecht: Kemink, 1867). Doedes is strongly convinced that the first edition did not appear until February of 1563, and that the date of the preface does not correspond to the completion of the first printing, 19-20.

4. *Bekenntnisschriften und Kirchenordnungen der nach Gottes Wort reformierten Kirche*, ed. Wilhelm Niesel (Zurich: Evangelischer Verlag, 1938), 139.

5. Ibid., 138-39.

6. On the profusion of catechisms in the Holy Roman Empire in the early modern period, see Gerald Strauss, *Luther's House of Learning* (Baltimore: Johns Hopkins University Press, 1978), 164-65.

7. Doedes, *De Heidelbergsche Catechismus*, 25-26.

8. "An den Christlichen Leser. Was im ersten truck ubersehen, als fürnemlich folio 55. Ist jetzunder auss befelch Churfürstlicher Gnaden. addiert worden." Doedes, *De Heidelbergsche Catechismus*, 26.

different understandings of the key sacrament of Communion. Although the Catechism was intended primarily as a pedagogical text, the effort to distinguish the Reformed from the Catholic position inevitably led to a polemical approach. Indeed, the newly-inserted material ended with the following sentence: "Thus the Mass is basically nothing but an idolatrous denial of the one sacrifice and suffering of Jesus Christ."[9] Not surprisingly, this strong statement led to equally strong attacks from confessional opponents. Yet the overall intent of the Catechism continued to be to educate the faithful. For instance, at the end of the Catechism text, the second edition also contained twenty-two folios of Christian prayers for use in the home and at church.[10]

The third edition differed from the second chiefly in terms of its more expanded answer to what became question 80, regarding the difference between the Lord's Supper and the Mass. The answer to that question in the third edition was about twice as long as the answer inserted into the second edition. The third edition became the definitive version on which both later German editions and translations in other languages were usually based.[11] Given that the debate over the presence of Christ in the sacrament of Communion was one of the major points of contention both between Catholics and Protestants, and between Reformed and Lutheran Protestants, it is not surprising that question and answer 80 were worked and reworked until the Palatine authorities were satisfied. The answer was reinforced in the third edition both by adding a section on the true significance of the Lord's Supper and by adding yet more criticism of the Mass, ending with the statement that the Mass was "a condemnable idolatry."[12]

As for the fourth edition, while its text replicated that of the third edition, the most significant visible difference was a change in the title, which now read *Kirchenordnung, wie es mit der christlichen Lehre, heiligen Sacramenten, und Ceremonien, inn des durchleuchtigsten Herrn Friedrichs Pfaltzgraven bey Rhein . . . . gehalten wirdt.* Indeed, the volume contained more than simply the text of the Catechism. Instead, the Catechism took its place amid a range of church ordinances, including instructions on celebrating baptisms and the Lord's Supper. Thus, the Catechism was not intended as a stand-alone work but rather was understood as a key part of the ordinances and other texts that helped to shape the Reformed church.[13] The general preface to this work was dated November 15, 1563.[14] In it, Elector Frederick reiterated the need for a consistent approach to religious training and indicated that the newly written church ordinances were to be used as faithfully as the Catechism.[15] The Catechism itself was prefaced in the

9. Klooster, *The Heidelberg Catechism*, 186.

10. Doedes, *De Heidelbergsche Catechismus*, 26-27.

11. For information on the pattern of the early editions, see D. Nauta's comprehensive list in "Die Verbreitung des Katechismus, Übersetzung in andere Sprachen, moderne Bearbeitungen" in *Handbuch zum Heidelberger Katechismus*, ed. Lothar Coenen (Neukirchen: Neukirchener Verlag, 1963), 40-41.

12. Klooster, *The Heidelberg Catechism*, 188.

13. *Bekenntnisschriften*, 137.

14. Nauta, 'Die Verbreitung', 41.

15. *Bekenntnisschriften*, 140-41.

fourth edition by two paragraphs, one laying out the importance of catechetical training and the other setting out how the Catechism was to be used in practice in the churches. The first paragraph even managed to include yet another attack on Catholic practices by contrasting the Catholic sacrament of confirmation unfavorably with the healthy religious training for young people provided by the Heidelberg Catechism.[16]

After the success of its first year, the Heidelberg Catechism was regularly reprinted in German in its first hundred years. It was published in a range of formats, from quarto- to octavo-sized and continued to be paired with the entire body of the Palatine church ordinances in most instances. Places of publication for these German editions included not only Heidelberg but also Neustadt an der Hardt (1584), Herborn (1588 and 1603), Amsterdam (1646), and Basle (1659).[17] The variety of places of publication indicates how important the Catechism was for a wide range of German-speaking Reformed communities, both within the German lands and beyond their borders. The Neustadt an der Hardt edition of 1584 is particularly significant because it was brought out just after the end of the reign of the Lutheran Elector Palatine, Ludwig VI. Johann Casimir, Ludwig's brother, who was Reformed, had retreated to Neustadt during the time of his brother's rule and had recreated a Calvinist center of learning and a Calvinist court.[18] The Heidelberg Catechism had become such a significant feature of Reformed identity that, after Ludwig's death in 1584, it was felt necessary to reprint it in Neustadt in 1584, in spite of the fact that there had already been at least five previous editions in German published in prior years. Specific German editions of the Catechism were also prepared for school children (1609 and 1611), as well as for those who wanted a simplified book: The 1659 edition of the Heidelberg Catechism advertised on the title page that it came "without the church ceremonies."[19]

In contrast to those who may have wanted a simpler text, others became acquainted with the Catechism in a more scholarly form, namely in Latin. Because Latin was the international language of learning in the sixteenth century, putting a text into Latin enabled the work to cross over geographic boundaries with ease, thus making it accessible to those who knew Latin across Europe. Given that the Heidelberg Catechism was translated into Latin already in 1563, it is clear that one aim of the Catechism's creators was to bring the work to the attention of the wider scholarly world. Heidelberg printers reissued the text in 1566, 1570, 1571, and 1575. Significantly, a Latin version was also printed in 1584 in Neustadt an der Hardt. The same printer produced both the German version discussed above and the Latin translation. Latin versions of the Catechism were also printed in Antwerp (1584), Leiden (1587 and 1626), Hanau

16. Ibid., 148-49.
17. See finding list at the end of this contribution.
18. For information on the Palatinate during this period and on the rivalry between Ludwig VI and Johann Casimir, see Volker Press, *Calvinismus und Territoriaalstaat: Regierung und Zentralbehörden der Kurpfalz 1559-1619* (Stuttgart: Ernst Klett, 1970), 267-321.
19. See finding list at the end of this contribution.

(1603, 1614, and 1656), Oxford (1629), and Edinburgh (1657).[20] The Heidelberg Catechism's dual role as provider of both religious education and academic training came through most clearly in the series of editions produced after 1600, in which the Latin and Greek versions of the text were printed on facing pages. These versions were clearly intended for students, who could simultaneously improve their knowledge of the ancient languages and their understanding of the Reformed faith through the use of a single text. Latin-Greek versions of the Heidelberg Catechism were published in Geneva in 1609; in Hanau in 1610, 1614, and 1625; in Frankfurt in 1625; in Amsterdam in 1623 and 1638; and in Utrecht in 1660.[21]

While the German versions of the Heidelberg Catechism were intended primarily for the German market, the Latin and Latin-Greek versions were destined for a geographically widespread clientele. However, there were also those who lived outside the German lands who wished to gain access to the Catechism, yet knew neither German nor Latin. For these readers, the Heidelberg Catechism began to appear in translated versions as early as 1563. The range of languages into which the Catechism was translated, the speed at which this translation process was done, and the large number of reprints all point to the popularity of the Heidelberg Catechism as a key document in the creation and upholding of Reformed identity. Indeed, had the Catechism not been perceived as important, there would have been no need or incentive to have it reprinted so often in so many languages in the sixteenth and seventeenth centuries.

Among the most prolific translators of the Catechism were the Dutch. The earliest Dutch version appeared in 1563 in Emden on the German-Dutch border. Another edition, printed by Michael Schirat, appeared in Heidelberg in the same year. At least twenty-two Dutch editions appeared prior to 1600, including six editions in 1566 alone. Printers in most Dutch cities, including Delft, Deventer, Antwerp, Rotterdam, Amsterdam, Harderwyk, and Utrecht produced the Dutch-language Catechism.[22] Given that printers preferred to reprint popular texts for a local market rather than going to the trouble and expense of shipping copies from one place to the next, it seems clear that there was a steady clientele for this work across the Reformed Dutch communities. Over time its move from cities in the southern provinces of the Netherlands, which reverted to Spanish Catholic control by the end of the sixteenth century, to cities in the north reflects the history of Calvinism in the Netherlands. Though there were Dutch Calvinists in the southern provinces in the 1560s and 1570s, by the end of the century most had sought refuge in the north where Calvinism was the official faith. The early importance of Emden as a printing center for Reformed works in Dutch, including the Catechism, should not be discounted. Emden was in the German lands rather than in the Low Countries, but its geographic location on the border between the two areas made it an ideal location for Dutch Calvinist refugees fleeing the persecution orchestrated by the Spanish Catholic authorities. The

20. See finding list at the end of this contribution
21. See finding list at the end of this contribution.
22. See finding list at the end of this contribution.

presence of the Dutch in large numbers in Emden from the 1560s onward led to a dramatic increase in Dutch publications for this emerging market, especially in works designed to sustain the faith of the exiles. The Heidelberg Catechism fit well in this category.[23]

While the Dutch translations of the Heidelberg Catechism appeared in large numbers during the first hundred years of its existence, versions of the Catechism in other European languages took longer to appear and were reprinted less frequently. In part, this difference was due to greater linguistic hurdles. While Dutch and German are clearly distinct languages, they do share common roots, thus simplifying the translating task. The jump from German to French or English was correspondingly greater. Furthermore, both the Huguenots in France and supporters of Calvinism in England had access to other catechetical texts that suited them well, whether it was Calvin's Genevan Catechism of 1542 for French-speakers or the 1549 catechism of the Church of England for English-speakers. Thus, the Heidelberg Catechism in French or in English was competing with other well-established texts.[24] Additionally, at least in the case of France, the traditional source of church-related texts had been Geneva since the mid-sixteenth century. Thus, French Protestants were not accustomed to turning to the German lands for works to sustain their devotional or pedagogical tasks. Hence, it should not be surprising to find that the Heidelberg Catechism was only translated into French and published four times during its first hundred years: once in 1590 in Haarlem, once in 1607 in an unspecified location, once in 1640 in Amsterdam, and once in 1650 in Delft. The 1607 edition may have been intended for readers who were bilingual because it offered the text of the Catechism in German and French on facing pages. Significantly, in all three cases where the place of publication is known, the printers were in the Netherlands. While part of the reason for printing the Catechism in French outside France may have been a result of the effectiveness of French Catholic censorship, a significant contingent of the readership for this work may in fact have been French-speaking Calvinists who had originally come from the southern provinces of the Low Countries. When the southern provinces were brought back to Catholicism and obedience to the rule of Spain, those who did not want to live under these circumstances fled north, to the newly-independent Dutch provinces, bringing their faith and their language with them. These French-speaking Dutch

23. For an excellent discussion of the printing industry in Emden and its links to Dutch Calvinism, see Andrew Pettegree, *Emden and the Dutch Revolt* (Oxford: Oxford University Press, 1992), 87-108.

24. On the use of Calvin's catechism in Geneva and France see E. Arnaud, *Notice Historique sur les deux catéchismes officiels de l'Eglise Réformée de France: Calvin & Ostervald* (Paris: Grassart, 1885). For catechetical texts in England, see David Siegenthaler, "Religious Education for Citizenship: Primer and Catechism" in *The Godly Kingdom of Tudor England: Great Books of the English Reformation*, ed. John Booty (Wilton: Morehouse-Barlow, 1981), 241-45.

established communities of faith known as the Walloon churches. Hence, the French-language editions of the Heidelberg Catechism may very well have been intended for Calvinists in the Netherlands rather than for those in France.[25]

As for English versions of the Heidelberg Catechism, these were somewhat more numerous than the French translations. The first English edition appeared in 1572 and was printed in London, with subsequent editions printed in 1578 (London), 1588 (Oxford), 1591 (Edinburgh), 1615 (Edinburgh, two editions), 1617 (London), and 1652 (Amsterdam).[26] The Edinburgh editions' importance for the Scottish Calvinists was reinforced by the statement on the 1591 title page that this Catechism had been "authorized by the Kinges Maiestie, for the use of Scotland."[27] In 1615, the title page of one edition was even more specific: "Appointed to be printed for the use of the Kirke of Edinburgh."[28] In the second edition of 1615, although the Catechism was not mentioned on the title page, it was bound together with the Psalter, a calendar, and the Book of Common Order. In this instance, the Heidelberg Catechism in its English translation was integrated into the same sort of volume as the fourth German edition of the Catechism was in 1563. In Scotland, as in Heidelberg, the Catechism was considered sufficiently important to be included among the primary liturgical texts of the church.

While translations of the Heidelberg Catechism into English, French, and Dutch provided sufficient access to the work for Calvinists from these linguistic groups, other translations, albeit done less frequently, show how geographically extensive the impact of this Catechism was. For instance, the Heidelberg Catechism appeared four times in Hungarian in its first hundred years, in Pápa in 1577, in Debrecen in 1604, in Herborn in 1607, and in Oppenheim in 1612.[29] Once again, the Catechism was published together with other liturgical texts in some instances: the 1607 edition brought together the Catechism and the Hungarian Psalter, while the 1612 version was printed together with the Hungarian Bible. As in the case of Scotland, the Heidelberg Catechism received official support in Hungary. Among the church bodies that ordered congregations to use the Heidelberg Catechism were the Upper Danubian Reformed Church province in 1619, the Western Danubian Reformed Church province in 1630, and the National Synod of the Hungarian Reformed Church in 1646. One should note, however, that the 1646 National Synod also stated that churches could legitimately use a native Hungarian catechism by János Siderius.[30] Other eastern European areas with significant Calvinist populations also ensured that the Heidelberg Catechism would be available in the local language, as in the case of

---

25. See finding list at the end of this contribution. See also Nauta, "Die Verbreitung," 50-51.
26. See finding list at the end of this contribution.
27. See finding list at the end of this contribution.
28. See finding list at the end of this contribution.
29. See finding list at the end of this contribution. See also Graeme Murdock, "Calvinist catechizing and Hungarian Reformed identity" in *Confessional Identity in East-Central Europe*, ed. Maria Crăciun, Ovidiu Ghitta, and Graeme Murdock (Aldershot: Ashgate, 2002), 88.
30. Murdock, "Calvinist catechizing," 88-89.

the Czech version published for the use of Bohemian Calvinists in 1619.[31] Indeed, the timing of this publication is significant because it occurred at the start of the Thirty Years' War when largely Protestant Bohemia was under attack by the forces of the Catholic Holy Roman Emperor. The ties with Heidelberg were reinforced by the Bohemian offer of the crown to the Palatine Elector, Friedrich V. Hence, the publication of the Heidelberg Catechism in Bohemian may well have been intended to reinforce the bond between the Bohemian Calvinists and their German fellow believers.[32] A further edition of the Heidelberg Catechism was also produced for Romanian Calvinists and was published in 1648. The Romanian pastor who translated the work, István Fogarasi, noted that it was intended primarily to help Romanian Calvinists, some of whom were recent converts from the Orthodox church, learn the basics of the faith.[33] In an area in which Calvinists were the minority and the Orthodox Church predominated, it was important for the Calvinists to turn to works such as the Heidelberg Catechism to provide a solid doctrinal foundation for their communities.

Calvinists in eastern Europe were not the only ones who sought to provide the Heidelberg Catechism in the language of those living in confessionally divided areas. Others who found themselves in equally difficult situations also turned to the Catechism as one of the elements to help shape their Reformed identity. Such was the case, for instance, in Graubünden in the southeastern Swiss lands where a version of the Heidelberg Catechism was made available in Romansch in 1613.[34] Published in Zurich, the work was intended for Calvinists who lived in the confessionally mixed area and who were subject to pressure from Catholic forces. Once again, the Catechism served not only as a teaching tool but also as a reminder to the Calvinists in Graubünden that they were part of a larger community of belief.[35]

Significantly, the Catechism in Romansch was printed together with a commentary by Zacharias Ursinus, one of Heidelberg's foremost theologians and a contributor to the text of the Catechism itself.[36] Ursinus' commentary, the *Corpus doctrinae Christianae ecclesiarum* was first published in Latin in 1591, after his

---

31. See finding list at the end of this contribution.

32. For information on the connections between international Calvinism and events in Bohemia in the later sixteenth and early seventeenth centuries, see Joachim Bahlcke, "Calvinism and estate liberation movements in Bohemia and Hungary (1570-1620)" in *The Reformation in Eastern and Central Europe*, ed. Karin Maag (Aldershot: Scolar Press, 1997), 72-91.

33. Maria Crăciun, "Building a Romanian Reformed community in seventeenth-century Transylvania" in *Confessional Identity in East-Central Europe*, 114.

34. See finding list at the end of this contribution.

35. For a brief summary of the religious situation in Graubünden in the early seventeenth century, and the links between Graubünden and other Reformed centers, see the introduction to the *Registres de la Compagnie des Pasteurs de Genève*, ed. Nicolas Fornerod, Philippe Boros, Gabriella Cahier, and Matteo Campagnolo (Geneva: Droz, 2001), 35-41.

36. For discussions on the authorship of the Catechism, see Lyle Bierma's contribution in this volume.

death, and was brought to press by his colleague, the theologian David Pareus.[37] The commentary was based on the lectures Ursinus gave at Heidelberg University on the doctrines of the Catechism. Like the Catechism itself, Ursinus' work was intended to provide doctrinal instruction, but, in doing so, it also served to help differentiate the Reformed views from those of competing confessional groups, such as Lutherans and Catholics.[38] The *Corpus doctrinae Christianae* proved to be highly successful in presenting the doctrinal implications of the Catechism to a wide readership. At least thirteen Latin editions of the work appeared between 1591 and 1663, published in cities such as Heidelberg and Neustadt, as well as in Geneva, where three editions appeared in 1612, 1616, and 1623. The English edition of Ursinus' commentary, published as *The Summe of Christian Religion*, was also extremely popular—at least twenty-three editions appeared between 1587 and 1663. The overall polemical context of the work was unmistakable. For instance, the 1645 edition brought together Ursinus' commentary and a separate text by David Pareus. The title page noted that Ursinus' work offered the opportunity to see "debated and resolved the questions of whatsoever points of moment have been or are controversed in divinitie."[39] All the English editions were published either in London, the English printing center, or in Oxford, undoubtedly for the university market. Nine editions of the commentary also appeared in Dutch between 1606 and 1657 under the title *Het Schat-Boeck der verklaringhen over de catechismus der christelicke religie die in de Gereformeerde Kercken ende scholen van Hoogh- en Neder-Duytslandt gheleert wordt*. The Dutch versions were printed in Amsterdam and in Leiden, the seat of the Dutch United Provinces' most important university.[40]

Yet, the commentary on its own only reached a certain audience, namely readers who had both the education and the patience to wade through between five hundred and a thousand pages of text, depending on the translation and the specific edition. Indeed, although Ursinus' commentary did engage in polemic to the extent that it laid out the Reformed doctrinal position and refuted the views of other confessions, much of the controversy over the Heidelberg Catechism was published in shorter and more readily accessible works.

---

37. Heinrich Graffmann, "Die Erklärung des Heidelberger Katechismus in Predigt und Unterricht des 16. bis 18. Jahrhunderts" in *Handbuch zum Heidelberger Katechismus*, ed. Lothar Coenen (Neukirchen: Neukirchener Verlag, 1963), 65-66. Graffmann provides a concise and helpful analysis of Ursinus' approach in his commentary.

38. For an analysis of Ursinus's commentary, see Derk Visser, *Zacharias Ursinus: The Reluctant Reformer: His Life and Times* (New York: United Church Press, 1983), 191-223.

39. Zacharias Ursinus, *The summe of Christian religion, delivered by Zacharias Ursinus first, by way of catechism, and then afterwards more enlarged by a sound and judicious exposition, and application of the same: wherein also are debated and resolved the questions of whatsoever points of moment have been, or are controversed in divinitie* (London: James Young, 1645).

40. To find out more about any of the editions listed here, readers are advised to turn to one of the most comprehensive collections of editions of Ursinus' commentaries, held by the Hekman Library at Calvin College and Calvin Theological Seminary. Rare sixteenth and seventeenth century editions of the Latin, English, and Dutch versions are complemented by the early versions available through the Early English Books Online, to which the Hekman Library subscribes.

Most of those who wrote against the Catechism in the sixteenth century came from the Lutheran camp. They opposed the work, and Reformed doctrine more generally, chiefly because of controversies over the Lord's Supper and because of disagreements regarding the correct understanding of the meaning of this sacrament. The first and most striking characteristic of these polemical works against the Heidelberg Catechism is the speed at which they were produced. In most instances, they appeared already in 1563 and 1564, only weeks or months after the Catechism itself. The rapid pace of publication was clearly dictated by the Lutherans' desire to make a swift response to limit the impact of the Catechism. Indeed, one can conclude that opponents perceived the Catechism as a danger because they were so quick to rush into print to attack it. Among the Lutheran theologians who wrote against the Heidelberg Catechism was Matthias Flacius Illyricus, one of the leading Lutheran hard-liners. Flacius Illyricus expressed his opposition in an undated tract, probably issued in 1563, entitled *Widerlegung eines kleinen deutschen calvinischen Catechismi.* In it, he described the Catechism as a poisonous work full of errors. His strategy involved establishing a list of what he saw as errors and using the standard polemical tool of quoting selectively from the original text and demolishing the quotations in his commentary.[41] He was joined in his stance by another leading Lutheran polemicist, Tilemann Heshusius, who brought out his *Trewe Warnung für den Heidelbergischen Calvinischen Catechissmum* in 1564. Heshusius also referred to the Heidelberg Catechism as poisonous and was particularly worried about the impact of the Catechism on youth who would then, according to Heshusius, be brought up absorbing these errors and be led along false paths.[42] Each of these vernacular works came to less than seventy-five folios, making them accessible to a general readership in the German lands both in terms of language and in terms of purchase cost.

The Reformed theologians, meanwhile, were equally quick to rebut the Lutheran criticisms in print. In 1564 alone, Zacharias Ursinus published three tracts refuting the charges made against the Heidelberg Catechism. One of the works, the *Gründlicher Bericht vom heiligen Abendmahl* concentrated specifically on controversies over the Lord's Supper, while the second, *Antwortt auff etlicher Theologien Censur über die am rand dess Heydelberger Catechismi auss heiliger Scrifft angezogene Zeugnusse* dealt with criticisms by the Catechism's opponents regarding the choice of biblical texts that had appeared as supporting references in the margins of the Catechism. In his third tract, *Verantwortung wider die ungegründten aufflagen unnd verkerungen,* Ursinus refuted the range of charges brought against

41. Matthias Flacius Illyricus, *Widerlegung eines kleinen deutschen calvinischen Catechismi, so in disem M.D.Lxiij. Jar, sampt etlichen andern irrigen Tractetlin ausgangen* (Regensburg: Heinrich Geissler, [1563]). Flacius Illyricus' work is available in the IDC microfiche series, "The Reformation in Heidelberg."

42. Tileman Heshusius, *Trewe Warnung für den Heidelbergischen Calvinischen Catechissmum: sampt Widerlegung etlicher Irthumen desselben* ([Eisleben: Urban Gaubisch], 1564). Heshusius' work is also available in the IDC microfiche series, "The Reformation in Heidelberg."

the Catechism by its detractors.[43] Each of these tracts again made efforts to be brief; none came to more than 170 folios. Two of the three works mentioned above, namely the first and the third, came out in the name of the entire theological faculty of the University of Heidelberg, thus reinforcing the communal character of the response.[44]

Overall, the flurry of publications that greeted the first editions of the Heidelberg Catechism is evidence of the Catechism's significant impact. While its detractors concentrated on labeling the work as poisonous and inspired by the Devil, its supporters insisted on the importance of providing access to true doctrine as compared with the "dreams and sophistries" of their opponents.[45] Indeed, the proponents of the Heidelberg Catechism could find encouragement over the longer term from the number of ruling bodies of the Reformed churches across Europe that gave the Catechism semiofficial or official recognition as key confessional statements. We have already seen how Scottish Calvinists gave the Heidelberg Catechism their approval even prior to the start of the seventeenth century. Similar support came from the Hungarians and from the Dutch Calvinists who adopted the Heidelberg Catechism as one of their official doctrinal standards at the Synod of Dordt in 1618. In the end, the extensive dissemination of the Heidelberg Catechism and supporting works in its first hundred years, in a wide range of languages, is testimony to the enduring significance of the work for the shaping of the Reformed churches' identity in the sixteenth and seventeenth centuries.

Finding list of Heidelberg Catechism editions, 1563-1663

German

1. *Catechismus, oder, Christlicher Underricht, wie der in Kirchen und Schulen der churfürstlichen Pfaltz getrieben wirdt*. Heidelberg: Johann Mayer, 1563.
2. *Catechismus, oder, Christlicher Underricht, wie der in Kirchen und Schulen der Churfürstlichen Pfaltz getrieben wirdt: Was im ersten Truck ubersehen, als*

---

43. Information on Ursinus' tracts appears in Klooster, *The Heidelberg Catechism*, 208.

44. *Gründtlicher Bericht vom Heiligen Abendmal unsers Herren Jesu Christi, aus einhelliger Lere der Heiligen Schrift, der alten rechtgläubigen christlichen Kirchen und auch der Augspurgischen Confession gestellt durch der Universitet Heydelberg Theologen* (Heidelberg: Johann Mayer, 1564); Zacharias Ursinus, *Antwort auff etlicher Theologen Censur uber die am Rand dess Heydelbergischen Catechismi, auss Heiliger Schrifft angezogene Zeugnusse . . .* (Neustadt an der Hardt: Matthaeus Harnisch, [1584]). According to Klooster, the first edition of this work appeared in 1564: Klooster, *The Heidelberg Catechism*, 208. *Verantwortung wider die ungegründten Aufflagen unnd Verkerungen, mit welchen der Catechismus christlicher Lere, zu Heidelberg im Jar M.D.LXIII aussgangen, von etlichen unbillicher Weise beschweret ist* (Heidelberg, Johann Mayer, 1564). See the catalogue for the IDC microfiche series, "The Reformation in Heidelberg."

45. See Zacharias Ursinus, *Verantwortung wider die ungegründten Aufflagen und Verkerungen, mit welchen der Catechismus christlicher Lere, zu Heidelberg im Jar M.D.LXIII. aussgangen, von etlichen unbillicher Weise beschweret ist*, fol. 7v.

fürnemlich Folio 55, ist jetzunder auss Befelch churfürstlicher Gnaden addiert worden. Heidelberg: Johann Mayer, 1563.

3. *Catechismus, oder, Christlicher Vnderricht: wie der in Kirchen vnd Schulen der Churfürstlichen Pfaltz getrieben wirdt.* 3d ed. Heidelberg: Johann Mayer, 1563.

4. *Kirchenordnung, wie es mit der christlichen Lehre, heiligen Sacramenten, unnd Ceremonien, inn dess durchleuchtigsten Herrn Friderichs Pfaltzgraven bey Rhein . . . gehalten wirdt.* Heidelberg, Johann Mayer, 1563.

5. *Catechismus Oder, Kurtzer underricht Christlicher Lehr, Wie der in der Chur vnd Fürstlichen Pfaltz Kirchen vnd Schulen getrieben wirt, sampt den Kirchen Cermonien, Gebeten, und gantzen vollkom[m]enen zeugnussen Biblischer Schrifft.* Neustadt an der Hardt: Matthaeus Harnisch, 1584.

6. *Catechismus, Oder Kurtzer underricht Christlicher Lehr, wie der in Kirchen vnd Schulen der Chur unnd Fürstlichen Pfaltz getrieben wirdt: Sampt den Kirchen Cermonien und Gebeten.* Herborn: Christoff Raben, 1588.

7. *Kirchenordnung: wie es mit der christlichen Lehre, heyligen Sacramenten, und Ceremonien, in des durchleuchtigsten, hochgebornen Fürsten vnd Herrn, Herrn Friderichs Pfaltzgraffen bey Rhein, des Heyligen Römischen Reichs Ertztruchsessen vnd Churfürsten, Hertzogen in Bayern, Churfürstenthumb gehalten wirdt.* Heidelberg: Gothard Vögelin, 1601.

8. *Catechismus, Oder Kurtzer Underricht Christlicher Lehr, wie der in Kirchen und Schulen der Chur unnd Fürstlichen Pfaltz getrieben wirdt: Sampt den Kirchen Cermonien und Gebeten.* Herborn: Christoff Raben, 1603.

9. *Catechismus oder, Kurtzer unterricht christlicher lehr wie der in kirchen und schulen der churfürstlicher Pfaltz verordnung kürtzlich erklärt und mit zeugnussen der Schrift bestetiget: für die schuljugend in ihrer churfürstlichen gnaden landen.* Heidelberg: Gotthard Vögelin, 1609.

10. *Catechismus, Oder Kurtzer underricht Christlicher Lehr, wie der in Kirchen unnd Schulen der Churfürstl. Pflatz getriben wird: Aus Churfürstl. Pfaltz verordnung kürtzlich erklärt, un[d] mit zeugnussen der Schrift bestätiget: für die Schuljugend in Irer Churfürstl. Gnaden Landen.* Amberg: [s.n.], 1611.

11. *Catechismus, oder Kurtzer Underricht Christlicher Lehr wie der in Kyrchen und Schulen der Churfürstlichen Pfaltz getrieben wird. Samt den Kyrchen-Ceremonien und Gebäten.* Amsterdam: Ludwig Elzevier, 1646.

12. *Catechismus, oder Kurtzer underricht Christlicher Lehr: wie der in Kirchen und Schulen der churfürstlichen Pfaltz getrieben wird. Ohne die Kirchen-Ceremonien.* Basle: Theodor Falckeisen, 1659.

Latin

13. *Catechesis religionis christianae, quae traditur in ecclesiis et scholis Palatinatus.* Heidelberg: Michael Schirat and Johann Mayer, 1563.

14. *Catechesis Religionis Christianae, Quae Tradita In Ecclesiis & Scholis Palatinatus, sub Friderico III. Electore, & traditur nunc quoque in ditione illustris. Princ. Iohan. Casimiri Comitis Palatini, &c.* Neustadt an der Hardt: Matthaeus Harnisch, 1584.

15. *Catechesis religionis Christianae, quae traditur in ecclesiis et scholis Palatinatus.* Heidelberg: Jacob Mylius and Heinrich Avenae, 1585.
16. *Catechesis religionis christianae, quae in ecclesiis et scholis Palatinatus, sub Frederico III electore tradebatur.* Leiden: Jan Paets Jacobszoon, 1587.
17. *Catechesis religionis Christianae, quae in ecclesiis et scholis Electoralis Palatinatus traditur.* Hanau: Wilhelm Antonius, 1603.
18. *Catechesis Religionis Christianae.* Hanau: [s.n.] 1614.
19. *Catechesis Religionis Christianae.* Neustadt an der Hardt: [s.n.], 1615.
20. *Catechesis Religionis Christianae, de novo edita.* Leiden: [s.n.], 1626.
21. *Catechesis religionis christianae.* Oxford: [s.n.], 1629.
22. *Catechesis Religionis Christianae, quae iin Ecclesiis & scholis reformatis docetur.* Hanau: [s.n.], 1656.
23. *Catechesis Religionis Christianae, quae iin Ecclesiis & scholis reformatis docetur.* Edinburgh, 1657.

Dutch

24. *Catechismus, oft christelicke onderrichtinghe, ghelijck die in kercken ende scholen der cheur vorstelicken Paltz . . . gheleert wort. Uut de Hoochduydtsche sprake . . . overgeset.* S.l. [Emden], s.n. [Gillis van der Erven], 1563.
25. *Catechismus ofte onderwysinge in de christlycke leere, also die in den kercken ende scholen kuervoerstlicken Paltz geleert werdt. In de Nederduytsche spraecke overgeset.* Heidelberg: Michael Schirat, 1563.
26. *Catechismus, ofte onderwysinghe in de christelicke leere, ghelyck die in kercken ende scholen der cheur vorstelicken Paltz . . . gheleert wordt . . . Uut de Hoochduydtsche sprake . . . overgeset.* Emden, s.n. [Gillis van der Erven], 1565.
27. *Catechismus ofte onderwijsinghe in de christelicke leere, gelijck in die kercken ende scholen der cheur vorstelicken Paltz . . . gheleert wordt. Uut de Hoochduytsche sprake . . . overgeset.* S.l. [Delft], s.n. [Harman Schinckel], 1566.
28. *Catechismus, ofte onderwijsinghe in de christelijcke leere, ghelijck die in kercken ende scholen der chuer-vorstelijcken Paltz ghedreven oft gheleert wordt. Uut de Hoochduytsche sprake in Nederduytsch . . . overgeset.* S.l. [Emden], s.n.[Gillis van der Erven], 1566.
29. *Catechismus, ofte onderwijsinghe in de christelijcke leere, gelijc die in die kercken ende scholen der chuervorstelijcken Paltz ghedreven oft gheleert wordt. Uut de Hoochduytsche sprake int Nederduytsche . . . overghesedt.* S.l. [Emden], s.n. [Gillis van der Erven], 1566.
30. *Cathechismus, ofte onderwijsinghe in de christelicke leere, gelijc die in kercken ende scholen der cheur-vorstelicken Palts . . . geleert wordt. Uut de Hoochduytsche sprake . . . overgeset.* Emden, Willem Gailliart, 1566.
31. *Kerckenordeninge: gelijck als die Leere, heylige Sacramenten, ende Ceremonien, in des doorluchtichsten, hoochghebooren Vorst ende Heere, Heer Frederick Paltzgrave by den Rijn, des Heyligen Roomschen Rijcks, Eertzdrost ende Cuervorst, Hartoch in Beyeren, [et]c. Chuervorstendooms by den Rijn, gheholden wort.* [Emden?: s.n.], 1566.

32. *Catechismus offte christlicke onderwijsinghe der heylsamen leere godlickes woordts, gelijck de in kercken ende scholen der chuerforstlicken Paltz, ende oock nu ter tijt in veelen christlicken ghemeinten der Nederlande . . . gheleert wordt. Uut hoochduytsch . . . overgheset.* S.l. [Deventer], [Simon I Steenberch], 1567.

33. *Catechismus ofte Onderwijsinghe inde Christelijcke leere, also die in de kercken . . . der Kueruorstelicken Paltz gheleert wert.* Amsterdam: [s.n.], 1567.

34. *Catechismus ofte onderwijsinghe inde Christelycke religie.* Antwerp: [s.n.], 1580.

35. *Catechismus ofte onderwijsinghe in de christelijcke leere, ghelijck die in kercken ende schoolen der cheur-vorstelijcken Paltz . . . gheleert wert.* Rotterdam: Dirck Mullem, [1582].

36. *Catechismus, welcke in den Gereformeerden Evangelischen Kercken ende Scholen der Keur-Vorstelijcken Pfaltz ende deser Nederlanden, geleert ende gheoeffent wordt.* Amsterdam: G. de Bouma, 1628.

37. *Christelicke Catechismus der Nederlantsche Ghereformeerde Kercken.* Harderwyck: G. de Bouma, 1646.

38. *Christelicke Catechismus.* Utrecht: [s.n.], 1647.

39. *Christelicke catechismus der Nederlantsche Gherefarmeerde Kerchen . . . Wt-gegevn door Gellium de Bouma . . . Hier achter is oock by-ghevoeght, Voor-bereydinghe tot het H. Avondtmael-ghestelt in Maniere van t'samen-spzaeck door Godefridum Udemas.* Amsterdam: Gerrit Goedesbergh, 1651.

English

40. *The catechisme, or maner to teach children and others the Christian faith: Used in all the landes and dominions that are under the mighty Prince Frederike, the Palsgrave of the Rhene.* London: Richard Johnes, 1572.

41. *The cathechisme or manner how to instruct and teach children and others in the Christian faith.* London: Henry Middleton, 1578.

42. *A catechisme, or short kind of instruction, whereby to teach children, and the ignoraunter sort, the Christian religion.* Oxford: Joseph Barnes, 1588.

43. *A catechisme of Christian religion, taught in the schooles and churches of the Low-Countrie and dominions of the Countie Palatine: with the arguments, and use of the several doctrines of the same catechisme by Jeremias Bastingius. And now authorized by the Kinges Majestie, for the use of Scotland.* Edinburgh: Robert Waldegrave, 1591.

44. *A catechisme of Christian religion . . . Appointed to be printed for the use of the Kirke of Edinburgh.* Edinburgh: Andrew Hart, 1615.

45. *The CL Psalmes of David, in prose and meeter: with their whole usuall tunes, newly corrected and amended: Hereunto is added the whole Church Discipline, and an exact Kalendar for xxv. yeeres: and also the Song of Moses in meeter, never before this time in print.* Edinburgh: Andrew Hart, 1615.

46. *A catechism of Christian religion: Allowed to be taught in the churches and schooles within the Countie Palatine.* London: Humphrey Lownes, 1617.

47. *A catechisme of Christian religion.* Amsterdam: John Frederick Stam, 1652.

French

48. *Catechisme, ou instruction en la religion chrestienne, comme elle a este dressee pour les eglises et escoles du Palatinat. Avec plusieurs prieres et cantiques ecclesiastiques. Catechismus ofte onderwijsinge in de christelijcke leere,* . . . Haarlem, Gillis Rooman, 1590.

49. *Catechisme des points principaux de la religion chrestienne. Hauptstuck christlicher Lehre. In Frantzösischer unnd Teutscher Sprachen verfertigt.* [S.l.]: Jacob Stoer, 1607.

50. *Catechisme, ou Instruction en la religion chrestienne, comme elle a esté dressé pour les Eglises et Escoles du Palatinat.* Amsterdam: [s.n.], 1640.

51. *Catechisme ou instruction en la religion Chrestienne comme elle a este dressee pour les eglises et escoles du Palatinat.* Delft:[s.n.], 1650.

Other

52. [Czech] *Katechysmus Nabozenstuj* [s.l.]: [s.n.], 1619.

53. [Greek and Latin] *Catechesis Religionis Christianae, quae in Ecclesiis et scholis Electoralis Palatinatus traditur.* Geneva: [s.n.], 1609.

54. [Greek and Latin] *Catechesis Religionis Christianae, quae in Ecclesiis et scholis Electoralis Palatinatus traditur.* Hanau: [s.n.], 1610.

55. [Greek and Latin] *Catechesis Religionis Christianae, quae in Ecclesiis et scholis Electoralis Palatinatus traditur.* Hanau: [s.n.], 1614.

56. [Greek and Latin] *Catechesis quae in ecclesiis et scholis Belgicarum provinciarum traditur.* . . . Amsterdam: H. Laurentius, 1623.

57. [Greek and Latin] *Catechesis Religionis Christianae, quae in Ecclesiis et scholis Electoralis Palatinatus traditur.* Frankfurt: [s.n.], 1625.

58. [Greek and Latin] *Catechesis Religionis Christianae Graeco-Latina,* . . . Hanau: [s.n.], 1625.

59. [Greek and Latin] *Ekklesion tes Belgikes exomologesis kai katechesis [Greek transliterated]* = *hoc est, Ecclesiarum Belgicarum confessio.* Utrecht: Hermann Ribbius, 1660.

60. [Hungarian] *A keresztyén hitröl való tudománynak roved kérdésekben foglaltatott summáj.* Pápa: [s.n.], 1577.

61. [Hungarian] *Catechesis, azaz kerdesök es feletök az kerestyeni tudomannak agairol.* Debrecen: [s.n.], 1604.

62. [Hungarian] *Kis Catechismus, avagy az keresztyén Hütnec részeiröl rövid kér desekben es feleletekben foglaltatot tudomány.* Herborn: [s.n.], 1607.

63. [Hungarian] *Szent Biblia...az palatinatusi katekizmussal.* Oppenheim: [s.n.], 1612.

64. [Latin-German] *Catechismus Latino-Germanicus: Oder, Kurtzer Lateinischer vnd Teutscher Vnderricht Christlicher Lehr, wie der in Pfältzischen Kirchen vnd Schulen gebreuchlich: Also ohne Kirchen ceremonien gedruckt, dass das grobe allein den vndern, vnd darbeneben das klein den obern Classen, mit erhaltung des völligen Textes vnd gantzer meinung.* . . . Herborn: [s.n.], 1614.

65. [Romansch] *Informatiun Chrastiauna: cun sias explicatiuns sün tuotts principaels puonks da vaira religiun.* Zurich: Typis Vuolphianis, 1613.

5

Bibliography of Research on the Heidelberg Catechism since 1900

Paul W. Fields

This bibliography contains secondary sources on the history and theology of the Heidelberg Catechism published from 1900 to the present. Five titles from the nineteenth century are also included because they are regularly referred to by authors cited in this list. The bibliography is divided into three sections: Books and Theses, Book Sections, and Journal Articles.

Books and Theses

Barger, H. H. *De Heidelbergsche catechismus als catechetisch leerboek*. Utrecht: Kemink en Zoon, 1914.

Barth, Karl. *Die christliche Lehre nach dem Heidelberger Katechismus*. Zollikon-Zurich: Evangelischer Verlag, 1948.

———. *Einfuhrung in den Heidelberger Katechismus*. Vol. 63, Theologische Studien. Zurich: EVZ-Verlag, 1960.

———. *The Heidelberg Catechism for Today*. Richmond: John Knox Press, 1964.

———. *Learning Jesus Christ through the Heidelberg Catechism*. Grand Rapids: Eerdmans, 1964.

Bartha, Tibor. *Der Heidelberger Katechismus in Ungarn*. Budapest: Verlag der Presseabteilung der Synodalkanzlei der Reformierten Kirche von Ungarn, 1967.

Berg, J. F. *The History and Literature of the Heidelberg Catechism and of Its Introduction into the Netherlands*. Philadelphia: William and Alfred Martien, 1863.

Beyer, Ulrich. *Abendmahl und Messe; Sinn und Recht der 80. Frage des Heidelberger Katechismus*. Beiträge zur Geschichte und Lehre der Reformierten Kirche, vol. 19. Neukirchen-Vluyn: Neukirchener Verlag des Erziehungsvereins, 1965.

Bierma, Lyle D. *The Doctrine of the Sacraments in the Heidelberg Catechism: Melanchthonian, Calvinist, or Zwinglian?* Studies in Reformed Theology and History, ed. David Willis, New Series, no. 4. Princeton: Princeton Theological Seminary, 1999.

Bouwmeester, G. *Zacharias Ursinus en de Heidelbergse Catechismus*. The Hague:

Willem de Zwijgerstichting, 1954.

Braselmann, Werner. *Friedrich der Fromme und sein Heidelberger Katechismus.* Konstanz: Christliche Verlagsanstalt, 1963.

Bruggen, J. van. *Annotations to the Heidelberg Catechism.* Neerlandia, Alta: Inheritance Publications, 1991.

Bruggink, Donald J. *Guilt, Grace, and Gratitude: A Commentary on the Heidelberg Catechism Commemorating Its 400th Anniversary.* New York: Half Moon Press, 1963.

Coenen, Lothar. *Handbuch zum Heidelberger Katechismus.* Neukirchen-Vluyn: Neukirchener Verlag, 1963.

Dijk, Klaas. *De voorzienigheid Gods.* Amsterdam: De Standaard, 1927.

Doekes, L. *Vierhonderd jaar Heidelbergse Catechismus: de Heidelbergse Catechismus herdacht in een landelijke samenkomst.* Amsersfoort: n.p., 1963.

Exalto, K. *De enige troost: inleiding tot de Heidelbergse Catechismus.* Kampen: Kok, 1979.

Feenstra, J. A. *Het eigendom des Heeren: korte verklaring van de Heidelbergse catechismus.* Kampen: Kok, 1952.

Felke, E. *Das Siegel des Bundes Betrachtungen zum Heidelberger Katechismus.* Worms: Druck und Verlag des Korrespondenzblattes der Freunde des Heidelberger Katechismus, 1921.

Frick, Max. *Reformierter Glaube: eine Darstellung der biblischen Lehre an Hand des Heidelberger Katechismus.* Zurich: Reformierten Schweizer Zeitung, 1932.

Good, James I. *The Heidelberg Catechism in Its Newest Light.* Philadelphia: Publication and Sunday School Board of the Reformed Church in the United States, 1914.

Gooszen, M. A. *De Heidelbergsche catechismus: textus receptus met toelichtende teksten; bijdrage tot de kennis van zijne wordingsgeschiedenis en van het Gereformeerd protestantisme.* Leiden: Brill, 1890.

Graffmann, Heinrich. *Der Unterricht nach dem Heidelberger Katechismus im Zeitalter der Orthodoxie und des Pietismus.* Monatshefte für Evangelische Kirchengeschichte des Rheinlandes, ed. Presseverband der Evangelischen Kirche im Rheinland, vol. 9. Cologne: Rheinland-Verlag, 1960.

———. *Unterricht im Heidelberger Katechismus.* 3 vols. Neukirchen: Buchhandlung des Erziehungsvereins, 1951.

Gruch, Jochen. *Deutschsprachige Drucke des Heidelberger Katechismus 1563-1800.* Beiträge Zur Katechismusgeschichte, vol. 1. Cologne: Sz-Verlag, 1996.

Haitjema, Theodorus Lambertus. *De Heidelbergse catechismus: als klankbodem en inhoud van het actuele belijden onzer kerk.* Wageningen: Veenmon en Zonen, 1962.

Halaski, Karl. *Die Botschaft des Heidelberger Katechismus: eine Handreichung zum 400 jährigen Jubiläum des Heidelberger Katechismus.* Nach Gottes Wort Reformiert, vol. 16. Neukirchen-Vluyn: Neukirchener Verlag des Erziehungsvereins, 1963.

Hartvelt, G. P. *Alles in Hem.* Aalten De Graafschap: De Graafschap, 1966.

Henss, W. *Der Heidelberger Katechismus im konfessionspolitischen Kräftespiel seiner Frühzeit: Historisch-bibliographische Einführung der ersten vollständigen deutsch[e]n Fassung, der Sogenannten 3. Auflage von 1563 und der dazugehörigen lateinischen Fassung.* Zürich: Theologischer Verlag, 1983.

Herrenbrück, Walter, and Udo Smidt. *Warum wirst du ein Christ genannt? Vorträge und Aufsätze zum Heidelberger Katechismus im Jubiläumsjahr.* Neukirchen-Vluyn: Neukirchener Verlag, 1965.

Hoeksema, Herman. *The Triple Knowledge: An Exposition of the Heidelberg Catechism.* 3 vols. Grand Rapids: Reformed Free Press, 1972.

Hollweg, Walter. *Neue Untersuchungen zur Geschichte und Lehre des Heidelberger Katechismus.* Beiträge zur Geschichte und Lehre der Reformierten Kirche, vol. 13. Neukirchen: Neukirchener Verlag, 1961.

Jacobs, Paul. *Theologie reformierter Bekenntnisschriften in Grundzügen.* Neukirchen: Neukirchener Verlag, 1959.

Klaas, Walter. *Die Stimme der Väter: Eine Erwägung des Heidelberger Katechismus, seiner Fragen und Antworten.* Siegen: Schneider, 1949.

Klooster, Fred H. *The Heidelberg Catechism and Parallels in Lutheran and Reformed Catechisms and Confessions.* Grand Rapids: Calvin Theological Seminary, 1976.

———. *The Heidelberg Catechism: Origin and History.* Grand Rapids: Calvin Theological Seminary, 1981.

———. *A Mighty Comfort: The Christian Faith according to the Heidelberg Catchism.* Grand Rapids: CRC Publications, 1990.

———. *Our Only Comfort: A Comprehensive Commentary on the Heidelberg Catechism.* 2 vols. Grand Rapids: Faith Alive Christian Resources, 2001.

Knap, J. J. *De Heidelbergsche catechismus: toepasselijk verklaard voor de gemeente des Heeren.* Groningen: J. B. Wolters, 1912.

Kolthoff, E. *Kurze Erklärung des Heidelberger Katechismus zur Vorbereitung auf den Unterricht.* Bentheim: E. W. Bronger, 1937.

Lang, August. *Der Heidelberger Katechismus und vier verwandte Katechismen.* 1907. Reprint, Darmstadt: Wissenschaftliche Buchgesellschaft, 1967.

———. *Der Heidelberger Katechismus. Zum 350jährigen Gedachtnis seiner Entstehung.* Schriften Des Vereins Fur Reformationsgeschichte, 31. Jahrg., 1. Stuck, Nr. 113. Leipzig: Verein fur Reformationsgeschichte, 1913.

Le Roux, Johann. *Die Heidelbergse Kategismus of Onderwysing in Die Christelike Leer: 'N Maklik-Verstaan Grafiese Uiteensetting.* Pretoria: The Author, 1998.

Lekkerkerker, A. F. N. *Gesprekken over De Heidelberger.* Wageningen: Zomer & Keunings, 1964.

Masselink, Edward J. *The Heidelberg Story.* Grand Rapids: Baker, 1964.

Metz, Wulf. *Necessitas satisfactionis? Eine systematische Studie zu den Fragen 12-18 des Heidelberger Katechismus und zur Theologie des Zacharias Ursinus.* Studien zur Dogmengeschichte und systematischen Theologie, vol. 26. Zurich: Zwingli-Verlag, 1970.

Neuser, Wilhelm. *Die Tauflehre des Heidelberger Katechismus: eine aktuelle Lösung des Problems der Kindertaufe.* Theologische Existenz Heute, vol. 139. Munich: Chr. Kaiser, 1967.

Obendiek, Harmannus. *Das Zeugnis der Wahrheit nach dem Heidelberger Katechismus.* Neukirchen: Verlag der Buchhandlung des Erziehungsvereins,

[1940].

Oberholzer, J. P. *Die Heidelbergse Kategismus, in Vier Teksuitgawes, Met Inleiding En Teksvergelyking.* Pretoria: Kital, 1986.

Olevianus, Caspar. *A Firm Foundation: An Aid to Interpreting the Heidelberg Catechism.* Translated and edited by Lyle D. Bierma. Grand Rapids: Baker Books, 1995.

O'Malley, J. Steven. *Pilgrimage of Faith: The Legacy of the Otterbeins.* Metuchen, N.J.: Scarecrow Press, 1973.

Oorthuys, G. *De eeuwige jeugd van Heidelberg; de Heidelbergsche Catechismus, een leerboek voor onzen tijd.* Amsterdam: Uitgevers-Maatschappij Holland, 1939.

Ott, Heinrich. *Dogmatik und Verkündigung: ein Programm dogmatischer Arbeit, dargestellt im Anschluss an die Fragen 1 bis 11 des Heidelberger Katechismus.* Zurich: EVZ Verlag, 1961.

Pery, Andre. *Der Heidelberger Katechismus: Erläuterungen zu seinen 129 Fragen und Antworten.* Neukirchen: Neukirchener Verlag, 1963.

———. *Le Catéchisme de Heidelberg: un commentaire pour notre temps.* Geneva: Labor et Fides, 1959.

Praamsma, Louis. *Before the Face of God: A Study of the Heidelberg Catechism.* 2 vols. Jordan Station, Ont.: Paideia Press, 1987.

Richards, G. W. *The Heidelberg Catechism: Historical and Doctrinal Studies, The Swander Memorial Lectures - 1911.* Philadelphia: Reformed Church in the United States, 1913.

Stam, Clarence. *Living in the Joy of Faith: The Christian Faith as Outlined in the Heidelberg Catechism.* Neerlandia, Alta: Inheritance, 1991.

Sudhoff, Karl Jakob. *Theologisches Handbuch zur Auslegung des Heidelberger Katechismus: Ein Commentar für geistliche und geförderte Nichttheologen.* Frankfurt am Main: Heyder and Zimmer, 1862.

Thelemann, Otto. *An Aid to the Heidelberg Catechism.* Grand Rapids: Douma Publications, 1959.

Ursinus, Zacharias. *The Commentary of Dr. Zacharias Ursinus on the Heidelberg Catechism.* Translated by G. W. Williard. 1852. Reprint, Phillipsburg, N.J.: Presbyterian and Reformed, 1985.

Van Baalen, Jan Karel. *The Heritage of the Fathers: A Commentary on the Heidelberg Catechism.* Grand Rapids: Eerdmans, 1948.

———. *Our Birthright and the Mess of Meat: Isms of Today Analyzed and Compared with the Heidelberg Catechism.* Grand Rapids: Eerdmans, 1929.

Van Senden, Hermann. *Der Heidelberger Katechismus im Unterricht: Ein Jahrgang Stundenbilder.* Neukirchen: Moers, 1928.

Verboom, Willem. *De Theologie van De Heidelbergse Catechismus—twaalf thema's: de context en de latere uitwerking.* Zoetermeer: Boekencentrum, 1996.

Verhey, Allen. *Living the Heidelberg: The Heidelberg Catechism and the Moral Life.* Grand Rapids: CRC Publications, 1986.

Visser, Derk. *Controversy and Conciliation: The Reformation and the Palatinate 1559-1583.* Allison Park: Pickwick Publications, 1986.

Winter, Friedrich. *Confessio Augustana und Heidelberger Katechismus in vergleichender Betrachtung.* Berlin: Evangelische Verlagsanstalt, 1954.

Woelderink, Jan Gerrit. *De inzet van de catechismus: verklaring van de zondag I-VII van de Heidelberger.* Franeker: T. Wever, 1960.

Book Sections

Asendorf, Ulrich. "Luther's Small Catechism and the Heidelberg Catechism—the Continuing Struggle: The Catechism's Role as a Confessional Document in Lutheranism." In *Luther's Catechisms—450 Years: Essays Commemorating the Small and Large Catechisms of Dr. Martin Luther,* edited by David P. Scaer et al., 1-7. Fort Wayne: Concordia Theological Seminary, 1979.

Barna, Nagy. "A Heidelbergi Kate Jelentkezese, Tortenete Es Kiadasai Magyarorszagon a Xvi. Es Xvii, Szazadban." In *A Heidelbergi Kate Tortenete Magyarorszagon,* edited by Bartha Tibor, 15-91. Budapest: Magyarorszagi reformatus egyhaz zsinati irodajanak sajtoosztalya, 1965.

Beintker, Michael. "Glaubensgewissheit nach dem Heidelberger Katechismus." In *Certitudo salutis: Die Existenz des Glaubens zwischen Gewissheit und Zweifel: Symposion aus Anlass des 75. Geburtstags von Hans Helmut Esser,* edited by Michael Beintker, 55-69. Münster: Lit, 1996.

Berkhof, Hendrikus. "The Catechism as an Expression of Our Faith." In *Essays on the Heidelberg Catechism,* edited by Bard Thompson, 93-122. Philadelphia: United Church Press, 1963.

———. "The Catechism in Historical Context." In *Essays on the Heidelberg Catechism,* edited by Bard Thompson, 76-92. Philadelphia: United Church Press, 1963.

Berkouwer, G. C. "Der Weg durch die Zeit: Ein Bekenntnis aus dem 16. in der Welt des 20. Jahrhunderts." In *Handbuch zum Heidelberger Katechismus,* edited by Lothar Coenen, 249-62. Neukirchen-Vluyn: Neukirchener Verlag, 1963.

Bierma, Lyle D. "Vester Grundt and the Origins of the Heidelberg Catechism." In *Later Calvinism: International Perspectives,* edited by W. Fred Graham, 289-311. Kirksville: Sixteenth Century Journal Publishers, 1994.

———. "What Hath Wittenberg to Do with Heidelberg? Philip Melanchthon and the Heidelberg Catechism." In *Melanchthon in Europe: His Work and Influence beyond Wittenberg,* edited by Karin Maag, 103-21. Grand Rapids: Baker, 1999.

Bruggink, Donald J. "The Holy Sacraments." In *Guilt, Grace, and Gratitude: A Commentary on the Heidelberg Catechism Commemorating Its 400th Anniversary,* edited by Donald J. Bruggink, 136-65. New York: Half Moon Press, 1963.

Burggraaff, Winfield. "God the Father." In *Guilt, Grace, and Gratitude: A Commentary on the Heidelberg Catechism Commemorating Its 400th Anniversary,* edited by Donald J. Bruggink, 66-79. New York: Half Moon Press, 1963.

Büsser, F. "Die Bedeutung des Gesetzes." In *Handbuch Zum Heidelberger Katechismus,* edited by Lothar Coenen, 159-70. Neukirchen-Vluyn: Neukirchener Verlag, 1963.

Coenen, Lothar. "Gottes Bund und Erwählung." In *Handbuch Zum Heidelberger Katechismus,* edited by Lothar Coenen, 128-34. Neukirchen-Vluyn: Neukirchener Verlag, 1963.

————. "Jugend- Und Erwachsenenunterricht mit dem Heidelberger Katechismus." In *Handbuch Zum Heidelberger Katechismus*, edited by Lothar Coenen, 200-212. Neukirchen-Vluyn: Neukirchener Verlag, 1963.

————. "Wort Gottes und Heiliger Geist." In *Handbuch Zum Heidelberger Katechismus*, edited by Lothar Coenen, 81-90. Neukirchen-Vluyn: Neukirchener Verlag, 1963.

Cook, James I. "Prayer." In *Guilt, Grace, and Gratitude: A Commentary on the Heidelberg Catechism Commemorating Its 400th Anniversary*, edited by Donald J. Bruggink, 209-26. New York: Half Moon Press, 1963.

De Jong, Jerome B. "The Misery of Man." In *Guilt, Grace, and Gratitude: A Commentary on the Heidelberg Catechism Commemorating Its 400th Anniversary*, edited by Donald J. Bruggink, 23-38. New York: Half Moon Press, 1963.

Den Hartogh, Gerrit. "Zacharias Ursinus en de Heidelbergse Catechismus." In *Voorzienigheid in donker licht: herkomst en gebruik van het begrip 'Providentia Dei' in de reformatorische theologie, in het bijzonder bij Zacharias Ursinus*, 24-64. Heerenveen: Groen, 1999.

Dijkstra, H. "Die Betekenis Van Die Heidelbergse Kategismus as Leerboek Vir Die Verbondsonderrig Van Die Kerkjeug." In *God Bou Op Deur Sy Woord.*, edited by C. J. H. Venter, 190-208. Potchefstroom: PU vir CHO, 1988.

Eenigenburg, Elton M. "God the Son." In *Guilt, Grace, and Gratitude: A Commentary on the Heidelberg Catechism Commemorating Its 400th Anniversary*, edited by Donald J. Bruggink, 80-110. New York: Half Moon Press, 1963.

Endre, Toth. "A Heidelbergi Kate a Magyar Reformatus Gyulekezetekben Es Iskolakban." In *A Heidelbergi Kate Tortenete Magyarorszagon*, edited by Bartha Tibor, 263-99. Budapest: Magyarorszagi reformatus egyhaz zsinati irodajanak sajtoosztalya, 1965.

Fries, P. "The Heidelberg Catechism in Modern Reformed Theology: O. Noordmans, A Cast Study." In *Controversy and Conciliation: The Reformation and the Palatinate, 1559-1583*, edited by Derk Visser, 205-13. Allison Park: Pickwick Publications, 1986.

Geza, Kathona. "A Heidelbergi Kate Deformalodasa Az Antitrinitarizmussal Vivott Harcokban." In *A Heidelbergi Kate Tortenete Magyarorszagon*, edited by Bartha Tibor, 95-129. Budapest: Magyarorszagi reformatus egyhaz zsinati irodajanak sajtoosztalya, 1965.

Goerlich, Andreas. "Paul Schneider und der Heidelberger Katechismus." In *Reformiertes Erbe, Festschrift für Gottfried W. Locher zu seinem 80. Geburtstag*, edited by Heiko A. Oberman et al., 91-102. Zurich: Theologischer Verlag, 1993.

Goeters, J. F. Gerhard. "Christologie und Rechtfertigung nach dem Heidelberger Katechismus." In *Das Kreuz Jesu Christi als Grund des Heils*, edited by Ernst Bizer, 31-47. Gutersloh: Mohn, 1967.

————. "Entstehung und Frühgeschichte des Kategismus." In *Handbuch Zum Heidelberger Katechismus*, edited by Lothar Coenen, 3-23. Neukirchen: Neukirchener Verlag, 1963.

Goetzmann, Jürgen. "Das Werk Jesu Christi und unser Dienst in der Kirche." In *Warum wirst du ein Christ gennant? Vorträge und Aufsätze zum Heidelberger*

Katechismus Im Jubiläumsjahr 1963, edited by Walter Herrenbrück and Udo Smidt, 113-20. Neukirchen-Vluyn: Neukirchener Verlag des Erziehungsvereins, 1965.

Graffmann, Heinrich. "Erklärung des Heidelberger Katechismus in Predigt und Unterricht des 16. bis 18. Jahrhunderts." In *Handbuch Zum Heidelberger Katechismus*, edited by Lothar Coenen, 63-77. Neukirchen-Vluyn: Neukirchener Verlag des Erziehungsvereins, 1963.

Gyenge, E. "Der Glaube: Seine Gewissheit und Bewahrung." In *Handbuch Zum Heidelberger Katechismus*, edited by Lothar Coenen, 113-27. Neukirchen: Neukirchener-Vluyn, 1963.

Hageman, Howard. "The Catechism in Christian Nurture." In *Essays on the Heidelberg Catechism*, edited by Bard Thompson, 158-79. Philadelphia: United Church Press, 1963.

———. "Guilt, Grace, and Gratitude." In *Guilt, Grace, and Gratitude: A Commentary on the Heidelberg Catechism Commemorating Its 400th Anniversary*, edited by Donald J. Bruggink, 1-19. New York: Half Moon Press, 1963.

———. "The Lasting Significance of Ursinus." In *Controversy and Conciliation: The Reformation and the Palatinate, 1559-1583*, edited by Derk Visser, 227-39. Allison Park: Pickwick Publications, 1986.

Halaski, Karl. "Die Wegweisung des Heidelberger Katechismus für die Leitung unserer Gemeinden." In *Warum wirst du ein Christ gennant? Vorträge und Aufsätze zum Heidelberger Katechismus im Jubiläumsjahr 1963*, edited by Walter Herrenbrück and Udo Smidt, 189-200. Neukirchen-Vluyn: Neukirchener Verlag des Erziehungsvereins, 1965.

Heideman, Eugene P. "God the Holy Spirit." In *Guilt, Grace, and Gratitude: A Commentary on the Heidelberg Catechism Commemorating Its 400th Anniversary*, edited by Donald J. Bruggink, 111-35. New York: Half Moon Press, 1963.

Herrenbrück, Walter. "Der Trinitätstheologische Ansatz des Heidelberger Katechismus." In *Warum wirst du ein Christ genannt? Vorträge und Aufsätze zum Heidelberger Katechismus im Jubiläumsjahr*, edited by Walter Herrenbrück and Udo Smidt, 48-67. Neukirchen-Vluyn: Neukirchener Verlag, 1965.

Hesse, Hermann. "Zur Sakramentslehre des Heidelberger Katechismus nach den Fragen 65-68." In *Theologische Aufsätze: Karl Barth zum 50. Geburtstag*, 467-89. Munich: Kaiser, 1936.

Hesselink, I. John. "The Dramatic Story of the Heidelberg Catechism." In *Later Calvinism: International Perspectives*, edited by W. Fred Graham, 273-88. Kirksville: Sixteenth Century Journal Publishers, 1994.

———. "The Law of God." In *Guilt, Grace, and Gratitude: A Commentary on the Heidelberg Catechism Commemorating Its 400th Anniversary*, edited by Donald J. Bruggink, 169-208. New York: Half Moon Press, 1963.

Hollweg, Walter. "Bearbeitete Caspar Olevianus den deutschen Text des Heidelberger Katechismus?" In *Neue Untersuchungen zur Geschichte und Lehre des Heidelberger Katechismus*, 124-52. Neukirchen: Neukirchener Verlag, 1961.

———. "Die Beiden Konfessionen Theodor von Bezas: Zwei bisher unbeachtete Quellen zum Heidelberger Katechismus." In *Neue Untersuchungen zur*

Geschichte und Lehre des Heidelberger Katechismus, 86-123. Neukirchen: Neukirchener Verlag, 1961.

————. "Zur Quellenfrage des Heidelberger Katechismus." In *Neue Untersuchungen zur Geschichte und Lehre des Heidelberger Katechismus,* 38-47. Neukirchen-Vluyn: Neukirchener Verlag, 1968.

Hutter, Ulrich. "Zacharias Ursinus und der Heidelberger Katechismus." In *Martin Luther und die Reformation in Ostdeutschland und Südosteuropa: Wirkungen und Wechselwirkungen,* 79-105. Sigmaringen: Thorbecke, 1991.

Huyssteen, P. H. van. "Die Heidelbegse Kategismus of Onderwysing in Die Christelike Leer." In *Die Berymde Psalms En Skrifberymings,* edited by P. H. van Huyssteen, 521-66. Kaapstad: NGKB, 1987.

Jacobs, Paul. "Heidelberger Katechismus—Reformatorisches Bekenntnis." In *Warum wirst du ein Christ gennant? Vorträge und Aufsätze zum Heidelberger Katechismus im Jubiläumsjahr 1963,* edited by Walter Herrenbrück and Udo Smidt, 40-47. Neukirchen-Vluyn: Neukirchener Verlag des Erziehungsvereins, 1965.

Klooster, Fred H. "Calvin's Attitude to the Heidelberg Catechism." In *Later Calvinism: International Perspectives,* edited by W. Fred Graham, 311-31. Kirksville: Sixteenth Century Journal Publishers, 1994.

————. "The Priority of Ursinus in the Composition of the Heidelberg Catechism." In *Controversy and Conciliation: The Reformation and the Palatinate 1559-1583,* edited by Derk Visser, 73-100. Allison Park: Pickwick, 1986.

Koch, Karl. "Der Heidelberger Katechismus als Bekenntnis und Lehrbuch." In *Warum wirst du ein Christ gennant? Vorträge und Aufsätze zum Heidelberger Katechismus im Jubiläumsjahr 1963,* edited by Walter Herrenbrück and Udo Smidt, 177-88. Neukirchen-Vluyn: Neukirchener Verlag des Erziehungsvereins, 1965.

Korn, W. E. "Die Lehre Von Christi Person Und Werk." In *Handbuch zum Heidelberger Katechismus,* edited by Lothar Coenen, 91-104. Neukirchen: NeuKirchen-Vluyn, 1963.

Kreck, Walter. "Rechter und Falscher Respekt vor dem Bekenntnis der Väter." In *Warum wirst du ein Christ gennant? Vorträge und Aufsätze zum Heidelberger Katechismus im Jubiläumsjahr 1963,* edited by Walter Herrenbrück and Udo Smidt, 67-78. Neukirchen-Vluyn: Neukirchener Verlag des Erziehungsvereins, 1965.

Locher, G. W. "'Das Vornehmste Stück der Dankbarkeit': Das Gebet im Sinne der Reformation nach dem Heidelberger Katechismus." In *Handbuch zum Heidelberger Katechismus,* edited by Lothar Coenen, 171-85. Neukirchener: Neukirchen-Vluyn, 1963.

Marcel, P. Ch. "Die Lehre von der Kirche und den Sakramenten." In *Handbuch zum Heidelberger Katechismus,* edited by Lothar Coenen, 135-58. Neukirchen: Neukirchener Verlag, 1963.

Mihaly, Bucsay. "A Heidelbergi Kate Magyarazatanak Tortenete 1791-Tol Napjainkig." In *A Heidelbergi Kate Tortenete Magyaro,* edited by Bartha Tibor, 207-60. Budapest: Magyarorszagi reformatus egyhaz zsinati irodajanak sajtoosztalya, 1965.

Miller, A. "The Theology of the Heidelberg Catechism: Then and Now." In *Controversy and Conciliation: The Reformation and the Palatinate, 1559-1583*, edited by Derk Visser, 215-25. Allison Park: Pickwick Publications, 1986.

Modis, L. "Bibliographie der ungarischen Literatur des Heidelberger Katechismus 1563-1963." In *Der Heidelberger Katechismus in Ungarn*. Budapest: Verlag der Presseabteilung der Synodalkanzlei der Reformierten Kirche von Ungarn, 1967.

Nauta, D. "Die Verbreitung des Katechismus, Übersetzung in andere Sprachen, moderne Bearbeitungen." In *Handbuch Zum Heidelberger Katechismus*, edited by Lothar Coenen, 39-62. Neukirchen: Neukirchener Verlag, 1963.

Neuser, Wilhelm. "Heidelberger Katechismus." In *Handbuch der Dogmen-und Theologiegeschichte*, edited by Carl Andresen, 286ff. Göttingen: Vandenhoeck & Ruprecht, 1978.

Niesel, Wilhelm. "Vorwort zum Heidelberger Katechismus." In *Die Bekenntnisschriften und Kirchenordnungen der nach Gottes Wort reformierten Kirche*, edited by Wilhelm Niesel, 148ff. Zurich: Zollikon, 1938.

———. "Das Zeugnis von der Kraft des Heiligen Geistes im Heidelberger Katechismus." In *Warum wirst du ein Christ gennant? Vorträge und Aufsätze zum Heidelberger Katechismus im Jubiläumsjahr 1963*, edited by Walter Herrenbrück and Udo Smidt, 79-93. Neukirchen-Vluyn: Neukirchener Verlag des Erziehungsvereins, 1965.

Nordholt, Gerhard. "Die zum Katechismus gehörende Gestalt der Gemeinde und des Gottesdienstes (unter Berücksichtigung der kurpfälzischen Kirchenordnung)." In *Handbuch zum Heidelberger Katechismus*, edited by Lothar Coenen, 24-38. Neukirchener: Neukirchen-Vluyn, 1963.

———. "Kirchenzucht als notwendige Funktion der Christusgemeinschaft." In *Handbuch zum Heidelberger Katechismus*, edited by Lothar Coenen, 213-27. Neukirchen: Neukirchen-Vluyn, 1963.

Olson, O. "The 'Fractio Panis' in Heidelberg and Antwerp." In *Controversy and Conciliation: The Reformation and the Palatinate, 1559-1583*, edited by Derk Visser, 147-53. Allison Park: Pickwick Publications, 1986.

Osterhaven, M. Eugene. "Man's Deliverance." In *Guilt, Grace, and Gratitude: A Commentary on the Heidelberg Catechism Commemorating Its 400th Anniversary*, edited by Donald J. Bruggink, 41-66. New York: Half Moon Press, 1963.

Osterhaven, O. "The Experimentation of the Heidelberg Catechism and Orthodoxy." In *Controversy and Conciliation: The Reformation and the Palatinate, 1559-1583*, edited by Derk Visser, 197-203. Allison Park: Pickwick Publications, 1986.

Sandor, Czegledy. "A Heidelbergi Kate Magyarorszagi Magyarazatainak Tortenete 1791-Ig." In *A Heidelbergi Kate Tortenete Magyarorszagon*, edited by Bartha Tibor, 131-68. Budapest: Magyarorszagi reformatus egyhaz zsinati irodajanak sajtoosztalya, 1965.

Schmitz, Otto. "Die Botschaft Des Heidelberger Katechismus 1563-1963." In *Warum wirst du ein Christ gennant? Vorträge und Aufsätze zum Heidelberger Katechismus im Jubiläumsjahr 1963*, edited by Walter Herrenbrück und Udo Smidt, 156-65. Neukirchen-Vluyn: Neukirchener Verlag des

Erziehungsvereins, 1965.

Schoener, Karlheinz. "Der Heidelberger und Die Heidelberger." In *Warum wirst du ein Christ gennant? Vorträge und Aufsätze zum Heidelberger Katechismus im Jubiläumsjahr 1963*, edited by Walter Herrenbrück and Udo Smidt, 201-15. Neukirchen-Vluyn: Neukirchener Verlag des Erziehungsvereins, 1965.

Schweizer, Eduard. "Scripture and Tradition: An Answer." In *Essays on the Heidelberg Catechism*, edited by Bard Thompson, 139-56. Philadelphia: United Church Press, 1963.

———. "Scripture and Tradition: The Problem." In *Essays on the Heidelberg Catechism*, edited by Bard Thompson, 124-38. Philadelphia: United Church Press, 1963.

Smidt, Udo. "Der Heidelberger Katechismus im Zeugnis." In *Warum wirst du ein Christ gennant? Vorträge und Aufsätze zum Heidelberger Katechismus im Jubiläumsjahr 1963*, edited by Walter Herrenbrück and Udo Smidt, 144-55. Neukirchen-Vluyn: Neukirchener Verlag des Erziehungsvereins, 1965.

Soedarmo, Raden. "Der Schritt in die andere Welt: Der Katechismus als europäisches Geistesgut im Werden der jungen Kirchen, dargestellt am Beispiel Indonesiens." In *Handbuch zum Heidelberger Katechismus*, edited by Lothar Coenen, 231-48. Neukirchen-Vluyn: Neukirchener Verlag, 1963.

Staedtke, Joachim. "Entstehung und Bedeutung des Heidelberger Katechismus." In *Warum wirst du ein Chirst genannt? Vorträge und Aufsätze zum Heidelberger Katechismus im Jubiläumsjahr*, edited by Walter Herrenbrück and Udo Smidt, 11-23. Neukirchen-Vluyn: Neukirchener Verlag, 1963.

Tamas, Esze. "A Heidelbergi Kate Tortenete Magyarorszagon a Xviii. Szazadban." In *A Heidelbergi Kate Tortenete Magyarorszagon*, edited by Bartha Tibor, 169-203. Budapest: Magyarorszagi reformatus egyhaz zsinati irodajanak sajtoosztal, 1965.

Teylingen, E. G. van. "Der Katechismus in der Predigt." In *Handbuch zum Heidelberger Katechismus*, edited by Lothar Coenen, 189-99. Neukirchen-Vluyn: Neukirchener Verlag, 1963.

Thompson, Bard. "Historical Background of the Catechism." In *Essays on the Heidelberg Catechism*, edited by Bard Thompson, 8-30. Philadelphia: United Church Press, 1963.

Van der Hoeven, A. "The Catechism and the Mercersburg Theology." In *Essays on the Heidelberg Catechism*, edited by Bard Thompson, 53-74. Philadelphia: United Church Press, 1963.

———. "The Reformed Church in the Palatinate." In *Essays on the Heidelberg Catechism*, edited by Bard Thompson, 31-52. Philadelphia: United Church Press, 1963.

———. "Ursinus en Olevianus, Heidelbergse Catechismus." In *Kerkelijke klassieken: Inleidende beschouwingen over geschriften van oude en nieuwe kerkvaders*, edited by H. Berkhof et al., 247-76. Wageningen: Veenman, 1949.

Visser, Derk. "St. Anselm's *Cur Deus Homo* and the Heidelberg Catechism (1563)." In *Anselm Studies II*, edited by Thomas A. Losoncy et al., 607-34. White Plains: Kraus International Publications, 1988.

———. "Zacharias Ursinus 1534-1583." In *Shapers of Religious Traditions in*

Germany, Switzerland, and Poland, 1560-1600, edited by Jill Raitt, 121-39. New Haven: Yale University Press, 1981.

———. "Zacharias Ursinus (1534-1583): Melanchthons Geist im Heidelberger Katechismus." In *Melanchthon in seinen Schülern*, edited by Heinz Scheible, 373-90. Wiesbaden: Harrassowitz, 1997.

Visser, L. L. J. "Die Lehre von Gottes Vorsehung und Weltregiment." In *Handbuch zum Heidelberger Katechismus*, edited by Lothar Coenen, 105-12. Neukirchen: Neukirchener-Vluyn, 1963.

Weber, Otto. "Analytische Theologie: Zum geschictlichen Standort des Heidelberger Katechismus." In *Warum wirst du ein Christ gennant? Vorträge und Aufsätze zum Heidelberger Katechismus im Jubiläumsjahr 1963*, edited by Walter Herrenbrück and Udo Smidt, 24-39. Neukirchen-Vluyn: Neukirchener Verlag des Erziehungsvereins, 1965.

———. "Der Heidelberger Katechismus in der heutigen Gemeinde." In *Warum wirst du ein Christ gennant? Vorträge und Aufsätze zum Heidelberger Katechismus im Jubiläumsjahr 1963*, edited by Walter Herrenbrück and Udo Smidt, 129-43. Neukirchen-Vluyn: Neukirchener Verlag des Erziehungsvereins, 1965.

Wittetkindt, Ernst E. "Die Botschaft des Heidelberger Katechismus heute." In *Warum wirst du ein Christ gennant? Vorträge und Aufsätze zum Heidelberger Katechismus im Jubiläumsjahr 1963*, edited by Walter Herrenbrück and Udo Smidt, 166-76. Neukirchen-Vluyn: Neukirchener Verlag des Erziehungsvereins, 1965.

Wolf, Erik. "Ordnung der Liebe." In *Warum wirst du ein Christ gennant? Vorträge und Aufsätze zum Heidelberger Katechismus im Jubiläumsjahr 1963*, edited by Walter Herrenbrück and Udo Smidt, 94-112. Neukirchen-Vluyn: Neukirchener Verlag des Erziehungsvereins, 1965.

Journal Articles

Beam, S. Z. "The Heidelberg Catechism." *The Reformed Church Review* 4, no. 3 (Fourth Series, 1900): 336-42.

Beeke, Joel R. "Faith and Assurance in the Heidelberg Catechism and Its Primary Composers: A Fresh Look at the Kendall Thesis." *Calvin Theological Journal* 27, no. 1 (1992): 39-62.

———. "The Heidelberg Catechism and Its Authors." *Reformed Theological Journal* 18 (November 2002): 66-73.

Benrath, Gustav A. "Die Eigenart der pfalzischen Reformation und die Vorgeschichte des Heidelberger Katechismus." *Heidelberger Jahrbuch* 7 (1963): 13-32.

———. "Zacharias Ursinus als Mensch, Christ und Theologe." *Reformierte Kirchen-Zeitung* 124, no. 6 (1983): 154-58.

Berkhof, Hendrikus. "The Heidelberg Catechism as a Contemporary Expression of Our Faith." *Theology and Life* 6, no. 2 (1963): 128-43.

Bierma, Lyle D. "How Should Heidelberg Catechism Q/A 60 Be Translated?" *Calvin Theological Journal* 26, no. 1 (1991): 125-33.

———. "Olevianus and the Authorship of the Heidelberg Catechism: Another

Look." *Sixteenth Century Journal* 13, no. 4 (1982): 17-27.

———. "De pedagogische strategie van de heidelbergse catechismus," trans. Willem J. van Asselt, *Kerk en Theologie* 53, no. 4 (2002): 330-40.

Bout, H. "Enige momenten uit de Catechismus." *Theologia Reformata* 6, no. 1 (1963): 46-53.

Burchill, Christopher J. "On the Consolation of a Christian Scholar: Zacharias Ursinus (1534-83) and the Reformation in Heidelberg." *Journal of Ecclesiastical History* 37, no. 4 (1986): 565-83.

Butin, Phil. "Two Early Reformed Catechisms, the Threefold Office, and the Shape of Karl Barth's Christology." *Scottish Journal of Theology* 44, no. 2 (1991): 195-214.

Buys, Flip. "Diskussie Na Aanleiding Van Dijkstra: Die Persoonlike Toespitsing Van Die Heil in Die Heidelbergse Kategismus." *In die Skriflig* 15, no. 58 (1981): 54-60.

Cuno, F. W. "Können wir Olevianus mit Recht als Mitfaser des Heidelberger Katechismus neben Ursinus stellen?" *Reformierte Kirchen-Zeitung* 25 (1902): 213-21.

Dahlmann, A. E. "The Theology of the Heidelberg Catechism." *The Reformed Church Review* 17, no. 2 (Fourth Series, 1913): 167-81.

de Bruyn, P. J. "Die Verklaring Van Die Tien Gebooie Volgens Die Heidelbergse Kategismus." *In die Skriflig* 25, no. 2 (1991): 199-216.

Dijkstra, H. "Die Aard Van Die Persoonlike Toespitsing Van Die Heil in Die Hiedelbergse Kategismus ('N Steekproef)." *In die Skriflig* 14, no. 56 (1980): 40-53.

Dijkstra, H., and Jan J. van der Walt. "Die Religieuse Betekenis Van Die Doop in Die Gereformeerde Belydenisskrifte, Veral in Die Heidelbergse Kategismus." *In die Skriflig* 23, no. 2 (1989): 22-34.

Dreyer, Wim. "Die Ontstaan Van Belydenisskrifte Gedurende Die Sestiende En Sewentiende Eeu." *Hervormde Teologiese Studies* 53, no. 4 (1997): 1206-27.

Engelbrecht, B. J. "Die Heidelbergse Kategismus as Kerklike Simbool." *Hervormde Teologiese Studies* 1, no. 1 (1943/1944): 160-73.

———. "'N Vergelyking Tussen Die Teologie Van Die Nederlandse Geloofsbelydenis En Die Heidelbergse Kategismus." *Hervormde Teologiese Studies* 45, no. 3 (1989): 626-44.

Freese, R. "Der Heidelberger Katechismus im Gottesdiesnt." *Reformierte Kirchen-Zeitung* 98 (spring 1957): 473.

Gerbrandy, S. "Wat doen wij met de Heidelbergse Catechismus?" *Nederlands Theologisch Tijdschrift* 37, no. 4 (1983): 290-303.

Giese, H. "Eine Kurzform des Heidelberger Katechismus?" *Reformierte Kirchen-Zeitung* 98 (spring 1957): 502.

Goeters, J. F. G. "Caspar Olevianus als Theologe." *Monatshefte für evangelische Kirchengeschicte des Rheinlandes* 37, 38 (1988/1989): 287-319.

Graafland, Cornelius. "De geloofskennis in antwoord 21 van De Heidelbergse Catechismus: Catechismusverklaring in verleden en heden." *Theologia Reformata* 6, no. 1 (1963): 24-38.

Hadorn, W. "The Influence of the Heidelberg Catechism on the Religious and

Church Life and Piety of the People of Bern." *The Reformed Church Review* 18, no. 4 (Fourth Series, 1914): 472-81.

Hageman, Howard G. "The Heidelberg Catechism as a Means of Christian Nurture." *Theology and Life* 6, no. 3 (1963): 239-54.

————. "Tribute to the Heidelberg Catechism." *Reformed and Prebyterian World* 27, no. 5 (1963): 201-6.

Hartvelt, G. P. "De avondmaalsleer van de Heidelbergse Catechismus en haar toepassing in de prediking." *Homiletica en Biblica* 23, no. 6 (1964): 121-40.

Herlyn, G. "Die Lehre der Prädestination im Genfer und Heidelberger Katechismus." *Reformierte Kirchen-Zeitung* (1938).

Hesse, H. A. "Katechismuspredigt nach Frage 37 des Heidelberger." *Reformierte Kirchen-Zeitung* 96 (spring 1955): 161.

Hinke, William J. "The Early Catechisms of the Reformed Church in the United States." *The Reformed Church Review* 12, no. 4 (Fourth Series, 1908): 473-512.

————. "The Origin of the Heidelberg Catechism." *The Reformed Church Review* 17, no. 3 (Fourth Series, 1913): 152-66.

Hossius, H. "Zur sprachlichen Neufassung des Heidelberger Katechismus." *Reformierte Kirchen-Zeitung* 98 (spring 1957): 361.

Jacobs, P. "Ist der Heidelberger Katechismus in Gehalt und Gestalt zu verändern?" *Reformierte Kirchen-Zeitung* 99 (spring 1958): 142.

Jonker, H. "De theologische zin van de praktijk der catechese." *Theologia Reformata* 6, no. 1 (1963): 39-45.

Kiefer, J. Spangler. "An Appreciation of the Heidelberg Catechism." *The Reformed Church Review* 17, no. 2 (Fourth Series, 1913): 133-51.

Klooster, Fred H. "Heidelberg Catechism—an Ecumenical Creed." *Bulletin of the Evangelical Theological Society* 8, no. 1 (1965): 23-33.

————. "Missions: The Heidelberg Catechism and Calvin." *Calvin Theological Journal* 7, no. 2 (1972): 181-208.

————. "Heidelberg Catechism and Comparative Symbolics." *Calvin Theological Journal* 1, no. 2 (1966): 205-12.

————. "Recent Studies on the Heidelberg Catechism." *Calvin Theological Journal* 1, no. 1 (1966): 73-8.

Küther, Waldemar. "400 Jahre Heidelberger Katechismus (Part 1)." *Reformatio* 12, no. 3 (1963): 225-29.

————. "400 Jahre Heidelberger Katechismus (Part 2)." *Reformatio* 12, no. 4 (1963): 225-29.

————. "400 Jahre Heidelberger Katechismus." *Reformierte Kirchen-Zeitung* 104 (summer 1963): 135.

Lang, A. "Discourse on the Three Hundred and Fiftieth Anniversary of the Heidelberg Catechism at Lancaster, May 13, 1914." *The Reformed Church Review* 18, no. 4 (Fourth Series, 1914): 448-55.

————. "The Religious and Theological Character of the Heidelberg Catechism." *The Reformed Church Review* 18, no. 4 (Fourth Series, 1914): 456-71.

————. "Der theologische Charakter des Heidelberger Catechismus." *Theologische Studien und Kritiken* 89, no. 1 (1915): 138-57.

Locher, G. W. "'Das vornehmste Stück der Dankbarkeit': Das Gebet im Sinne der Reformation nach dem Heidelberger Katechismus." *Evangelische Theologie* 17 (summer 1957): 563.

Mattos, Alderi. "O Catecismo De Heidelberg: Sua Historia E Influencia." *Fides Reformata* 1, no. 1 (1994): 25-33.

McCord, James I. "The Heidelberg Catechism: An Ecumenical Confession." *Princeton Seminary Bulletin* 56, no. 2 (1963): 12-18.

Neuser, Wilhelm. "Die Erwählungslehre im Heidelberger Katechismus." *Zeitschrift für Kirchengeschichte* 75, no. 3-4 (1964): 309-26.

————. "Die Väter des Heidelberger Katechismus." *Theologische Zeitschrift* 35, no. 3 (1979): 177-94.

Niesel, Wilhelm. "Das Zeuginis von der Kraft des Heiligen Geistes im Heidelberger Katechismus." *Theologische Literaturzeitung* 88, no. 8 (1963): 561-70.

Nijenhuis, W. "Coornhert en de Heidelbergse Catechismus: Moment in de strijd tussen humanisme en reformatie." *Nederlands Theologisch Tijdschrift* 18, no. 4 (1964): 271-88.

Oberholzer, J. P. "Die Heidelbergse Kategismus in Afrikaans: 'N Eerste Blik Op Die Eerste Halfeeu." *Hervormde Teologiese Studies* 43, no. 1 & 2 (1987): 86-97.

————. "Die Heidelbergse Kategismus in Sy Eerste Jare." *Hervormde Teologiese Studies* 45, no. 3 (1989): 598-610.

O'Malley, J. Steven. "The Hermeneutics of the Otterbeins." *Methodist History* 25, no. 1 (1986): 17-28.

————. "The Otterbeins: Men of Two Worlds." *Methodist History* 15, no. 1 (1976): 3-21.

Otten, Heinz. "Das Bekenntnis der Einheit der Kirche nach dem Heidelberger Katechismus." *Evangelische Theologie* 5 (1938): 223-32.

Pont, A D. "Die Sekerheid Van Dei Geloof by Calvyn En Sommige Van Sy Navolgers." *Hervormde Teologiese Studies* 44, no. 2 (1988): 404-19.

Ranck, Henry H. "The Heidelberg Catechism for Catechization." *The Reformed Church Review* 12, no. 4 (Fourth Series, 1908): 513-26.

Richards, George W. "A Comparative Study of the Heidelberg, Luther's Smaller, and the Westminster Shorter Catechism." *The Reformed Church Review* 17, no. 2 (Fourth Series, 1913): 193-212.

Schulze, L. F. "Calvyn En Die Heidelbergse Kategismus." *In die Skriflig* 27, no. 4 (1993): 487-99.

————. "Die Teologiese Wortels En Struktuur Van Die Heidelbergse Kategismus: 'N Oorsig." *Hervormde Teologiese Studies* 50, no. 1 & 2 (1994): 194-210.

————. "Twee Kategismusse Uit Die 16de Eeu: 'Nspieël Van Aksentverskuiwing." *In die Skriflig* 25, no. 1 (1991): 3-27.

Spoelstra, Bouke. "Die Sogenaamde Kategismuspreek—Vanwaar, Waarom En Hoe." *In die Skriflig* 25, no. 3 (1991): 363-82.

————. "'N Oorsig Oor Die Diakoniologiese Rol Van Die Gereformeerde Belydenisskrifte in Kerkwees." *In die Skriflig* 25, no. 2 (1991): 217-42.

Staedtke, E. "Ziel und Methode der kirchlichen Erziehungsarbeit: Eine religionspädagogische Untersuchung über Frage 1 und 2 des Heidelberger Katechismus." *Reformierte Kirchen-Zeitung* 76 (spring 1926): 297, 305.

Steen, H. "Lehrplan für den Konfirmandenunterricht auf Grund des Heidelberger Katechismus." *Reformierte Kirchen-Zeitung* 96 (spring 1955): 457.

Steenkamp, J. J. "Ursinus, Die Opsteller Van Die Heidelbergse Kategismus, Olevianus En Die Heidelbergse Teologie." *Hervormde Teologiese Studies* 45, no. 3 (1989): 611-25.

Tanis, James R. "Heidelberg Catechism in the Hands of the Calvinistic Pietists." *Reformed Review* 24, no. 3 (1971): 154-61.

Thompson, Bard. "The Heidelberg Catechism and the Mercersburg Theology." *Theology and Life* 6, no. 3 (1963): 225-38.

Truxal, A. E. "A Symposium on the Heidelberg Catechism." *The Reformed Church Review* 17, no. 2 (Fourth Series, 1913): 213-49.

van der Linde, S. "De Heidelbergse Catechismus in het kader van het Gereformeerd Protestantisme." *Theologia Reformata* 6, no. 1 (1963): 5-23.

van Rooy, Harry F. "Die Gebruik Van Die Ou Testament in Die Belydenisskrifte, Hermeneuties Beoordeel." *In die Skriflig* 25, no. 1 (1991): 29-46.

Velthuysen, G. C. "Die Verhouding Tussen Die Heidelbergse Kategismus En De Kort Begrip Van Faulkelius—Met Besondere Verwysing Na Die Teologiese Klemverskuiwings in Laasgenoemde." *Hervormde Teologiese Studies* 45, no. 3 (1989): 645-54.

Venter, C. J. H. "'Jou Enigste Troos'": Pastorale Perspektiewe En Motiewe Uit Die Heidelbergse Kategismus." *In die Skriflig* 25, no. 1 (1991): 47-69.

Verhey, Allen D. "Prayer and the Moral Life According to the Heidelberg Catechism." *Reformed Review* 48, no. 1 (1994): 26-41.

Weber, Otto. "Der Heidelberger Katechismus und die Predigt." *Reformierte Kirchen-Zeitung* 103 (spring 1962): 468.

Willis, David. "Forgiveness and Gratitude: The Doctrine of Justification in the Heidelberg Catechism." *Harvard Divinity Bulletin* 28, no. 1 (1963): 11-24.

Zimmermann, Gunter. "Der Heidelberger Katechismus als Dokument des subjektiven Spiritualismus." *Archiv für Reformationsgeschichte* 85 (1994): 180-204.

Part 2:
Translations of Ursinus's Catechisms

Introduction

Lyle D. Bierma

Authorship, Date, and Purpose

Surviving source material on the origin of the *Catechesis minor*, or Smaller Catechism (SC), and so-called *Catechesis maior*, or Larger Catechism (LC), is nearly as sparse as the material on the origin of the Heidelberg Catechism (HC) itself. What few data do exist, however, have usually been thought to point to Zacharias Ursinus as the author of both documents. The LC has been linked to Ursinus ever since its first appearance in print in a volume of his theological treatises in 1584, the year after his death, and then again, under a different title, in Reuter's collection of Ursinus's works in 1612.[1] Reuter also included the first published version of the SC, to whose title were appended the words "written in the year 1562 by Dr. Zacharias Ursinus; produced now for the first time from the library and original manuscript [*autographo*] of the author."[2] In his introduction, Reuter informs the reader that the two catechisms had been composed by order of the magistrate—the larger for studious adults and advanced students and the smaller for the general population and children—and that once they had been approved, a significant part of the HC was taken from them.[3] This implied that Ursinus could have written the LC no earlier than September 1561, the time of his arrival in Heidelberg, and no later than sometime in 1562, the date Reuter ascribes to the companion SC.

Three centuries later, August Lang became the first to challenge some of these claims. He argued that the LC had probably originated in the context of Ursinus's teaching at the Sapience College *before* the commissioning of the HC and that it did not serve directly as a source for the text of the HC. He was also convinced that the SC was an abridgement of the LC but that there were still significant differences between the two catechisms in structure and content. These differences could best be explained by the influence on the SC of the same committee that oversaw production of the HC itself.[4] Indeed, as Neuser would

1. Quirinus Reuter, "Catechesis, hoc est, rudimenta religionis christianae," in *Zachariae Ursini . . . volumen tractationum theologicarum*, vol. 1 (Neustadt: Harnisch, 1584), 620-51; "Catechesis, Summa Theologiae, per quaestiones et responsiones exposita: sive capita religionis Christianae continens," in *D. Zachariae Ursini . . . Opera theologica*, ed. Quirinus Reuter (Heidelberg: Lancellot, 1612), 1:10-33.
2. "Catechesis minor, perspicua brevitate christianum fidem complectens," in *Ursini . . . Opera theologica*, ed. Reuter, 1:34-39.
3. *Ursini . . . Opera theologica*, ed. Reuter, 1:10-11.
4. August Lang, *Der Heidelberger Katechismus und vier verwandte Katechismen* (Leipzig: Deichert, 1907), LXXVII-LXXVIII. See also pp. LXXVIII-LXXXVII.

assert a half century later, the SC was not the work of Ursinus alone but was "a committee project."[5]

More recent research has helped to clarify this picture. In 1972, Erdmann Sturm called attention to important information he had discovered in the inaugural address Ursinus had delivered in September 1562 upon assuming the post of professor of Dogmatics at the University of Heidelberg. First, Ursinus indicates that the territorial catechism currently in preparation was just about ready. Second, he reports that it had been decided that his first course of university lectures should offer "a summary of doctrine" (*summam doctrinae*) that fell somewhere between a rudimentary catechism and a detailed treatment of the traditional theological loci. None of his extant writings fits the description of this "summary of doctrine" better than his "Catechesis, Summa Theologiae," the so-called *Catechesis maior*. That would suggest, then, that he developed the LC sometime in late 1562 and that whatever impact it might have had on the text of the HC, it was not specifically designed or employed as a draft for the new catechism. When one combines this with Ursinus's earlier statement in March 1562 that the (Heidelberg) catechism and church order were in the process of being drawn up, it is safe to conclude that the SC, a lay catechism that did serve as a draft for the HC, was penned sometime before the LC. Moreover, the fact that the SC was not an abridgement of the LC and was composed for a wholly different audience and purpose removes most of the grounds for questioning Reuter's old claim that Ursinus alone was the author.[6]

In sum, we can say in all likelihood (1) that Ursinus was the author of both the SC and LC; (2) that he composed the SC in late 1561 or early 1562 and the LC in late 1562; (3) that the SC was designed as a simple catechism for untutored adults and children, possibly commissioned but certainly employed as a preliminary draft for the HC; and (4) that the LC was designed as a midlevel theological text for university students, not commissioned for the writing of the HC but probably consulted late in the process.

Structure and Content

Like almost all catechisms of the Western church during the previous millennium, the SC and LC were essentially expositions of the fundamentals of Christianity as summarized in the Apostles' Creed, the Ten Commandments, the Lord's Prayer, and the sacraments. However, the two catechisms do not treat these topics in exactly the same order or under the same theme. The SC moves from the summary of the law (Q/A 7-10) to creed (13-44), to sacraments (53-71), to commandments (72-95), and to prayer (96-108); whereas the LC places the sacraments last in this series, in a section on the ministry of the church. Furthermore, the SC integrates these catechetical elements into the threefold

5. Wilhelm Neuser, "Die Erwählungslehre im Heidelberger Katechismus," *Zeitschrift für Kirchengeschichte* 75 (1964): 311.

6. Erdmann Sturm, *Der junge Zacharias Ursinus: Sein Weg vom Philippismus zum Calvinismus* (Neukirchen: Neukirchener Verlag, 1972), 239-41, 246.

scheme of misery (summary of the law), deliverance (creed, sacraments), and gratitude (commandments, prayer).[7] The LC, on the other hand, organizes its material around the theme of a twofold covenant—a covenant established at creation and a covenant of grace.[8] The summary of the law is a summary of the covenant of creation (Q/A 10-29), whereas the creed summarizes the gospel of the covenant of grace (30-132), the commandments provide a pattern of life for God's partners in this covenant (148-223), prayer fulfills one of the important requirements of worship in this covenant (224-63), and the ministry of the church, including the sacraments, is the means by which God receives believers into his covenant of grace and keeps them there (264-323).[9] If, as several have suggested, this reflects the combined influence of Melanchthon's doctrine of the law, Bullinger's doctrine of the covenant, and much of the structure and content of Calvin's Genevan Catechism,[10] then we find already in Ursinus's first major theological work a convergence of all three of the Protestant traditions in which he was nurtured.

Relation to the Heidelberg Catechism

Those familiar with the HC cannot help but notice a significant overlap with the structure and content of the SC—the primary textual foundation for the HC. The focus on comfort, the threefold division of the material, the order and integration of the major elements of catechesis, and much of the wording of the two documents are very similar. Indeed, parallels to the phrasing of no fewer than 90 of the SC's questions and answers can be found in 110 of the questions and answers in the HC.

One should be careful, however, not to exaggerate the similarity between the two documents. For one thing, there are also linguistic parallels between the HC and the Larger Catechism that have no counterparts in the SC (e.g., HC 32, LC 64). Such parallel wording can be found between at least twenty-eight questions and answers of the LC and twenty-two of the HC. Moreover, even though the texts of the SC and HC are often similar, they are not identical. As Hollweg has pointed out, the HC represents a considerable reworking of the text of the SC, involving such things as a more personal and practical focus (cf., e.g., HC 26 with SC 17); a positive restatement and contemporary application of some of the commandments (cf. HC 94 with SC 82); and the addition (e.g., HC 28), deletion (e.g., SC 55), and expansion (cf. HC 122, 127 with SC 101, 106) of certain

---

7. See SC 4-6. For the historical background to this threefold division, see chap. 3, pp. 81-86.

8. Sturm, *Zacharias Ursinus*, 253.

9. Cf. Lang, *Heidelberger Katechismus*, LXIV. For more on the covenant theme in the LC, SC, and HC, see chap. 3 in this volume, pp. 96-98.

10. Lang, *Heidelberger Katechismus*, LXIV-LXVI; J. F. Goeters, "Entstehung und Frühgeschichte des Katechismus," in *Handbuch zum Heidelberger Katechismus*, ed. Lothar Coenen (Neukirchen-Vluyn: Neukirchener Verlag, 1963), 13; Sturm, *Zacharias Ursinus*, 257-58.

questions and answers.[11] One could also add that the literary and theological links between the general theme of the HC (comfort), its threefold division, and its expositions of the creed, law, prayer, and sacraments are clearer and more carefully established than in the SC. It may be going too far to say that the HC was "something completely new,"[12] but it was certainly more than a lightly edited version of its predecessor.

Text and Translation

This translation of the SC and LC, the first ever in English, is based on the oldest published Latin texts of each catechism, which appeared, respectively, in posthumous collections of Ursinus's theological works in 1612 and 1584.[13] In many places, I have followed an unpublished English translation by Professor Fred Klooster and John Medendorp, one of his students at Calvin Seminary, but I have also frequently altered their wording based on my own reading of the Latin text.

To assist the reader in finding the parallels among the SC, the LC, and the HC, I have appended a footnote to each question and answer in the SC and LC, listing the appropriate cross references, if any. Such parallels may range all the way from entire questions and answers and nearly identical wording in both documents to just a phrase or two in a question and answer and a paraphrase of the wording. In translating Scripture quotations in the two catechisms, such as the Ten Commandments and the Lord's Prayer, I have adhered closely to the Latin text but adopted as much as possible the language of the *English Standard Version* of the Bible.

11. Walter Hollweg, "Bearbeitete Caspar Olevianus den deutschen Text zum Heidelberger Katechismus?" in *Neue Untersuchungen zur Geschichte des Heidelberger Katechismus* (Neukirchen: Neukirchener Verlag, 1961), 126-35. Hollweg concludes by saying that "zusammenfassend läßt sich also sagen, daß der Bearbeiter, der unserem Katechismus seine Endgestalt gab, das mit viel Überlegung, Weisheit, Originalität getan hat, so daß seine Arbeit durchaus also große und selbständige Leistung zu werten ist" (ibid., 135).

12. Ibid., 131.

13. See above, nn. 2 and 1. Goeters makes reference to an original German version of the SC but offers no supporting documentation. "Entstehung und Frühgeschichte," 12. A second, slightly altered edition of the LC was also included in the Reuter collection in 1612. I have used as the basis for the translation the reprints of the Latin texts in Lang, *Heidelberger Katechismus*, 200-18 (SC), 152-99 (LC).

The Smaller Catechism

1   Q. What is the comfort by which your heart is sustained in death as well as in life?

    A. That God has truly pardoned all my sins because of Christ and has given me eternal life, in which I may glorify him forever.[1]

2   Q. How are you sure of that?

    A. The Holy Spirit testifies to this in my heart through the Word of God, the sacraments, and the beginning of obedience to God.[2]

3   Q. What does God's Word teach?

    A. First, it shows us our misery; second, how we are delivered from it; and third, what gratitude ought to be shown to God for this deliverance.[3]

4   Q. How do we come to know our misery?

    A. From the divine law, which is summarized in the Decalogue.[4]

5   Q. How do we learn the way of deliverance?

    A. From the gospel, that is, the articles of the Christian faith, and the sacraments.[5]

6   Q. Where are we taught the gratitude we owe to God?

    A. In the Decalogue, and in the doctrine of the invocation of God.[6]

7   Q. What is the summary of the Decalogue?

    A. Christ summarized it with these words in Matthew 22: "You shall love the Lord your God with all your heart, and with all your soul, and with all your mind. This is the first and great commandment. And a second is like it—You shall love your neighbor as yourself. On these two commandments all the law and the prophets

1. LC 1; HC 1
2. LC 2, 5
3. LC 8-9; HC 2
4. LC 9; HC 3
5. LC 9
6. No parallels

depend." Concerning these commandments God said: "Cursed be everyone who does not abide by all the things written in the book of the law and do them."[7]

8   Q. But are you able to do this?

A. No. For although the first parents of the human race in Paradise were created righteous and holy and able to do this, by willful disobedience they robbed themselves and all their descendents of that grace of God, so that now we are all born children of wrath. And unless we are renewed by the Spirit of God, we can do nothing but sin against God and our neighbor.[8]

9   Q. What is sin?

A. All ignorance and doubt concerning God, every inclination and action—internal or external—that opposes the divine law, all of which makes us deserving of the wrath of God and eternal death.[9]

10   Q. How then can you escape eternal death?

A. Through the Son of God our Lord Jesus Christ, who for my sake became human, by his suffering and obedience satisfied for me most perfect and strict justice of God, and merited for me eternal life, which he has already begun in me through his Spirit and will perfectly restore after this life.[10]

11   Q. Does this satisfaction of Christ help all people?

A. No. Only those who accept it by true faith.[11]

12   Q. What is faith?

A. It is a firm assent by which we know that everything related to us in God's Word is true, and a deep-rooted assurance created by the Holy Spirit in the hearts of God's elect, by which each person is convinced that God has graciously granted him remission of sins, righteousness, and eternal life because of Christ's merit alone.[12]

7. LC 15; HC 4, 10
8. LC 18-22; HC 5-8
9. LC 23, 25
10. HC 16-18, 58
11. LC 37; HC 20
12. LC 38; HC 21

13   Q. What is the summary of those things which a Christian ought to believe?

       A. It is summarized in the Apostles' Creed.[13]

14   Q. What is that creed?

       A. "I believe in God the Father almighty, creator of heaven and earth. And in Jesus Christ, etc."[14]

15   Q. How many parts does this creed have?

       A. Three. The first has to do with the eternal Father and our creation; the second with the Son and our redemption; and the third with the Holy Spirit and our sanctification.[15]

16   Q. Since there is only one God, why do you speak of Father, Son, and Holy Spirit?

       A. Because that is how God has revealed himself in his Word, namely, that these three distinct persons are one, true and eternal God, who created heaven and earth, in whom we have been baptized, and whom we are commanded to worship.[16]

17   Q. What do you believe about the eternal Father?

       A. That the eternal Father is the first person of the Godhead, who from eternity generated the Son, his own image, through whom he made heaven and earth and all creatures out of nothing. He preserves and governs them according to the eternal decree of his will for his own glory and the salvation of his people, and works all good things in everything and through all creatures, even through the wicked when they sin out of their own corruption. Because of his only begotten Son, he has adopted me as his own child and takes care of my body and soul in such a way that nothing can happen to me apart from his fatherly will and in such a way that all things necessarily work together for my salvation.[17]

18   Q. What do you believe about the Son?

       A. That the Son is the second person of the Godhead, Word and image of the Father, equal with the Father, coeternal and consubstantial, generated by the Father from eternity, and sent so

13. LC 39; HC 22
14. LC 41, 56, 105; HC 23
15. LC 40; HC 24
16. LC 43; HC 25
17. LC 45-52, 54-55; HC 1, 26-27

that, having assumed a human nature, by his merit and omnipotence he might deliver from eternal death and restore to eternal life me and all who believe in him.[18]

19   Q. Why do you call him "Jesus," that is, "Savior"?

    A. Because I am most firmly persuaded that he alone by his merit and power is the author of perfect and eternal salvation for me and all who believe in him.[19]

20   Q. Why do you say "Christ," that is, "anointed"?

    A. Because he was ordained by his eternal Father and anointed by the Holy Spirit to be for me and all believers the chief prophet, who reveals the will of God to us; our only high priest, who reconciled us to God by his intercession and the one sacrifice of his body on the cross; and our king, who rules us by his Word and Spirit, preserves the salvation won for us, and gives us complete and eternal possession of it after this life.[20]

21   Q. Why do you call him God's "only begotten Son" when we, too, are God's children?

    A. Because by nature he alone, according to his divinity, is the Son of God, generated by the father from eternity, and one, eternal God with the Father and the Holy Spirit. However, by grace God has adopted me and all believers as his children.[21]

22   Q. Why do you call him "our Lord"?

    A. Because he was appointed by the Father to be head over all things in heaven and earth, and bought us for his own with his precious blood.[22]

23   Q. Why do you say "conceived by the Holy Spirit and born of the virgin Mary"?

    A. Because I have been taught by God's Word that through the operation of the Holy Spirit the Son of God assumed a human nature from the flesh and blood of the virgin Mary, so that he might at the same time be true God, as he was from eternity, and the true son of David, in all things like us his brothers, except for

18. LC 45, 57
19. LC 58; HC 29
20. LC 59-63; HC 31
21. LC 65; HC 33
22. LC 67; HC 34

sin, and so that by his most perfect obedience he might cover my sins in the sight of God.[23]

24   Q. Why did Christ have to be truly human?

A. Because the justice of God demanded that the human nature that had sinned make satisfaction for sin.[24]

25   Q. Why did he have to be true God at the same time?

A. So that he might be able to bear the weight of God's wrath against the sin of the whole human race and restore us to righteousness and eternal life.[25]

26   Q. What do you believe about Christ's suffering?

A. That all the torments and insults that he sustained in soul and body, as well as the experience and dread of God's wrath—unbearable for all creatures—are the sole and sufficient sacrifice by which he has redeemed me and all believers from eternal death and procured for us remission of sins, reconciliation with God, the Holy Spirit, righteousness, and eternal life.[26]

27   Q. But why did he suffer "under Pontius Pilate"?

A. So that being condemned by earthly judgment—even though he was innocent—he might deliver us from the condemnation of divine judgment, which we had merited.[27]

28   Q. Why was he crucified?

A. So that he might testify that the divine curse, to which we were liable, had been placed on him, since anyone who hung on a tree was cursed by God.[28]

29   Q. But why did he want to redeem us only by dying?

A. Because divine justice and truth did not allow sin to be atoned for and life restored to us without death.[29]

---

23. LC 69; HC 35-36
24. LC 74; HC 16
25. LC 75; HC 17
26. LC 79, 87; HC 37
27. LC 80; HC 38
28. LC 81; HC 39
29. LC 82; HC 40

30   Q. Why was he also buried?

A. In order to prove that he really had died, and to make our graves, like his, peaceful resting places for our bodies.[30]

31   Q. What do you believe about his descent into hell?

A. That in addition to bodily death he also experienced the pains of hell in his suffering, and that he humbled himself in utter shame and disgrace so that he might prepare heavenly joy and glory for us.[31]

32   Q. Since then Christ has suffered and died for us, why do we still suffer and die?

A. Our suffering and death are not a satisfaction for our sins but a training in Christian patience, a testing of our faith, a fatherly chastisement that calls us to continual repentance, a conformity with Christ, and finally a deliverance from sin and all miseries.[32]

33   Q. What do you believe about Christ's resurrection?

A. That by his divine power he called his body back to life and adorned it with eternal glory, so that the human Jesus Christ, at the appointed time, might raise from the dead also me and all who believe in him, and might make us participants in righteousness and every heavenly good that he merited for us by his death; and so that in the meantime he might make those of us who are his members more certain of our resurrection.[33]

34   Q. What do you believe about his ascension into heaven?

A. That he exalted his human nature above all the visible heavens, and is and remains in this nature not on earth but in heaven until the end of the world, so that he might appear as our intercessor before the Father, that he might assure us that, with our flesh located in heaven like a guarantee, he will lift us up to himself as a head does its members, and that he might send us his Spirit from heaven as a reciprocal guarantee, by whose power we meditate not on earthly things but on things above.[34]

---

30. LC 83; HC 41
31. LC 84; HC 44
32. LC 89; HC 42
33. LC 90; HC 45
34. LC 93, 96, 100; HC 46, 49

35   Q. But isn't Christ with us always until the end of the world, as he promised?

       A. Since Christ is true God and truly human, he is always with the church in his divinity, majesty, grace, and Spirit; but in his human nature he is not now on earth but in heaven.[35]

36   Q. But aren't the two natures in Christ separated if the human nature is not present wherever the divine is?

       A. Not at all. For since the divinity is infinite and is and remains present everywhere at the same time, it is not necessary that it be separated or divided from his body in order to be somewhere else.[36]

37   Q. Why do you say that he sits "at the right hand of God"?

       A. Because he ascended into heaven so that there, in his human nature, he might show that he is Lord over all creatures and head of the church, the one through whom the Father administers all things; and so that he might fill us with the gifts of his Spirit and most powerfully guard and preserve us from all his and our enemies.[37]

38   Q. What do you believe about his return to judge the living and the dead?

       A. That just as he ascended into heaven, he will again in his human nature truly descend from there on the last day in his Father's glory, and after all unbelievers are cast down into eternal punishment, he will deliver me and all the elect from all evil and take us to himself in the eternal and heavenly kingdom, which he has already taken possession of in my name.[38]

39   Q. What do you believe about the Holy Spirit?

       A. That the Holy Spirit is the third person of the Godhead, who proceeds from the Father and the Son, and is coeternal and consubstantial with both; and that he is sent into my heart and those of all the elect to sanctify us, works in us true faith and conversion to God, remains with us forever, and thus makes us participants in Christ and all his benefits.[39]

---

35. LC 94; HC 47
36. LC 95; HC 48
37. LC 98, 101; HC 50-51
38. LC 97, 102-3; HC 52
39. LC 45, 106, 109, 112; HC 53

40   Q. What do you believe about the "holy catholic church"?

        A. That the Son of God, from the beginning of the world to its end, out of the whole human race, has gathered and will continue to gather unto himself a community elected to eternal life, united by true faith through his Word and Spirit; and that I am a living member of his church and will remain so into all eternity.[40]

41   Q. Why do you call it "the communion of saints"?

        A. Because all believers share in the same Christ and the same benefits that Christ gives to his church; and because all individuals should gladly contribute their gifts to the enrichment of the whole body of the church.[41]

42   Q. What do you believe about "the remission of sins"?

        A. That because of Christ's satisfaction God has forever blotted out the memory of all my sins, receives me in grace, and imputes to me the obedience of Christ, so that I will never come under judgment.[42]

43   Q. What do you believe about "the resurrection of the body"?

        A. That this very body that I now have will return to my soul on the last day by the power of Christ, will be made like Christ's glorious body, and will live with him and all the elect forever.[43]

44   Q. What do you believe about "life everlasting"?

        A. That after this life I will enjoy perfect and eternal blessedness and joy in God, inasmuch as already now I experience in my heart the beginning of a true knowledge of God and joy of the Holy Spirit.[44]

45   Q. But what do you gain by this faith, when you believe all these things?

        A. That I am righteous before God and an heir to eternal life as certainly as I believe that I am.[45]

---

40. LC 113, 115, 125; HC 54
41. LC 116; HC 55
42. LC 126-27; HC 56
43. LC 128, 130; HC 57
44. LC 129, 131; HC 58
45. LC 132; HC 59

46   Q. How then are you justified before God?

     A. Through faith alone in Jesus Christ, by which I am certainly persuaded that, out of pure mercy and without any merit of my own, God gives and imputes to me the perfect satisfaction, righteousness, and holiness of Christ, as if I had never committed a sin, or as if I myself had made satisfaction for all my sins and had been as totally obedient as Christ was for me.[46]

47   Q. But why can't our good works count as righteousness before God, or at least partially so?

     A. Because all our works in this life, even the best, are imperfect and stained with sin. Therefore, if they were examined in God's judgment, they would have to be rejected by God and condemned along with us. For the righteousness that endures before God must be perfect and pure in every way and measure up to the divine law.[47]

48   Q. Why do you say that you are justified through faith alone?

     A. Because neither faith nor my other works are the righteousness by which I please God in this life, but only the suffering and obedience of Christ, which are given and imputed to me by God just as if I had done it myself, if only I receive it with a believing heart. For since this gift is invisible and spiritual, it cannot be accepted by us except with the hand of the heart, that is, by true faith.[48]

49   Q. Where does that faith come from in people?

     A. It is a gift of God, which he works in our hearts through his Spirit.[49]

50   Q. Why is it that this gift comes to you instead of to so many others who are lost forever?

     A. Because God elected me in Christ for eternal life before the foundations of the world were laid, and he now regenerates me by the special grace of his Spirit. For unless this had happened, the corruption of my nature is such that I would have knowingly and willingly perished in my sins just like the many reprobate.[50]

46. LC 133; HC 60
47. LC 138; HC 62
48. LC 137; HC 61
49. HC 65
50. No parallels

51   Q. Doesn't this view, in which you declare that you were elected to eternal life, make you careless and more negligent in the daily exercises of obedience?

    A. Not at all. Rather it kindles in me even more a desire to persevere and advance in piety, since without true conversion to God I cannot comfort myself with the assurance of my election. And the more certain I am of my salvation, the more I wish to show God that I am thankful.[51]

52   Q. But aren't you inclined to doubt your salvation when you hear that none are saved except those elected by God?

    A. Certainly not. In fact, precisely because of this, I have a firm comfort in every temptation. For if I seriously desire with my heart to believe and obey God, I ought to be convinced by this most compelling evidence, as it were, that I am numbered among those who have been elected to eternal life and that therefore I can never be lost, no matter how weak my faith is.[52]

The Sacraments

53   Q. By what means and instruments does the Holy Spirit work, nurture, and confirm faith in us?

    A. Through the preaching of the Word of God and the use of the sacraments.[53]

54   Q. What are sacraments?

    A. They are ceremonies instituted by God so that by these visible pledges and public testimonies, as it were, he might remind and assure all believers of the grace promised them in the gospel; and so that they, on their part, might obligate themselves to faith and a holy life and distinguish themselves from unbelievers.[54]

55   Q. Can anyone share in or be certain of salvation without the use of the sacraments?

    A. No one can who continues to despise them. For such a person lacks true faith and excludes himself from God's people and covenant. However, someone who is deprived of the sacraments

51. HC 64
52. LC 219
53. LC 264, 266; HC 65
54. LC 274-75, 277-78; HC 66

against his own will still shares in the grace promised to believers and their descendents.[55]

56   Q. How many sacraments did Christ institute?

      A. Two, baptism and the Supper.[56]

Baptism

57   Q. What is baptism?

      A. It is the washing done with water in the name of the Father, the Son, and the Holy Spirit, instituted by Christ, so that by this visible pledge and public testimony, as it were, he might remind and assure all of us who believe in him that not only for others but also for each one of us our sins have been washed away by his blood and Spirit; and so that we, on our part, might be obligated to advance each day in true conversion.[57]

58   Q. What does it mean to be washed by Christ's blood and Spirit?

      A. It means that because of the shed blood of Christ, we receive remission of sins and are given the Holy Spirit, by whose power we are able and desire more and more to resist sin and to serve God in newness and holiness of life.[58]

59   Q. How can it happen that the external, physical bath with water makes us more certain of this internal, spiritual washing?

      A. Because the Holy Spirit moves our hearts to a firmer belief through this promise of Christ, namely, that a washing away of sins most certainly happens to all who believe and are baptized.[59]

60   Q. Where is this promised to us?

      A. In the institution of baptism at the end of Matthew and Mark, when the Lord says the following: "Go and make disciples of all nations, and baptize them in the name of the Father, and the Son, and the Holy Spirit. Whoever believes and is baptized will be saved, but whoever does not believe will be condemned." The

55. LC 281
56. LC 283; HC 68
57. LC 284-85; HC 69
58. LC 286-87; HC 70
59. LC 289

same thing is promised in other places in sacred Scripture where baptism is called the bath of regeneration and the washing away of sins.[60]

61 Q. But does the water wash away sin?

A. By no means. This happens only by Christ's blood and Spirit.[61]

62 Q. Why then is this bath with water called regeneration and the washing away of sins?

A. Because it is a sure pledge and sign by which Christ testifies to all of us who believe in him that our souls have been cleansed from sin by his blood and Spirit as surely as we are washed with visible water, which usually removes dirt from the body.[62]

63 Q. Why ought infants to be baptized, since they have not yet been given faith?

A. First, since the Holy Spirit is effective also in them, he moves them to believe and obey God even though they do not yet believe in the same way that adults do. Second, because they, too, belong to the kingdom and covenant of God and the church of Christ, and therefore ought to be marked with the sign of divine grace. Third, because infants in the Old Testament were circumcised, and baptism has replaced circumcision.[63]

The Lord's Supper

64 Q. What is the Lord's Supper?

A. It is the breaking and eating of the bread of the Lord and the passing of his cup in the community of believers, with the proclamation of his death, instituted by Christ, so that by this visible pledge and public testimony, as it were, he might remind and assure all of us who do this in true faith that his body was broken on the cross and his blood shed not only for others but also for each one of us, and that it is eaten and drunk by us as the true food and drink of eternal life; and so that we, on our part, will be obligated to seek life in him alone, to live in a way befitting his members, and to love one another.[64]

60. LC 290; HC 71
61. HC 72
62. HC 73
63. LC 293-94; HC 74
64. LC 295; HC 75

65　Q. What does it mean to eat the body of Christ and to drink his blood?

　　A. It means to receive from God by true faith in Christ remission of sins and righteousness because of Christ's body handed over to death and his shed blood; and to be joined with Christ our head through the Holy Spirit, who at the same time dwells in Christ's body, which is and remains in heaven, and in us on earth—joined in such a way that we are flesh of his flesh and bone of his bone, and live with him and are governed by one and the same Spirit, just as members of our body are governed by one and the same soul.[65]

66　Q. How can it happen that the external, physical breaking and eating of the bread and partaking of the wine make us more certain of this internal, spiritual eating?

　　A. Because the Holy Spirit moves our hearts to a firmer belief through this promise of Christ, namely, that all believers who eat this broken bread and drink the cup that is shared most certainly eat the body of Christ broken for them on the cross and drink his shed blood.[66]

67　Q. Where is this promised to us?

　　A. In the institution of the Supper, where Christ calls bread and wine his body and blood. It is described by the gospel writers and the apostle Paul in this way: "Our Lord Jesus Christ on the night when he was betrayed took bread, and when he had given thanks, he broke it and gave it to the disciples and said, 'Take, eat, this is my body, which is broken for you. Do this in remembrance of me.' In the same way he also took the cup after and gave thanks and gave it to them saying, 'Drink of it, all of you. This cup is the new testament in my blood, which is shed for you and for many for the remission of sins. Do this, as often as you drink it, in remembrance of me.' For as often as you eat this bread and drink this cup, you proclaim the Lord's death until he comes." This same promise is given when Paul calls the bread that we break and the cup of blessing that we bless a communion with the body and blood of Christ.[67]

65. LCC 299-301; HC 76
66. LC 303-4
67. LC 305, 309; HC 77

68   Q. But do the bread and wine become the very body and blood of Christ?

A. No. For Christ has a single true, human body, which was born of the virgin Mary, crucified for us, died, was buried, raised, transported into heaven, and is now there at the right hand of God, not on earth, until Christ returns from heaven to judge the living and the dead.[68]

69   Q. Why then are this bread and this cup called the body and blood of Christ, or a communion with the body and blood of Christ, and a new testament?

A. Because the breaking and eating of this bread and partaking of this cup are a sure pledge and sign by which Christ testifies to all of us who believe in him that as surely as we eat this bread broken for us and drink this cup passed out to us, which nourish physical and temporal life, so surely were his body broken and blood shed for us; so surely are they for us the spiritual food and drink of eternal life; and so surely do we have communion with them and share in the new testament.[69]

70   Q. For whom is it suitable and profitable to come to this Supper?

A. Those who are truly converted to God and have it as their intention to celebrate the benefits of Christ and confirm their faith. For one who does not come in this way acts contrary to the institution of Christ, despises Christ and his benefits, and eats and drinks judgment on himself.[70]

71   Q. But whom should the church admit to the Lord's Supper?

A. Those who have been baptized in Christ and by their life and confession can be regarded as Christians. But according to the command of Christ, the church ought to separate itself from those who are not this way until they reform, so that God's covenant not be dishonored and the whole church become liable for their sin and condemnation.[71]

68. HC 78, 80
69. LC 306-8; HC 75, 79
70. LC 313-14; HC 81
71. LC 319; HC 82

The Decalogue

72 Q. Can anyone who has been given true faith but does no good works be righteous before God?

A. No. For only those who are led by the Spirit are the children of God. And it cannot happen that true gratitude to God not follow true faith.[72]

73 Q. What is that gratitude?

A. True conversion to God and the fruits of this conversion.[73]

74 Q. What is conversion?

A. Mortification of the old person and vivification of the new.[74]

75 Q. What is mortification of the old person?

A. It is to be truly sorry for offending God with our sins, and to detest and flee them more each day.[75]

76 Q. What is vivification of the new person?

A. It is to rest and rejoice in God, who has been reconciled through Christ, and to be inflamed more each day by an eagerness for holiness and righteousness.[76]

77 Q. But aren't there also sins that remain in believers?

A. There remain in all saints, so long as they live on earth, many very serious sins, defects with which we are born, and perverse inclinations, as well as many sins of ignorance and weakness. By virtue of their true conversion to God, they struggle against these sins their whole life, and therefore these sins are not imputed to them, their inchoate obedience is pleasing to God because of Christ, and they do not persevere in any sins against their conscience. For fornicators, idolaters, adulterers, thieves, coveters, drunkards, slanderers, and robbers will not inherit the kingdom of God.[77]

72. LC 140-41; HC 64, 86
73. LC 142
74. LC 143; HC 88
75. LC 144; HC 89
76. LC 145; HC 90
77. LC 212; HC 87

78   Q. What are the fruits of conversion?

      A. Good works.[78]

79   Q. What are good works?

      A. Those things that God commands us in the Decalogue.[79]

80   Q. What are the commandments of the Decalogue?

      A. First: Hear, O Israel. I am the Lord your God, who brought you out of the land of Egypt, the house of bondage. You shall have no other gods before me.

      Second: You shall not make for yourself a graven image or any likeness of things, etc.

      Third: You shall not take the name of the Lord your God in vain, etc.

      Fourth: Remember the Sabbath day, to keep it holy, etc.

      Fifth: Honor your father and mother, etc.

      Sixth: You shall not murder.

      Seventh: You shall not commit adultery.

      Eighth: You shall not steal.

      Ninth: You shall not bear false witness against your neighbor.

      Tenth: You shall not covet your neighbor's house; you shall not covet, etc.[80]

81   Q. How is the Decalogue divided?

      A. Into two tables. The first four commandments contain our duties of piety toward God. The second six include what we owe our neighbor.[81]

82   Q. What does the first commandment require?

      A. That we detest all idolatry with our whole heart and flee from it with the utmost zeal.[82]

---

78. LC 146
79. LC 147; HC 91
80. LC 155, 163, 179, 185, 191, 196, 200, 203, 206, 209; HC 92
81. LC 152-54; HC 93
82. LC 156, 162; HC 94

83   Q. What is idolatry?

A. It is to invent or have anything other than or in the place of the one, true God, who has revealed himself to us in his Word, on which our hope and trust depend; or anything that we love or fear more than him or honor contrary to his command.[83]

84   Q. What does the second commandment demand?

A. That we desire to worship God not by our own will but only by the prescription of God's Word, in spirit and in truth, so that we do not bring the most severe punishments upon ourselves and our posterity by false and idolatrous forms of worship.[84]

85   Q. Does God then forbid the making or possessing of all images?

A. No, only those which are for the purpose of representing or worshipping God, or which give occasion for or the appearance of idolatry.[85]

86   Q. But shouldn't images be permitted in Christian sanctuaries as "books" for the unlearned?

A. No. For God wants his church to be taught not by images and statues but by his Word. Therefore, those who dare to add statues to this aspect of divine worship sin against this commandment and do not escape the charge of idolatry.[86]

87   Q. What does the third commandment require?

A. That by God's name we neither curse anyone, nor swear falsely or rashly, nor give others the occasion to do so, nor use his name except with fear and reverence, so that we always honor his name and avoid God's terrifying indignation, which threatens especially those who dishonor it.[87]

88   Q. But can we occasionally swear by God's name if we do so piously?

A. Yes, when necessity clearly requires that the truth be confirmed and defended by this means for God's glory and our neighbors' good.[88]

---

83. LC 161; HC 95
84. LC 164, 168; HC 96
85. LC 165, 167, 169; HC 97
86. LC 168; HC 98
87. LC 180; HC 99-100
88. LC 181; HC 101

89   Q. What is enjoined upon us in the fourth commandment?

A. First, that the ministry of the church be maintained and cultivated, that the church meet at the times appointed to learn the Word of God, receive the sacraments according to the divine institution, call upon God with united and public prayers, and give alms, after all unnecessary hindrances to these have been removed. Second, that throughout our whole life we meditate on and practice what we have learned on those days, that is, that we rest from all our evil works and present our members to God as tools of righteousness.[89]

90   Q. What is commanded in the fifth commandment?

A. That each person diligently carry out the duties of his calling; that to our parents and all who are in authority over us or to some extent give us good instruction, we show reverence, love, due obedience, and gratitude; and that at the same time we bear with their weaknesses, so that we receive from God the good things of this life that serve our salvation.[90]

91   Q. What is sanctioned in the sixth commandment?

A. That no one harm his own body or life, or those of another, without a command of God, or avenge himself, or become angry without cause, or desire to do harm or avenge himself, or suggest such a desire by word or gesture; but that we love all people as ourselves and do good even to our enemies.[91]

92   Q. What does the seventh commandment ask for?

A. That, whether married or single, we avoid all filth and immodesty in our actions, gestures, words, thoughts, and desires, as well as everything that incites it, and that we always live chaste and holy lives.[92]

93   Q. What is prescribed for us in the eighth commandment?

A. That we neither take our neighbor's possessions for ourselves through trickery, nor desire to preserve or increase our own possessions to the detriment of others, nor thoughtlessly squander them; but rather that we prevent the misfortunes of others to the

---

89. LC 186-87, 189; HC 103
90. LC 192, 195; HC 104
91. LC 197-98; HC 105-7
92. LC 201-2; HC 108-9

best of our ability, faithfully carry out our work, and help those in need according to our means.[93]

94   Q. What does the ninth commandment prescribe?

     A. That we neither testify falsely against anyone, nor misrepresent, belittle, slander, mistrust, be quick to condemn, lie about, or chatter idly about others; but rather that in court and in all the affairs of life, we always speak and acknowledge the truth and guard our neighbor's reputation as much as we can.[94]

95   Q. What does the tenth commandment demand?

     A. That not even the slightest inclination or thought contrary to any of God's commandments ever tempt our hearts, but that with our whole heart we continually hate all sin and burn with a love for righteousness.[95]

Prayer

96   Q. Why is prayer to God necessary for Christians?

     A. First, because it is the most important part of our gratitude to God, without which true faith cannot exist. Second, because God does not want to give the Holy Spirit, eternal salvation, and all those things that benefit it to those who despise or do not acknowledge his gifts, but only to those who pray earnestly and incessantly and glorify him for these gifts.[96]

97   Q. What kind of prayer pleases God and is heard by him?

     A. When we petition the one true God in the name of Christ for whatever he has commanded us to ask for, not with a pretense of feeling in our hearts but with a true sense of our need and a deep-rooted assurance that he will listen to us, just as he promised us in his Word.[97]

---

93. LC 204-5; HC 110-11
94. LC 207-8; HC 112
95. LC 210; HC 113
96. LC 224; HC 116
97. LC 225, 231; HC 117

98   Q. What does God want us to ask for?

A. All good things spiritual and physical, to the extent that they serve God's glory and our salvation, which Christ summarized in six petitions in that prayer he taught his disciples.[98]

99   Q. What is that prayer?

A. Our Father, who art in heaven, etc.[99]

100   Q. Why do we address God with these words: "Our Father, who art in heaven"?

A. So that—having been reminded that we, with the entire church of saints, call upon this one true God, who is our Father in Christ and the Lord of heaven and earth, and who thus desires and is able through Christ to give us all things pertaining to our salvation inasmuch as these things befit good children—we might worship him with reverence and trust.[100]

101   Q. What is the first petition in this prayer?

A. That God's name be hallowed, that is, that we and all people rightly acknowledge and call upon God, and that all our thoughts, words, and deeds be directed toward the glory of God's holiness, goodness, and majesty.[101]

102   Q. What is the second petition?

A. That God's kingdom come, that is, that he rule us by his Word and Spirit, subject us more and more to himself, convert many people to himself, preserve his church, and destroy all the Devil's works, until the fullness of his kingdom comes, in which he will be all in all.[102]

103   Q. What is the third petition?

A. That God's will be done on earth as it is in heaven, that is, that we and all people renounce our own desires and subject ourselves in

98. LC 234; HC 118
99. LC 235; HC 119
100. LC 238-39, 241; HC 120
101. LC 244; HC 122
102. LC 246; HC 123

all things to the divine will, which alone is good; and furthermore that everyone carry out his duties as cheerfully and faithfully as the holy angels in heaven.[103]

104   Q. What is the fourth petition?

     A. That he give us this day our daily bread, that is, that he bless our labors and supply us with all that we need for this life, in such a way that from this we acknowledge him as the source of all good things and place all our trust in only his fatherly providence and daily blessing.[104]

105   Q. What is the fifth petition?

     A. That he forgive us our debts as we forgive our debtors, that is, that by virtue of his mercy because of the suffering and death of Christ he not impute to us miserable sinners whatever sins we commit and whatever corruption remains in us; that he turn away his wrath from us; and that he receive us in grace. This he will do if only we, too, erase from our minds the memory of wrongs done to us and love even our enemies.[105]

106   Q. What is the sixth petition?

     A. That he lead us not into temptation but deliver us from evil, that is, that he strengthen and defend us with the power of his Spirit against all the assaults of our mortal enemies—the Devil, the world, sin, and our flesh—so that we neither fall into sin nor go down to defeat in this spiritual battle, but so that, having finally won the complete victory through our Lord Jesus Christ, we may enjoy eternal happiness.[106]

107   Q. Why do you add these words, "For thine is the kingdom, and the power, and the glory forever"?

     A. Because I look for everything that I ask for from his goodness and power alone and wish to contribute to his glory.[107]

---

103. LC 248; HC 124
104. LC 250-51; HC 125
105. LC 255-57; HC 126
106. LCC 259; HC 127
107. LC 262; HC 128

108   Q. Why do you add the little word "Amen" to the end of the prayer?

       A. Because I know that God listens to my prayers just as surely as I really desire this.[108]

108. LC 263; HC 129

The Larger Catechism

1   Q. What firm comfort do you have in life and in death?

    A. That I was created by God in his image for eternal life, and after I willingly lost this in Adam, out of his infinite and gracious mercy God received me into his covenant of grace, so that because of the obedience and death of his Son sent in the flesh, he might give me as a believer righteousness and eternal life. It is also that he sealed his covenant, in my heart by his Spirit, who renews me in the image of God and cries out in me, "Abba, Father," by his Word and by the visible signs of this covenant.[1]

2   Q. How do you know that God has established such a covenant with you?

    A. Because I am truly a Christian.[2]

3   Q. Whom do you call truly a Christian?

    A. One who is grafted into Christ by true faith and baptized in him.[3]

4   Q. Is there then no true religion besides the Christian religion?

    A. None.[4]

5   Q. Why do you say that?

    A. Because the Holy Spirit testifies to this religion alone in the hearts of believers. This one alone offers certain deliverance from sin and death. This one alone convicts consciences of its purity and truth. Finally, since the beginning of the world God has confirmed this one alone by great miracles, by true predictions of future things, by protection against all enemies, and by the blood of so many holy martyrs.[5]

---

1. SC 1; HC 1
2. SC 2
3. HC 20
4. No parallels
5. SC 2

6   Q. Where is it described?

     A. In the books of the prophets and apostles.[6]

7   Q. What then does this religion have that distinguishes it from all others?

     A. All other religions teach something of the truth but only as it concerns external knowledge, and they add the worship of idols and various errors, even contrary to the judgment of sound reason. However, they teach nothing about the perfect righteousness that God requires in his Word or about the Mediator through whom this righteousness is obtained, and thus they leave people in the midst of despair and death. The Christian religion alone truly shows what kind of person God created, for what purpose, and how he might reach this goal.[7]

8   Q. How many parts are there to the summary of Christian doctrine?

     A. Four.[8]

9   Q. What are they?

     A. The summary of the divine law, or Decalogue; the summary of the gospel, or Apostles' Creed; the invocation of God, or the Lord's Prayer; and the institution of the ministry of the church.[9]

10   Q. What does the divine law teach?

     A. It teaches the kind of covenant that God established with mankind in creation, how he managed in keeping it, and what God requires of him after establishing a new covenant of grace with him—that is, what kind of person God created, for what purpose, into what state he has fallen, and how he ought to conduct his life after being reconciled to God.[10]

11   Q. What kind of person was created?

     A. Someone who is in the image of God.[11]

6. No parallels
7. No parallels
8. No parallels
9. SC 4-5
10. No parallels
11. HC 6

12 Q. What is this image?

A. A true knowledge of God and the divine will, and the inclination and desire of the whole person to live according to this knowledge alone.[12]

13 Q. For what purpose was humanity created?

A. To worship God in eternal happiness with one's whole life.[13]

14 Q. What is the worship of God?

A. It is obedience given to God according to his law, with the primary goal of treating him with honor.[14]

15 Q. What is the summary of this law and this obedience?

A. That we love the Lord our God with all our heart, all our soul, and all our strength. And our neighbor as ourselves.[15]

16 Q. What does it mean to love God with all one's heart, soul, and strength?

A. It means to acknowledge him alone as God, that is, as our creator, preserver, and savior, and before everything to obey him perfectly in body and soul our whole life long, in such a way that we would rather deny ourselves and give up every created thing than offend him in anything.[16]

17 Q. What does it mean to love our neighbor as ourselves?

A. It means to desire and do good for all people to the best of our ability, in so far as the perfect honor of God permits, just as we would wish to happen to us.[17]

18 Q. Can any of us accomplish this obedience?

A. With the exception of Christ alone, no one has ever been able or will ever be able to accomplish it in this life.[18]

12. SC 8; HC 6
13. HC 6
14. HC 6
15. SC 7; HC 4
16. No parallels
17. No parallels
18. SC 8; HC 5

19   Q. But why are we unable to accomplish it?

      A. Because we lost the image of God.[19]

20   Q. How was it lost?

      A. Through the fall of our first parents in Paradise.[20]

21   Q. What was this fall?

      A. By their own will they submitted to the Devil, disregarded the command and warnings of God, and ate the fruit of the forbidden tree.[21]

22   Q. What was the result of this fall?

      A. That all people by nature can do nothing but sin and are deserving of eternal damnation.[22]

23   Q. What is sin?

      A. Whatever is contrary to the law of God.[23]

24   Q. Are not even infants free from sin?

      A. They are not, for original sin is inborn and inheres in all people as long as we live on earth.[24]

25   Q. What is original sin?

      A. It is guilt because of the fall of our first parents, ignorance and doubt concerning God and his will, and the inclination to those things that God has forbidden—inborn because of the fall of our first parents and the cause of all internal and external evil actions.[25]

19. SC 8; HC 9
20. SC 8; HC 7
21. SC 8
22. SC 8; HC 8
23. SC 9
24. No parallels
25. SC 9

26   Q. What results from sin?

     A. Every sin merits the anger of God and temporal and eternal death.[26]

27   Q. What is temporal death?

     A. It is the separation of the soul from the body and all the miseries leading up to it.[27]

28   Q. What is eternal death?

     A. It is the terrifying awareness of divine wrath and judgment and the perpetual torment of soul and body.[28]

29   Q. Why does sin merit eternal punishment?

     A. First, because God's justice demands that the punishment fit the crime. For every sin is an infinite wrong because it is an offense against God, that is, the infinite Good. Therefore it merits infinite punishment. Second, because sin does not cease, its punishment cannot cease. But without the grace of Christ, no one stops sinning. Therefore, no one can ever be delivered from punishment.[29]

30   Q. Where then do you receive your hope of eternal life?

     A. From the gracious covenant that God established anew with believers in Christ.[30]

31   Q. What is that covenant?

     A. It is reconciliation with God, obtained by the mediation of Christ, in which God promises believers that because of Christ he will always be a gracious father and give them eternal life, and in which they in turn pledge to accept these benefits in true faith and, as befits grateful and obedient children, to glorify him forever; and both parties publicly confirm this mutual promise with visible signs, which we call sacraments.[31]

26. HC 10
27. No parallels
28. No parallels
29. HC 11
30. No parallels
31. No parallels

32   Q. Why is this covenant also called a testament?

     A. First, because the term testament began to be used in the church in place of covenant. Second, because just as a testament is not put into effect without the death of the testator, so this covenant could not be ratified without the death of Christ.[32]

33   Q. What is the difference between the Old and New Testaments?

     A. It is the same testament or covenant of God with all the elect from the time of the first promise announced in Paradise, concerning the seed of the woman who would crush the head of the serpent, to the end of the world. But they are called Old and New Testaments because some of the circumstances and signs of the covenant were changed. For, in the first place, in the Old Testament they believed in the Christ yet to come; in the New we believe in the Christ who has been revealed. Second, the Old Testament contained the promise of the preservation of the nation of Israel until Christ; in the New we have only the general promise of the preservation of the church under various governments. Third, the Old Testament had levitical ceremonies, for which, having been abolished in the New, Christ instituted baptism and his Supper. Fourth, the Old Testament was more obscure; the New is clearer.[33]

34   Q. Next, how do we know that God establishes such a covenant with humanity?

     A. From the gospel.[34]

35   Q. What does the gospel teach?

     A. What God promises us in his covenant of grace, how we are received into it, and how we know we are in it—that is, how we are delivered from sin and death, and how we are certain of this deliverance.[35]

36   Q. What is the difference between the law and the gospel?

     A. The law contains the natural covenant, established by God with humanity in creation, that is, it is known by humanity by nature, it

32. No parallels
33. No parallels
34. SC 5; HC 19
35. No parallels

requires our perfect obedience to God, and it promises eternal life to those who keep it and threatens eternal punishment to those who do not. The gospel, however, contains the covenant of grace, that is, although it exists, it is not known at all by nature; it shows us the fulfillment in Christ of the righteousness that the law requires and the restoration in us of that righteousness by Christ's Spirit; and it promises eternal life freely because of Christ to those who believe in him.[36]

37   Q. Does the gospel teach that God's covenant of grace extends to all people?

A. He certainly calls all to that covenant, but people do not become members of it unless they embrace it and keep it, that is, in true faith receive both the Christ who is offered to them and his benefits.[37]

38   Q. What is faith?

A. It is to assent firmly to every word of God related to us, and it is a firm assurance by which each person is convinced that God has graciously granted him remission of sins, righteousness, and eternal life because of Christ's merit, and through him; and which, having been awakened in the hearts of the elect by the Holy Spirit, makes us living members of Christ and produces in us true love and invocation of God.[38]

39   Q. What then is the summary of those things which the gospel presents to us to believe so that we may be members of the divine covenant?

A. It is summarized in the Articles of Faith, or Apostles' Creed.[39]

40   Q. How many main parts does this creed have?

A. Three. The first has to do with creation and preservation; the second with redemption; and the third with our sanctification.[40]

36. No parallels
37. SC 11; HC 20
38. SC 12; HC 21
39. SC 13; HC 22
40. SC 15; HC 24

41   Q. What is the first part?

     A. "I believe in God the Father almighty, creator of heaven and earth."[41]

42   Q. Who is God?

     A. God is one, spiritual, intelligent, eternal, and infinite essence; distinct from all creatures, truthful, good, just, pure, merciful, kind, absolutely free; and the source and cause of all good, of infinite power and wisdom, and angry with sin. He is eternal Father, who from eternity generated the Son, his own image; and Son, coeternal image of the Father; and Holy Spirit, who proceeds from the Father and the Son. This is how the Godhead was revealed by the trustworthy Word and divine testimonies: The eternal Father, together with the Son and the Holy Spirit, created, preserves, and governs by his providence heaven and earth and all creatures, gathers in all humanity an eternal church for himself because of and through the Son, and is the judge of the righteous and the unrighteous.[42]

43   Q. Since there is only one God, why do you speak of Father, Son, and Holy Spirit?

     A. Because that is how God has revealed himself in his Word and divine testimonies, namely, that the eternal Father, Son, and Holy Spirit are three persons, actually distinct from each other by certain properties, and nevertheless only one divine essence and one God, creator of heaven and earth, in whom we are baptized, and whom we are commanded to worship.[43]

44   Q. How are they one with each other?

     A. First of all, because they are a single essence and a single God. Second, because they are equal in everything—eternity, power, majesty, wisdom, and goodness.[44]

45   Q. How do they differ from each other?

     A. The eternal Father is the first person of the Godhead, who generated the Son from eternity and works all good in all creatures

41. SC 14; HC 23
42. No parallels
43. SC 16; HC 25
44. No parallels

through the Son and Holy Spirit. The Son is the second person of the Godhead, the image, wisdom, and Word of the Father, generated by the Father from eternity, through whom the Father created and preserves all things, sent from the bosom of the Father to reveal the gospel; to assume human nature; and to be the Mediator, Redeemer, Justifier, and Savior. The Holy Spirit is the third person of the Godhead, proceeding from the Father and the Son, who is sent to sanctify the hearts of believers in Christ.[45]

46   Q. What does it mean to believe in God?

     A. It means to be firmly convinced that this single, true God, who has revealed himself in the church, is the Lord of all creatures, so that by supreme right he can do with respect to them whatever he wishes; and yet that he so desires our good that we ought to expect from him everything that pertains to our salvation.[46]

47   Q. Why do you say, "Father"?

     A. First, because he is the eternal Father of our Lord Jesus Christ. Second, because he is the Father of believers, whom he adopted in Christ.[47]

48   Q. Why "almighty"?

     A. Because he can do and does do whatever he wishes in heaven and earth, so that nothing happens apart from his will and decree.[48]

49   Q. What does it mean to believe in God as both Father and almighty?

     A. It means to know with certainty that he is both willing and able to give most faithfully and abundantly all those things that pertain to our salvation.[49]

50   Q. Why do you add, "creator of heaven and earth"?

     A. Because he made all other things out of nothing, preserves them by his presence, and governs them by his providence, for his glory and the salvation of his own.[50]

45. SC 17-18, 39; HC 26
46. SC 17; HC 26
47. SC 17; HC 26
48. SC 17; HC 26
49. SC 17; HC 26
50. SC 17; HC 26

51   Q. Did God then also create evil things?

A. Everything God created was very good, but devils and people turned away from God by their own will and corrupted themselves.[51]

52   Q. What do you call the providence of God?

A. The eternal, immutable, most wise and supreme counsel of God, according to which all things happen and are directed to the glory of God.[52]

53   Q. Must one say, then, that even the wicked are ruled by God?

A. He indeed works out through them what he wills by his power and counsel, in such a way that they cannot even move without his will, but he neither sanctifies them nor leads them by his grace and Spirit.[53]

54   Q. Then is not God the cause of the sins they commit?

A. By no means. For God is able to arrange and carry out, even through the very wicked, nothing but the best and most righteous. For that the wicked themselves sin while God works good through them is due not to God's good will and just judgment but to the corruption that clings to them and has been brought about by them of their own accord.[54]

55   Q. What does it mean to believe in the creator of heaven and earth?

A. It means to be certain that we not only were created by God but also are nourished and sustained by him, and that we, all that is ours, and all creatures, are upheld and ruled by his hand in such a way that nothing can happen to us apart from his good and salutary will for us.[55]

56   Q. What is the second part of the Articles of Faith?

A. "And in Jesus Christ, his only begotten Son, our Lord, who was conceived by the Holy Spirit, born of the virgin Mary, suffered under Pontius Pilate, was crucified, died, and was buried; he

51. SC 17; HC 6
52. SC 17; HC 27
53. HC 28
54. SC 17
55. SC17; HC 27, 28

descended into hell. The third day he arose again from the dead. He ascended into heaven and is seated at the right hand of God the Father almighty. From there he will come to judge the living and the dead."[56]

57   Q. Who is Jesus Christ?

A. He is the eternal Son of God, one God with the eternal Father and Holy Spirit, who was made human for our salvation.[57]

58   Q. Why is he called "Jesus"?

A. Because by his merit and power he is the author of perfect and eternal salvation for all who believe in him.[58]

59   Q. What does the name "Christ" mean?

A. That he was anointed by the Father as prophet, priest, and king.[59]

60   Q. With what kind of anointing was he anointed?

A. With the fullness of all the gifts of the Holy Spirit.[60]

61   Q. Why is he called "prophet"?

A. Because through the ministry and the Holy Spirit in our hearts he has revealed to us the Father's will for us, and he fulfills the prophecies and types that pointed to him in the Old Testament.[61]

62   Q. What is his priesthood?

A. It is his procuring of the Father's grace for us by his intercession and by the sacrifice of his obedience and death.[62]

63   Q. What is his kingship?

A. It is the Son of God's establishing and preserving the ministry of the gospel from the very beginning, and through that ministry his converting and vivifying the elect, his sanctifying them by the

56. SC 14; HC 23
57. SC 18
58. SC 19; HC 29
59. SC 20; HC 31
60. SC 20; HC 31
61. SC 20; HC 31
62. SC 20; HC 31

Holy Spirit, defending them against devils, raising them to eternal life, and ushering them into the presence of the Father, so that from then on God might reign among them publicly and not through the ministry.[63]

64 Q. What then does it mean to believe in Jesus Christ?

A. It means that we have this comfort: that by him as our king we are given and ruled by the Holy Spirit and defended against all dangers; that by him as our high priest we are reconciled and brought to the Father, so that we can ask and expect all good things from him; and that by him as the true prophet we are illumined with the knowledge of the Father. Then indeed we are made kings with him, who have dominion with him over all creatures for eternity; and priests, who already now offer ourselves and all that is ours as thank offerings to God; and prophets, who truly know and glorify God.[64]

65 Q. Why do you say that Christ is God's "only begotten Son" when we, too, are God's children?

A. Because we, who were enemies of God by nature, have been adopted by God as his children by grace, by which the merit of Christ and the right of inheritance are imparted to those who are grafted into Christ. But Christ alone is God's Son by nature: according to his divinity generated from eternity from the essence of the Father, and according to his human nature by the personal union of his flesh with the Godhead.[65]

66 Q. What does it mean to believe in the Son of God?

A. It means to feel in one's heart by the testimony of the Holy Spirit that we have been adopted by God as children because of his only begotten Son.[66]

67 Q. Why do you call him "our Lord"?

A. Because he was appointed by the Father to be head over all things in heaven and earth and bought us for his own with his blood.[67]

---

63. SC 20; HC 31
64. HC 32
65. SC 21; HC 33
66. SC 21; HC 33
67. SC 22; HC 34

68   Q. What does it mean to believe in Christ our Lord?

       A. It means to know for certain that we belong to Christ in such a way that neither will he allow us to be snatched from his hand nor do we have permission to desert him for another.[68]

69   Q. What do you understand when you say, "conceived by the Holy Spirit, born of the virgin Mary"?

       A. That the Son of God, who is the eternal Word of the Father, assumed in the womb of the virgin Mary, without the seed of a man, a soul and human body, formed from the substance of the virgin and perfectly sanctified along with the soul from the very moment of conception by the power of the Holy Spirit—so that according to the promises given to the fathers he might be truly human, like us in all things except for sin, and the true seed of David.[69]

70   Q. How do you understand that the Word assumed flesh?

       A. In this way: that neither was the divine nature changed into the human nor the human into the divine, but that, as soon as the human nature was conceived in the womb of the virgin, these two natures were so united in one person that thereafter they could never be separated, and yet they retain their own distinct properties; and that one and the same Christ is true God and truly human and can do and experience both what is divine and what is human, yet each thing individually according to that nature to which it belongs—just as soul and body are one person.[70]

71   Q. Why was it necessary that Christ be true God and truly human?

       A. Because otherwise he could not be the mediator between God and humanity.[71]

72   Q. What then is the function of the mediator?

       A. To restore the covenant between God and humanity, who had rebelled against God.[72]

---

68. No parallels
69. SC 23; HC 35
70. No parallels
71. HC 15, 36
72. No parallels

73   Q. Why could this covenant not have been ratified without a mediator?

A. Because God's justice demanded that he be angry with humanity forever on account of their sin. Since, therefore, it was impossible for God to have any fellowship with the human race that would violate his justice, it was necessary that someone intervene who, by appeasing God for us, satisfying his justice, and taking away every future offense, might again unite separated humanity with God.[73]

74   Q. Why did this mediator of the covenant have to be truly human?

A. Because the justice of God required that sin be atoned for by suffering and death; and consequently, since the divine nature could not suffer and die, atonement had to come through a creature; and since humanity had sinned, atonement had to come through humanity, not some other creature.[74]

75   Q. Why did he have to be true God?

A. First, because one who is merely a creature would be destroyed under the weight of God's wrath against sin. Second, because one who is merely a creature would not be able to pay God the full price for sin. Third, because we cannot be led into the presence of God unless we are adorned with righteousness and eternal life. Therefore, it was necessary for the mediator to gather and preserve the church in this life, give it the Holy Spirit, and afterwards raise it to eternal glory—all of which are from God alone.[75]

76   Q. Why did he have to be conceived by the power of the Holy Spirit and not by the ordinary means of nature?

A. So that no stain of sin could be passed on to him.[76]

77   Q. Why did he have to be without any sin?

A. Because divinity could not assume a sinful nature, nor could one who is not himself completely free from sin be an intercessor and sacrifice for others that pleases God.[77]

73. No parallels
74. SC 24; HC 16
75. SC 25; HC 17
76. No parallels
77. No parallels

78   Q. What does it mean now to believe in Christ who was conceived by the Holy Spirit and born of the virgin Mary?

     A. It means to be certain in one's heart that although we are all conceived and born in sin and under the wrath of God, the Son of God was conceived and born truly human without sin, so that by his merit and communion he might make us pure and holy.[78]

79   Q. What do you understand when you say that he "suffered"?

     A. That Christ sustained all sorts of misery and pain in soul as well as body, not only in that final act of redemption in which he was arrested and crucified but also continuously from his mother's womb to the grave.[79]

80   Q. Why is the name of the ruler under whom he suffered mentioned?

     A. First, so that a Roman ruler might be evidence, as Christ was suffering, that that the royal scepter had now been withdrawn from the Jews, just as had been predicted, and that therefore no other Messiah ought to be expected. Second, so that we might be reminded that we have escaped not only punishment but also just condemnation by the divine judgment, because Christ was condemned for us by an earthly judge, even though he was innocent.[80]

81   Q. Why did God want him to die on a cross?

     A. So that he might show that the curse to which we were liable had been placed on him. For cursed was anyone who hung on a tree.[81]

82   Q. Why was he able to redeem us only by dying?

     A. Because divine justice and truth did not allow sin to be atoned for without death.[82]

---

78. HC 36
79. SC 26; HC 37
80. SC 27; HC 38
81. SC 28; HC 39
82. SC 29; HC 40

83   Q. Why did he also want to be buried?

       A. First, to testify that he had really died. Second, so that by his burial, as well as by his death, he might merit for us a blessed rest in our graves.[83]

84   Q. What do you understand by his descent into hell?

       A. That he experienced in his soul and conscience—yet short of despair—the pains of death and horror of God's wrath, by which the damned are driven to despair and eternally tormented.[84]

85   Q. But could God ever be angry with Christ or desert him?

       A. Never. But he hid his favor and help for a time in such a way that the human nature of Christ experienced the same distresses that plague those who are deserted and rejected by God.[85]

86   Q. Why was it necessary that he experience these torments?

       A. Because the sins of us all were cast upon him; for that reason he felt God's wrath against them as if he alone had committed all the sins of all people.[86]

87   Q. What benefit accrues to us from the suffering and death of Christ?

       A. The one sacrifice, by which he has merited for us reception into the covenant of divine grace, that is, remission of sins, the gift of the Holy Spirit, righteousness, and eternal life.[87]

88   Q. What does it mean then to believe in Christ who suffered, was crucified, died, and was cast into hell?

       A. It means that each person is firmly convinced that, because Christ has endured for us those things that we deserved, we have been delivered from the curse and eternal death and will enjoy with him blessing and eternal life; and that each person experiences in his heart the beginnings of the mortification of sin through the Holy Spirit.[88]

---

83. SC 30; HC 41
84. SC 31; HC 44
85. No parallels
86. No parallels
87. SC 26
88. HC 43

89   Q. But since Christ has suffered these things for us, why do we still suffer so many things and die?

A. We do indeed suffer in this life and die a bodily death, but our afflictions are not signs of God's wrath, nor ought they to be compared with our sins or our future glory. For they are placed on us by our heavenly Father so that we might be made like Christ our head, so that little by little our old person might be crucified and buried with Christ and finally completely destroyed, so that faith and the invocation of God might be exercised in us, and so that the presence of God might be seen in our protection and deliverance. Therefore, all these afflictions are bearable and beneficial for us, and the death of the body itself leads us into eternal happiness.[89]

90   Q. How do you understand that "the third day he rose again from the dead"?

A. That the divinity of Christ by its own almighty power called back to life his body, which he had not gotten rid of after he died, and adorned it with immortality and heavenly glory.[90]

91   Q. Why was it necessary that he come back to life?

A. First, it was necessary for himself, because it was impossible for the human nature united with the Word to remain in death. Second, it was necessary for us because it would not be enough for the mediator—God and human, Jesus Christ—to merit righteousness and life if he did not also give them to us by his power. But this could not have happened if he had not first conquered death in his body.[91]

92   Q. Who then may be said to believe in the risen Christ?

A. Those who feel in their hearts that because death has been overcome by Christ, they have already received from him the beginnings of righteousness and eternal life, and likewise can no more remain in bodily death than can he, that head of whom they are members.[92]

89. SC 32; HC 42
90. SC 33
91. SC 33; HC 45
92. SC 33; HC 45

93   Q. In what sense do you say that "he ascended into heaven"?

   A. That he lifted up his human nature above all the visible heavens and remains in that nature continuously to the end of the world, not on earth but in that infinite light in which God is plainly seen by the blessed angels and people.[93]

94   Q. Isn't then Christ with us always until the end of the world, as he promised?

   A. According to his human nature, he is not now on earth; but in his divinity, Spirit, power, and grace, he is never separated from us.[94]

95   Q. But aren't the two natures in Christ separated if the human nature is not present wherever the divine is?

   A. Certainly not. For since the divine nature is infinite, it is not necessary for it to be separated from his body in order to be somewhere else. For it perpetually exists and remains the same way inside and outside of his body simultaneously.[95]

96   Q. Why did he ascend into heaven?

   A. First, because it was necessary for the majesty of the human Christ that, when the time of humiliation had ended, he spend time not in this corruptible world but outside of it in heavenly glory. Second, so that by this extraordinary triumph he might testify to us of his victory over sin, death, and all his and our enemies. Third, so that to the end of the world the church might know that he was not an apparition and did not change into another nature or disappear after the resurrection, but that he perpetually remains truly human and has departed to a heavenly place where he now dwells bodily and visibly until he returns. Fourth, so that he might testify that the gates of heaven have been thrown open also for us, his brothers and members. Fifth, so that as intercessor and advocate he might prepare a place for us in the presence of God.[96]

93. SC 34; HC 46
94. SC 35; HC 47
95. SC 36; HC 48
96. HC 49

97   Q. Now say what it means to believe in Christ who has been raised above the heavens.

     A. It means to be really persuaded that Christ as our firstborn brother has taken possession of heaven in our name, so that he is now our advocate there before the Father and after a little while will take us there to himself.[97]

98   Q. What is the right hand of the Father where Christ is said to sit?

     A. It is the authority over heaven and earth by which the affairs of the universe are governed and the church gathered and preserved, and it is the visible manifestation of this glory to creatures.[98]

99   Q. Why is this called "the right hand of God"?

     A. The analogy is to rulers, who place at their right hand those to whom they entrust the duties of administering the government.[99]

100   Q. What does it mean then to sit at this right hand?

     A. It means that the Son of God is head of the church, angels, and people, and the person through whom the Father directly brings about all good in everything; and that he visibly manifests this glory in his human nature, which has been exalted above all the heavens and all creatures.[100]

101   Q. Explain what it means to believe in Christ who is seated at the right hand of the Father.

     A. It means to be persuaded in our hearts that Christ, our brother and our flesh, has taken over the government of the world, so that he might share it with us; and that in the meantime, until we fully take hold of it, he guards and rules us and fills us with his gifts and Spirit.[101]

97. SC 38; HC 49
98. SC 37; HC 50
99. No parallels
100. SC 34
101. SC 37; HC 51

102   Q. What is the meaning of these words, "From there he will come to judge the living and the dead"?

      A. That on the last day Christ will visibly return from heaven with divine power and majesty, just as when the disciples saw him ascending, and that he will judge all people who have lived from the beginning of the world and who are then left upon the earth, so that he might take to himself into the fellowship of heaven all who have truly believed in him, but cast out the rest into eternal fire along with the Devil and his angels.[102]

103   Q. What does it mean, then, to believe in Christ who will return as judge?

      A. It means to be sustained by this comfort: that after a little while Christ will return so that after all the wicked have been cast out into eternal punishment, he might deliver us from all evil in soul and body, show before all creatures that in him we are innocent, and take us to himself to be with him forever.[103]

104   Q. How can it be said that Christ was conceived, born, anointed, suffered, died, was raised, lifted up into heaven, and will return when you have confessed that he is true God and all these things do not happen to God?

      A. All these things are true of him according to the human nature but not according to the divine; just as from eternity he is omnipotent, immutable, infinite, and fills heaven and earth according to his divinity but not according to the human nature.[104]

105   Q. Recite the third part of the Articles.

      A. "I believe in the Holy Spirit, the holy catholic church, the communion of saints, the remission of sins, the resurrection of the body, and the life everlasting. Amen."[105]

102. SC 38; HC 52
103. SC 38; HC 52
104. No parallels
105. SC 14; HC 23

106   Q. Who is the Holy Spirit?

      A. He is the third person of the Godhead, one true God with the eternal Father and Son, who renews us in the image of God.[106]

107   Q. Why is he called "Spirit"?

      A. Not only because he is God, but especially because he is the person through whom the Father and Son revive and move our hearts.[107]

108   Q. Why "Holy"?

      A. Because he is God and makes us like God.[108]

109   Q. What is his work?

      A. The sanctification of the elect, by which they become participants in Christ and his benefits; and the distribution of gifts in the church, which bring about its edification.[109]

110   Q. What is the sanctification of the elect?

      A. It is that by the Holy Spirit through the ministry of the gospel the elect are taught the will of God for them, they are regenerated, and through faith made temples of God and members of Christ, so that they might mortify the works of the flesh, walk and advance in newness of life, feel comfort and joy in God, and be preserved for eternal life.[110]

111   Q. Do any gifts of the Holy Spirit affect also those who are not elected to eternal life?

      A. They do affect many in the church who are not saints but are without true faith and conversion—thus to their condemnation.[111]

112   Q. What does it mean to believe in the Holy Spirit?

      A. It means to be convinced and to feel in one's heart that the Spirit of Christ, one true God with the Father and Son, has begun true

106. SC 39; HC 53
107. No parallels
108. No parallels
109. SC 39; HC 53
110. No parallels
111. SC 39

faith and conversion in us, is the author of all that pertains to our sanctification, and will remain with us forever.[112]

113   Q. What is that church that you believe exists?

A. It is a community of persons elected by God for eternal life and born again by the Holy Spirit, who embrace the pure doctrine of the gospel with true faith, use the sacraments according to the divine institution, fulfill the obedience owed to the ministry, and are given righteousness and eternal life because of and through Christ.[113]

114   Q. Why do you say "holy"?

A. Because Christ, who has redeemed the church with his blood and clothed it with his righteousness, also renews it by his Spirit for holiness and uprightness of life, which is begun in this life but will be completed in the future.[114]

115   Q. Why "catholic"?

A. Because in all times and from all peoples and all parts of the world, there are and will be to the very end some believers in Christ who make up this church.[115]

116   Q. Why "the communion of saints"?

A. Because all the saints have been called to communion in the same Christ and in the same benefits of Christ, and because they contribute whatever gifts each has received from God to the enrichment of the whole church.[116]

117   Q. What is the basis for this communion of the saints in Christ?

A. The Holy Spirit, who lives in Christ and in all the saints, is the invisible and indissoluble bond that joins them to Christ and works in them eternal life and righteousness like that in Christ, so that having been made one body with Christ, they might receive life and blessing from him—just as members depend on the head and

---

112. SC 39
113. SC 40; HC 54
114. No parallels
115. SC 40; HC 54
116. SC 41; HC 55

branches on the vine—and so that they might be joined to one another as closely as possible by the same Spirit.[117]

118   Q. Can the church be distinguished from other people by the human eye?

     A. No, the Lord alone recognizes his own.[118]

119   Q. How then can we unite with it?

     A. It is necessary that we join the visible church.[119]

120   Q. What is that visible church?

     A. It is the community of persons who by their words and external deeds profess the uncorrupted doctrine of the gospel, the proper use of the sacraments, and the obedience owed to the ministry, even though some in it are saints and others hypocrites.[120]

121   Q. Is then this visible church different from the church of the saints?

     A. It is partly different and partly not. For the entire church of the saints is contained in this visible church, but not the entire visible church is holy, because it has many hypocrites mixed in with it.[121]

122   Q. Since the church of the saints is included in the visible church, how is it not also visible?

     A. It is called invisible not because the saints are not visible to the eye but because in this life we cannot distinguish them with enough certainty from hypocrites.[122]

123   Q. Is it then necessary that all who will be saved be in the church of the saints before they leave this life?

     A. Yes, for whomever God has elected to eternal life he also calls to the communion of Christ in this life. But those who are separated from it will not inherit the kingdom of God.[123]

117. No parallels
118. No parallels
119. No parallels
120. No parallels
121. No parallels
122. No parallels
123. No parallels

124   Q. But how will each of us know whether we are in the church of the saints?

      A. If we experience the beginnings of true faith and conversion to God in us and show it by our lives.[124]

125   Q. What does it mean to believe "a holy catholic church, the communion of saints"?

      A. It means not to doubt that, from the beginning of the world to the end, a church elected for eternal life has been gathered and preserved on the earth by the Son of God through the Holy Spirit and ministry of the gospel, and that we are and forever will remain living members of that church.[125]

126   Q. What do you understand by "the remission of sins"?

      A. That because of the intercession and merit of Christ, God does not impute to believers in Christ any of their sins, nor does he condemn them because of their sins or punish them with eternal punishment.[126]

127   Q. How do you believe "the remission of sins"?

      A. I know for certain that because of the satisfaction of Christ, all my sins have been forgiven me in such a way that God will never call me into judgment for them.[127]

128   Q. What "resurrection of the body" do you profess?

      A. That when Christ returns to judge, all who have died since the beginning of the world will receive their same bodies that they had in this life, but now immortal and imperishable, and all who are then living on the earth will be renewed in a sudden change—the godly to happiness and glory, and the ungodly to torment and eternal disgrace.[128]

124. No parallels
125. SC 40; HC 54
126. SC 42; HC 56
127. SC 42; HC 56
128. SC 43; HC 57

129 Q. What is "the life everlasting" of which you speak?

A. It is the clear knowledge and glory of God, eternal joy in God, and the fullness of all good.[129]

130 Q. What does it mean to believe in "the resurrection of the body"?

A. It means to be firmly convinced that on the last day the bodies that we now have will be completely restored and our souls will be returned to them through the power of Christ, so that we might enjoy in soul and body eternal life and glory with Christ.[130]

131 Q. What does it mean to believe in "the life everlasting"?

A. It means to experience in our hearts already now the beginnings of eternal life, and to hold most steadfastly to this comfort—that after this life we will enjoy it more fully, and then perfectly once our bodies have been raised by Christ.[131]

132 Q. What then do we obtain by this faith when we believe all these things?

A. That all the things that God promised believers in his covenant are valid for us, that is, that we are justified and heirs to eternal life.[132]

133 Q. How are we justified before God in this life?

A. Through faith alone in Christ, when God out of his gracious mercy, for us who believe, forgives our sins, imputes to us the satisfaction of Christ as if we ourselves had done it, and on that account receives us in grace without any of our own merits and gives us the Holy Spirit and eternal life.[133]

134 Q. How is what you say consistent—that we are justified by the mercy of God, by the merit of Christ, and by our faith?

A. These are entirely consistent with each other and have the same meaning. For it is the mercy of God alone that welcomes us who are unrighteous as righteous. It is the death and righteousness of

129. SC 44; HC 58
130. SC 43; HC 57
131. SC 44; HC 58
132. SC 45; HC 59
133. SC 46; HC 60

Christ by which we are pleasing to God when that righteousness is imputed to us by his mercy. And it is faith by which we receive the righteousness of Christ granted to us by God.[134]

135 Q. Why is it necessary that the satisfaction and righteousness of Christ be imputed to us in order for us to be righteous before God?

A. Because God, who is immutably righteous and true, wants to receive us into the covenant of grace in such a way that he does not go against the covenant established in creation, that is, that he neither treat us as righteous nor give us eternal life unless his law has been perfectly satisfied, either by ourselves or, since that cannot happen, by someone in our place.[135]

136 Q. Why does God want to impute this righteousness only to believers?

A. Because he justifies and saves us so that we may acknowledge and glorify his benefits, which would not happen if we did not believe that they were given to us by him.[136]

137 Q. But why do you say that through faith alone we are justified?

A. Because we are righteous before God not by the merit or value of our faith or any other of our works but only by receiving the righteousness given by God. But since this gift is spiritual, it can be received only by the soul and heart, that is, by believing.[137]

138 Q. But why aren't our works the righteousness, or part of the righteousness, that has value before God?

A. Because before regeneration all our works are sins. And even though after regeneration we begin to do good works, as long as we are in this life they are always tainted by some imperfection. But the law of God places under a curse all who do not perfectly keep it. Therefore, whatever part—even the smallest part—of our righteousness we might attribute to our good works, in that respect it will be impure and defective and thus will not hold up in the judgment of God.[138]

134. No parallels
135. HC 12
136. No parallels
137. SC 48; HC 61
138. SC 47; HC 62

139 Q. But since a temporal and eternal reward is so often promised for good works, don't they merit anything before God?

A. No creature's good works, with the sole exception of Christ's obedience, can merit anything before God. For even if we had done everything we should, we would still be unworthy servants and owe more than we had done; God would not owe us even the slightest thing. Therefore, reward accompanies good works by virtue of the divine promises; it is not owed or merited, but given graciously and out of mercy.[139]

140 Q. If, therefore, good works contribute nothing to our righteousness, can we be justified even though none are found in us?

A. No, we cannot.[140]

141 Q. What causes you to say this?

A. First, because the covenant of God is valid only for those who keep it. We are obligated not only to believe in Christ but also to live holy lives before God, incipiently in this life and perfectly in the next. Second, because God gave his Son over to death for us and received us in grace, not so that we might have license to wallow in our sins but so that we might be thankful for his benefits by walking in newness of life. Third, because whomever God justifies because of Christ he also regenerates to new life by the Holy Spirit. So then he does not impute Christ's merit to those who are not ruled by the Spirit of Christ. Fourth, because it is impossible that there be true faith without its fruits. One who does not have these fruits, therefore, can neither boast of faith nor take comfort in partnership in the divine covenant.[141]

142 Q. What then is the fruit of faith to which God's covenant of grace obligates us, and by which true faith is recognized?

A. True conversion to God.[142]

143 Q. What is conversion to God?

A. Mortification of the flesh and vivification by the Spirit.[143]

139. HC 63
140. SC 72
141. SC 72, HC 64, 86
142. SC 73
143. SC 74; HC 88

144   Q. What is mortification of the flesh?

A. It is sorrow for God's being offended by our sins and a hatred for and earnest flight from sin.[144]

145   Q. What is vivification by the Spirit?

A. It is joy in God, who is gracious to us through Christ, and a love and burning desire for righteousness for the glory of God.[145]

146   Q. What accompanies this conversion?

A. Good works.[146]

147   Q. What are good works?

A. They are internal and external actions commanded by God in the Decalogue and done by those who have been reconciled to God through Christ, for this main purpose—in order that obedience and gratitude be shown to God for the benefits received from him.[147]

The Law

148   Q. Do Christians, who have already been received into God's covenant, also need the teaching of the Decalogue?

A. Yes, for the law of God must be preached both to those converted through the gospel and to those not yet converted.[148]

149   Q. Why is the law preached before the gospel to those not yet converted?

A. So that, terrified by the knowledge of sin and of the wrath of God, they might be stirred up to seek deliverance; and so that they might be prepared to hear the gospel and be converted to God.[149]

144. SC 75; HC 89
145. SC 76; HC 90
146. SC 78
147. SC 79; HC 91
148. No parallels
149. No parallels

150 Q. But why must the law still be proclaimed to the converted after the gospel has been preached?

A. First, so that they may learn what worship God approves and requires of his covenant partners. Second, so that seeing how far they are in this life from the perfect fulfillment of the law, they may continue in humility and aspire to heavenly life.[150]

151 Q. Since Christ abolished the law, why are we bound to the Decalogue?

A. Christ fulfilled the civil and ceremonial laws of Moses in such a way that no one is obligated to keep them anymore; moreover, it is not even right to reintroduce into the church the ceremonies that pointed to the future appearance of Christ. He even abrogated the Decalogue in himself for believers in such a way that it no longer condemns them. But the clearer now to us that God's grace in Christ is, the more we owe him obedience.[151]

152 Q. How many parts are there to the Decalogue?

A. It has two tables: the first consists of four commandments, and the second of six.[152]

153 Q. What does the first table teach?

A. How we ought to be and act toward God.[153]

154 Q. What does the second table teach?

A. How we ought to be and act toward others.[154]

155 Q. What is the first commandment?

A. "Here, O Israel: I am the Lord your God, who brought you out of the land of Egypt, out of the house of bondage. You shall have no other gods before me."[155]

150. No parallels
151. No parallels
152. SC 81; HC 93
153. SC 81; HC 93
154. SC 81; HC 93
155. SC 80; HC 92

156 Q. What does God forbid in this commandment?

A. That we neither neglect nor give to another the worship we owe him.[156]

157 Q. What is the worship that he demands we render to him?

A. That we acknowledge him as our God according to his Word, firmly believe every word of his, place all our trust in him alone, look to him for all good things, love and honor him above all, humble ourselves before him, and patiently endure what he inflicts upon us.[157]

158 Q. When Moses speaks to the people of Israel, does he also address us?

A. No less than he did them. First, because God was not producing then for the first time the law summarized in the Decalogue, but he was repeating and clarifying for the people of Israel not only what he required of them but also that for which all rational creatures had been made. Second, inasmuch as we have been engrafted into Christ, who is the natural seed of Abraham, we are the spiritual children of Abraham and Israel.[158]

159 Q. Why does God call himself "Lord"?

A. To remind us that he has full authority to rule us since he is the creator and sustainer of all things.[159]

160 Q. Why does he call himself our God, who brought Israel out of Egypt?

A. First, so that we might remember that this God alone is the true God, who revealed himself from the beginning in the church by his sure Word and clear divine testimonies. Second, so that when we consider that we have been saved and delivered from all evil by him, we might realize that we owe him gratitude and obedience.[160]

156. No parallels
157. HC 94
158. No parallels
159. No parallels
160. No parallels

161   Q. What is an "other god"?

A. Anything besides the God revealed in the church in which people place any trust, or which they love or fear more than or equal to God, or to which they show an honor and reverence for the purpose of worshipping God that is outside of or contrary to the Word of God.[161]

162   Q. Why is "before me" added?

A. So that we flee all idolatry, not only in the sight of others but also in our hearts, since all things are exposed to the eyes of God.[162]

163   Q. What is the second commandment?

A. "You shall not make for yourself a graven image, or any likeness of anything that is in the heaven above, or that is in the earth below, or that is in the water under the earth. You shall not bow down to them or serve them. For I the Lord your God am strong and jealous, visiting the iniquity of the fathers upon the children to the third and fourth generation of those who hate me, but showing mercy to thousands of those who love me and keep my commandments."[163]

164   Q. What is the meaning of this commandment?

A. That we not try to worship God in any other way than he has commanded in his Word.[164]

165   Q. Are all sculptured and painted images whatsoever forbidden by this law?

A. No, only those that are made for the purpose of portraying or worshipping God.[165]

161. SC 83; HC 95
162. SC 82
163. SC 80; HC 92
164. SC 84; HC 96
165. SC 85; HC 97

166 Q. Why doesn't God want to be portrayed in visible form?

A. For this reason: since he is an eternal and incomprehensible spirit, every representation of him in corporeal, corruptible, mortal form is a lie about God and a diminishing of his majesty.[166]

167 Q. What does it mean to worship God by means of images?

A. It means in the worship of God to turn to them, either in soul or body, as if God would listen to us better if he were worshipped by means of them; or by thought, gesture, utterance of the divine name, or any external sign whatsoever to show them honor as if they represented God; or to desire in any way to worship God by using them.[167]

168 Q. Why is it not right to worship God by means of images?

A. Because it belongs to divine authority alone and not to any creature to institute the form of divine worship and the testimonies of the divine presence. Indeed, to represent God differently than he is, is a serious insult to him.[168]

169 Q. Why does God forbid not only that such images be worshipped but even that they be made?

A. So that we don't appear to approve of idolaters by having these images, which can be a kind of idolatry or the occasion for it, and so that we don't upset God by providing the occasion for anyone else to sin.[169]

170 Q. So this commandment isn't talking only about images?

A. No, but also about all humanly devised worship of God.[170]

171 Q. Why does God add a threat and a promise to this commandment?

A. So that he may more effectively deter us from idolatry, which is among the worst of sins.[171]

---

166. No parallels
167. SC 85
168. SC 84, 86; HC 98
169. SC 85
170. No parallels
171. No parallels

172   Q. Why does he call himself "strong"?

      A. So that we many fear his power to punish.[172]

173   Q. Why "jealous"?

      A. Because he never allows his honor to be given with impunity to another by means of the magnitude of this sin.[173]

174   Q. Why does he threaten punishments even for the descendants of sinners?

      A. First, so that he might show the magnitude of the sin, which would bring down punishment not only on those by whom it is done but also on their descendants if God chose to act according to the strictness of his justice. Second, so that people might abstain from sin at least out of concern for their descendants.[174]

175   Q. But does the justice of God allow descendants to be punished for the sins of the parents?

      A. Yes, for by virtue of the depravity of our nature, we would all continue in the sins of our parents if God did not look upon us with his matchless mercy.[175]

176   Q. Why does he promise to bless the descendants of the upright?

      A. First, so that he might express to the upright the magnitude of his mercy, by which he deals kindly not only with them but also with their descendants, and accordingly move us more to gratitude and zeal for his honor. Second, so that he might draw us to piety through the happiness promised our descendants.[176]

177   Q. Then do all the descendants of the upright receive mercy from God?

      A. By this promise God did not bind his grace to physical succession, but he does distribute spiritual and bodily blessing to the

172. No parallels
173. No parallels
174. No parallels
175. No parallels
176. No parallels

descendants of the upright as he saw fit to do from eternity to show forth his glory.[177]

178   Q. Why does he say that he will bless the thousandth generation but punish only the fourth?

A. To testify that he rejoices not in the damnation but the salvation of people and that he punishes only as a manifestation of his justice.[178]

179   Q. What is the third commandment?

A. "You shall not take the name of the Lord your God in vain. For the Lord will not hold him guiltless who takes the name of the Lord his God in vain."[179]

180   Q. What is forbidden by this commandment?

A. That we say anything false or blasphemous about God, make mention of him lightly, dishonor his name by scandals, curse anyone by his name, but especially that we swear falsely, rashly, or against his Word.[180]

181   Q. And what is required?

A. That we proclaim divine truth as much as we are able, glorify God with word and deeds, thank him, pray to him, and swear through him alone, where defense of the truth and human concord demand it.[181]

182   Q. What is a scandal?

A. It is an evil teaching or deed that makes someone else worse off.[182]

183   Q. What is an oath?

A. It is calling upon God to be a witness that we do not intend to deceive in what we are asserting, and to punish us if we have deceived.[183]

177. No parallels
178. No parallels
179. SC 80; HC 92
180. SC 87; HC 99
181. SC 88; HC 101
182. No parallels
183. HC 102

184 Q. Why did he add a threat to this commandment?

A. To show that profaning his name is among the most serious of sins.[184]

185 Q. What is the fourth commandment?

A. "Remember the Sabbath day, to keep it holy. Six days you shall labor, and do all your work, but the seventh day is a Sabbath to the Lord your God. On it you shall not do any work, you, or your son, or your daughter, your male servant, or your female servant, or your livestock, or the sojourner who is within your gates. For in six days the Lord made heaven and earth, the sea, and all that is in them, and rested the seventh day. Therefore the Lord blessed the Sabbath day and made it holy."[185]

186 Q. What does this law require?

A. That a certain time, free of activities that would hinder this, be devoted to the public ministry of the church—a time in which the true doctrine about God is taught and learned, the sacraments are rightly administered and used, and public invocation of and confession to God are made; and that obedience and honor be given to this ministry, and each individual earnestly desire to maintain it in his own place.[186]

187 Q. What does it forbid?

A. All contempt, denigration, and willful hindrance of the ministry.[187]

188 Q. Why does God want a certain time designated for the ministry of the church?

A. First, because of our weakness, since at other times we rarely apply ourselves totally to meditation on divine things. Second, so that rest from labor may be given those under another's power.[188]

184. HC 100
185. SC 80; HC 92
186. SC 89; HC 103
187. SC 89
188. No parallels

189   Q. Why did God designate the seventh day for ministry among the people of Israel?

A. Because on the seventh day he stopped creating things. Therefore, by making this day holy, he wanted to remind his people that they, too, should rest from their works, that is, their sins, and devote themselves to the contemplation of divine works.[189]

190   Q. Are we also bound to the seventh day?

A. We are not, because by his coming Christ abolished the Mosaic ceremonies. But we should observe to the best of our ability the time and order necessary for ministry that have been established by the church, without, however, considering them part of the worship of God.[190]

191   Q. What is the fifth commandment?

A. "Honor your father and your mother, that you may grow old in the land that the Lord your God will give you."[191]

192   Q. What is required in it?

A. That all people faithfully carry out the tasks to which they have been called by God, and that children show to parents, and subjects to magistrates and all who are in authority, reverence, love, and obedience in all things not forbidden by God, and gratitude and patience in putting up with whatever weaknesses they have. But parents and all in authority must see to it that their children and those entrusted to them live in piety and peace.[192]

193   Q. What is forbidden?

A. All negligence in our duties; all contempt of authorities; and all ingratitude, solicitude, and obedience that is either feigned or in conflict with any command of God.[193]

---

189. SC 89; HC 103
190. No parallels
191. SC 80; HC 92
192. SC 90; HC 104
193. No parallels

194   Q. Why does God add a promise to this command?

A. So that he might encourage us to keep it and show how much he values it, since without it human society cannot exist.[194]

195   Q. Does God then always prolong this life for those who obey their parents?

A. God fulfills this and other promises of earthly things for us in such a way as he knows will help our salvation.[195]

196   Q. What is the sixth commandment?

A. "You shall not murder."[196]

197   Q. What is forbidden by this law?

A. Not only every injury to life or body, whether ours or someone else's, and all personal revenge, but also unjust anger, hatred, and desire for harm or revenge, as well as the expression of such a desire with words and gestures.[197]

198   Q. What does it require?

A. That we love all people as ourselves and protect their lives and well-being as much as we can.[198]

199   Q. Does the magistrate then sin when he kills criminals or inflicts other punishments?

A. He does not sin at all, for he is God's servant for wrath on one who does evil. On the contrary, he would be seriously sinning if he neglected his duty, not only because he would be giving evildoers license to attack others but also because by not punishing wrong, he would be drawing God's anger and punishment on himself and all his people.[199]

194. No parallels
195. SC 90
196. SC 80; HC 92
197. SC 91; HC 105-6
198. SC 91
199. HC 105

200   Q. What is the seventh commandment?

      A. "You shall not commit adultery."[200]

201   Q. What does it forbid?

      A. Not only adultery, but also obscenity and shameful behavior in actions, gestures, words, thoughts, and desires—in short, lack of self-control and anything which might give occasion to aimless passions.[201]

202   Q. What does it require?

      A. That all persons, whether single or married (for those suited for it), practice chastity and modesty, not only externally with their bodies but also in word, gesture, soul, and heart—in short, self-control, without which chastity cannot be maintained.[202]

203   Q. What is the eighth commandment?

      A. "You shall not steal."[203]

204   Q. What is forbidden by it?

      A. Taking others' goods for ourselves, whether by violence or deceit; trying or wishing in any way to get rich at the expense of others; and thoughtlessly squandering our means.[204]

205   Q. But what does it require?

      A. That we desire to protect everyone's possessions and meet our neighbor's need according to the measure of our means.[205]

206   Q. What is the ninth commandment?

      A. "You shall not bear false witness against your neighbor."[206]

200. SC 80; HC 92
201. SC 92; HC 108-9
202. SC 92; HC 108-9
203. SC 80; HC 92
204. SC 93; HC 110
205. SC 93; HC 111
206. SC 80; HC 92

207   Q. What is prohibited by this law?

     A. Not only ruining anyone in court by perjury, but also all belittlement, misrepresentation, mistrust, evil condemnation, and finally idle chatter, flattery, and lies of every kind.[207]

208   Q. But what does it require of us?

     A. That we be zealous for truth and fidelity in court, in contracts, and in every word and that we think and speak well of others as much as we can, and guard their good reputation.[208]

209   Q. What is the tenth commandment?

     A. "You shall not covet your neighbor's house; you shall not covet your neighbor's wife, or his male servant, or his female servant, or his ox, or his donkey, or anything that is your neighbor's."[209]

210   Q. What is taught by this law?

     A. It adds a clarification to the other commandments, namely, that our souls and hearts ought not to be tempted by any thought or inclination contrary to God's law, but burn continually and wholly with hatred for all sin and a love for righteousness.[210]

211   Q. Can anyone perfectly fulfill in this life the obedience required in these commandments?

     A. No one, not even the holiest, except for Christ alone. For throughout our lives all of us carry around the remnants of sin and have barely a small beginning of that obedience which God's law requires.[211]

212   Q. But can people be holy and righteous before God if they continue to commit all sorts of sins?

     A. By no means. For those who continue in sin against their conscience will not inherit the kingdom of God. But in the saints in this life there remain original sin and many sins of ignorance,

207. SC 94; HC 112
208. SC 94; HC 112
209. SC 80; HC 92
210. SC 95; HC 113
211. HC 114

omission, and weakness, against which they still fight and for which they obtain pardon before God through Christ if they are truly sorry for them.[212]

213 Q. Since the obedience even of those who are born again is not complete and the law condemns all who are not perfectly obedient, how can this imperfect obedience be pleasing to God?

A. It is pleasing to God not because it is the kind of obedience that is pleasing by itself, but because the sins that contaminate it are forgiven for believers, and in Christ believers are loved by God as children.[213]

214 Q. But since we are not justified before God by this obedience, why does he require it?

A. First, so that we might offer our gratitude to him who freely justifies and saves us. Second, so that in our reconciliation it will still be clear that God is an enemy of sin, since he receives in grace only those who repent.[214]

215 Q. Since in the future we can do nothing by ourselves but sin, how can we make a beginning in faith and the new life and persevere in them?

A. Only by the Spirit of God, who renews and rules us.[215]

216 Q. Does this grace reach all people, or is it accessible to all?

A. Certainly not, but only those whom God from eternity has elected in Christ for eternal life, in order that he might reveal his mercy in them.[216]

217 Q. Isn't God then unjust when he condemns those to whom he does not give this grace that would enable them to repent and believe?

A. Not at all. For first of all, no one has given anything to God first that puts God in his debt; God may do with his own what he wishes. Second, all people deserve to be abandoned and rejected by God forever because of their corruption received from Adam, so

212. SC 77; HC 87
213. No parallels
214. HC 86, 115
215. HC 8
216. No parallels

that no one is saved except by the infinite mercy of God. Third, those not regenerated by the Spirit of Christ don't even have any desire to be so. Therefore, since they are lost by their own volition, they have no excuse for questioning God. Fourth, it was by its own will and not by any fault of God that the human race lost its ability to obey God and cast itself into necessary sinning.[217]

218   Q. But since by ourselves we are incapable of thinking anything good, surely we shouldn't indulge in unbelief and other sins while we await being forcibly changed by the Holy Spirit?

A. It is neither right to do that, nor is anyone elect who does it. For first of all, when we do that, our consciences condemn us. Second, if God takes us from this life while we are persevering in the intention to sin, we will perish forever. Third, the Holy Spirit does not force or pressure us to believe and repent unwillingly, but through the hearing and reflecting on God's Word he renews and moves our wills and hearts so that we sincerely desire to be governed by him.[218]

219   Q. But inasmuch as no one is saved except those whom God from eternity has elected to salvation, how can you be convinced that the promise of grace pertains to you when you don't know whether you are elect?

A. Because by true faith I embrace the grace of God offered to me, and by that most compelling evidence I know that I have been elected by God to eternal life and will always be kept by him. For if he had not elected me from eternity, he would never have given me the Spirit of adoption.[219]

220   Q. But how can you apply the promised grace to yourself through faith, when you are stained in so many ways by so many sins?

A. First, because God has shown his mercy in such a way that he wishes to remit all the sins of a believer, no matter how many and how great they are. Second, because the merit of Christ is infinitely greater than all sins, not only mine but also those of all people. Third, because God commands me to believe in Christ, no matter how much I have sinned, and affirms at the same time that not to believe is a greater sin than all the others that could be

217. No parallels
218. No parallels
219. SC 52

committed by someone. Therefore, just because I have offended my God with so many and such great sins, I ought not to add this, by far the greatest of sins, so that I ungratefully trample on God's mercy and the blood of his Son shed for me.[220]

221 Q. But since your faith is so weak, how do you know that you are justified through it?

A. Because God receives in grace all who are endowed with true faith, however weak it is, and brings to completion the work he has begun in them.[221]

222 Q. But how do you know that your faith is true and not just historical faith or conjecture?

A. First, because I experience in my heart this testimony of the Holy Spirit that I am earnestly seeking and receiving the grace of God offered in Christ, that I abhor nothing more than this greatest of sins, that is, not to believe in Christ, and that I am consequently one of the children of God. Second, because I experience that a true conversion to God has begun in me.[222]

223 Q. How then do we obtain and retain the grace of the Holy Spirit to keep God's covenant?

A. When we earnestly and persistently ask this of God, diligently learn God's Word, use the sacraments as divinely instituted, and are zealous for holiness of life.[223]

The Invocation of God

224 Q. Why is the invocation of God necessary for Christians?

A. First, because it is among the most important parts of the worship of God that the covenant of grace requires of us. Second, because this is the way God wants the elect to acquire and retain both the grace of the Holy Spirit necessary for keeping his covenant and all the rest of his benefits. Third, because it is a testimony in their hearts to the divine covenant. For whoever rightly calls upon God

220. No parallels
221. SC 52
222. No parallels
223. No parallels

has been given the Spirit of adoption as children and has been received into God's covenant.[224]

225   Q. What is true invocation of God?

      A. It is a burning desire of the soul by which, according to his command and promises, we ask for and expect spiritual and physical gifts from God alone because of Christ; or it is giving thanks to God for gifts received.[225]

226   Q. Why ought we to call upon God alone?

      A. Because he alone is the source and primary author of all good things to everyone and because there is no one to hear and help those who pray from all places except almighty God.[226]

227   Q. May we not then ask for things also from other people?

      A. We may, but only those things that can be given by them, and only by those who are present and, as it were, instruments of divine beneficence toward us.[227]

228   Q. Is it enough to pray with the mouth?

      A. By no means. For unless we pray with an understanding of what we are asking, both out of a true sense of our misery and with an anxious and ardent desire for the grace of God, our prayers are not only in vain but also provoke God to wrath.[228]

229   Q. But where does this burning desire for prayer come from?

      A. The Holy Spirit must kindle it in our hearts. Therefore, this grace of the Holy Spirit ought to be one of the main things that we ask for from God.[229]

230   Q. But shouldn't we also sometimes pray with our mouths?

      A. To be sure, and even often. First, because the Lord commanded it when he said, "When you pray, say." Second, because our tongues

224. SC 96; HC 116
225. SC 97; HC 117
226. No parallels
227. No parallels
228. No parallels
229. HC 115

and words ought also to glorify God through invocation and thanksgiving. Third, because praying aloud often keeps our attention.[230]

231 Q. Must we be convinced that our prayers are always heard by God?

A. Yes, because God has both promised that we will receive whatever we ask for in faith and commanded that we ask with this confidence.[231]

232 Q. How can we have this confidence when our unworthiness is so great?

A. Since God has offered Christ to us as a mediator, who presents to the Father the prayers of those who call upon the Father in his name, he has promised that he will hear us because of Christ; and it is certain that when Christ prays for us and with us, the Father cannot deny him anything.[232]

233 Q. Then why don't we receive everything we ask for?

A. We receive everything that pertains to our salvation and in the way that is best for us. If, however, out of ignorance we ask for something other than that, it is better that it not be given to us.[233]

234 Q. But what ought we to ask for and with what form of prayer?

A. Christ prescribed to his disciples the best form of prayer, which summarizes everything that ought to be asked of God.[234]

235 Q. What is that prayer?

A. "Our Father, who art in heaven, hallowed be your name. Your kingdom come, your will be done, on earth as it is in heaven. Give us this day our daily bread, and forgive us our debts as we also forgive our debtors. And lead us not into temptation, but deliver us from evil. For yours is the kingdom and the power and the glory, forever. Amen."[235]

230. No parallels
231. No parallels
232. No parallels
233. No parallels
234. SC 98; HC 118
235. SC 99; HC 119

236   Q. How many parts does it have?

A. It contains a preface and six petitions.[236]

237   Q. What is the preface?

A. "Our Father, who art in heaven."[237]

238   Q. Why did the Lord attach this preface to our prayers?

A. First, so that when we are about to pray, we may distinguish our invocation from the prayers of unbelievers by turning ourselves to this God who has made himself known in the church. Second, so that when we consider whom and what kind of God we are calling upon, we may be encouraged to call upon him with reverence and trust.[238]

239   Q. Why do we call God "Father"?

A. So that when we consider that we have been adopted by God as children because we are members of Christ, we will both call upon him through Christ and be convinced that we will be heard as by a gracious Father.[239]

240   Q. Why do we say "our"?

A. First, so that we consider that we ought to pray not only for ourselves but also for others, especially for those who are members with us of the one body of Christ and children of the same Father in heaven. Second, so that we pray more boldly when we consider that the whole church of the saints, including Christ himself, the firstborn among his brothers, is praying with us.[240]

241   Q. Why is "who art in heaven" added?

A. First, so that we do not think anything earthly or temporal about God but realize that his majesty is so great that neither our senses nor our souls can grasp it. Second, so that when we remember that our God has dominion over heaven and earth, is everywhere

236. SC 98
237. No parallels
238. SC 100; HC 120
239. SC 100; HC 120
240. No parallels

present, and hears and helps those who call upon him, we address him with fear and trust. Third, so that we do not direct the worship of God to any place or thing beyond his command.[241]

242 Q. What is the first petition?

A. "Hallowed be your name."[242]

243 Q. What is the "name" of God?

A. Whatever is believed and preached about God in accordance with his Word.[243]

244 Q. What then are we asking for in this petition?

A. That people acknowledge, invoke, and glorify God in the way that his holiness, goodness, and majesty require.[244]

245 Q. What is the second petition?

A. "Your kingdom come."[245]

246 Q. What are we asking for with these words?

A. That God sanctify believers more and more by his Spirit, add to their number, and restrain those who fight against him, until, when all obstacles have been removed, it becomes plain that all things are subject to his will.[246]

247 Q. What is the third petition?

A. "Your will be done, on earth as it is in heaven."[247]

248 Q. What is being asked in this petition?

A. That we and all people desire and choose what is pleasing to God, but that if we desire anything contrary to his wishes, it not be

241. HC 121
242. No parallels
243. HC 122
244. SC 101; HC 122
245. No parallels
246. SC 102; HC 123
247. No parallels

granted; and that each one carry out his duties as promptly and willingly as the holy angels in heaven.[248]

249   Q. What is the fourth petition?

       A. "Give us this day our daily bread."[249]

250   Q. What do you understand by the word "bread"?

       A. Whatever is necessary to maintain the present life.[250]

251   Q. Why do we ask this of God when he commanded that it be procured by our labor?

       A. We indeed ought to work, but neither our labor nor its fruits do us any good without divine blessing.[251]

252   Q. Why do we say "our"?

       A. Because it becomes ours by the gift of God, and for that reason we ought to be content with what he has given.[252]

253   Q. Why does the Lord want us to ask for "daily bread" and that it be given us "this day"?

       A. In order that we be content with what is sufficient for our need.[253]

254   Q. What is the fifth petition?

       A. "And forgive us our debts as we also forgive our debtors."[254]

255   Q. What are we asking for with these words?

       A. That God, out of his gracious mercy because of Christ, pardon all our sins, turn away his wrath from us, and receive us in grace.[255]

248. SC 103; HC 124
249. No parallels
250. SC 104; HC 125
251. SC 104; HC 125
252. No parallels
253. No parallels
254. No parallels
255. SC 105; HC 126

256 Q. Do all need to ask for this remission?

A. All—even the most holy. For Christ prescribed this form of prayer for all believers, since there is no righteous person on the earth who does not also sin.[256]

257 Q. Why did the Lord add, "As we also forgive our debtors."

A. First, so that we enter into prayer with true faith, conversion to God, and love for our neighbor; if, in fact, we do not sincerely forgive others, we ought not to expect forgiveness from God, but we are asking for his vengeance upon our sins. Second, so that when we truly forgive others, we might have the sure testimony of the Holy Spirit in our hearts that we are children of God and might obtain remission of our sins from God.[257]

258 Q. What is the last petition?

A. "And lead us not into temptation, but deliver us from evil."[258]

259 Q. What are we praying for in this petition?

A. That God outfit us with the power of his Spirit against the Devil and our flesh, so that we not fall into sin; and that when we are finally set free from all our sins, miseries, and death, he give us eternal life and happiness.[259]

260 Q. What do you understand by "temptation"?

A. The cunning and deceits of the Devil with which he continually plots against us all and, by virtue of our weakness, would turn us away from God if we were not protected by the Father's hand.[260]

261 Q. How does God lead into temptation when Scripture attributes this to the Devil?

A. The Devil tempts people to sin. But those whom God wishes to punish he deprives of his grace, strikes with blindness, and hands over to the Devil to be driven into sin and destruction.[261]

256. SC 105; HC 126
257. SC 105; HC 126
258. No parallels
259. SC 106; HC 127
260. No parallels
261. No parallels

262   Q. Why is there added, "For yours is the kingdom and the power and the glory, forever"?

      A. First, so that we may testify that our prayers rely not on our own confidence but on the goodness and power of God alone. Second, so that we may be reminded that we ought to ask God for all good things for this main purpose: that the kingdom, the power, and the glory be ascribed to him. Third, so that we may begin and close our prayer with praise to God.[262]

263   Q. What is the meaning of the little word "Amen"?

      A. It signifies a desire that what we are asking for really happen and a confidence that it really will.[263]

The Ministry of the Church

264   Q. What is the ministry of the church?

      A. It is the public preaching of God's Word, the administration of the sacraments, and church discipline—instituted by Christ for bringing to completion the salvation of the elect.[264]

265   Q. Why did God institute the ministry of the church?

      A. So that through it he might receive us into his covenant, keep us in it, and really convince us that we are and forever will remain in it.[265]

266   Q. Why do you say that we are received and kept in God's covenant through the ministry?

      A. Because it is the instrument of the Holy Spirit by which he works and confirms in the hearts of the elect the faith and conversion that God requires of us in his covenant.[266]

---

262. SC 107; HC 128
263. SC 108; HC 129
264. SC 53; HC 65
265. No parallels
266. SC 53; HC 65

267 Q. Isn't the Holy Spirit's own honor taken away when sanctification is attributed to the ministry?

A. No, for the strength and power by which we are sanctified are all from the divine Spirit; the ministry is merely his instrument by which he moves the souls and hearts of the elect whenever and however it seems right to him—not because he could not do otherwise but because it pleased the divine wisdom, through the foolish preaching of the cross, to save those who believe.[267]

268 Q. What should ministers preach?

A. Nothing but the Word of God contained in the law and the gospel.[268]

269 Q. But how can we be certain that the Word of God is being proclaimed by ministers?

A. If they proclaim the teaching recorded in the books of the Old and New Testaments, and if what they say conforms to the Articles of the Faith and the commandments of God; in short, if they teach us to seek our entire salvation in Christ alone.[269]

270 Q. Isn't it enough to learn God's Word privately?

A. It is indeed necessary for our salvation to meditate on it day and night, but if we want to be Christians, we must also make use of the public ministry when we are not prevented by circumstance.[270]

271 Q. Why is this necessary?

A. First, because of God's command. Second, so that God may be publicly glorified by the whole church in the sight of all people and creatures. Third, so that the unity of the church might be preserved and displayed.[271]

267. No parallels
268. No parallels
269. No parallels
270. No parallels
271. No parallels

272   Q. What does the Holy Spirit bring about through the preaching of God's Word?

A. First, he teaches us what God promises us in his covenant and what he in turn requires from us. Next, he persuades us to believe and obey him more and more each day.[272]

273   Q. But how does the Holy Spirit work in us through hearing and meditating on God's Word?

A. When we learn it for the purpose of believing and obeying him in all things.[273]

The Sacraments

274   Q. What are sacraments?

A. They are signs of the covenant between God and believers in Christ, or seals of the righteousness of faith.[274]

275   Q. Say that more clearly.

A. Sacraments are ceremonies instituted by God and added to the promise of grace, so that he might represent to them the grace promised in the gospel, that is, the communication of Christ and all his benefits; and so that, by these visible pledges and public testimonies, as it were, he might assure all those who use these ceremonies in true faith that this promise certainly belongs to them and will be valid for them forever; and so that those using them might, on their part, bind themselves to perseverance in true faith and piety toward God.[275]

276   Q. Then does God present and assure us of the same benefits in the Word and the sacraments?

A. Yes, the same ones. For the signs of the covenant cannot testify to anything other than what is promised in the covenant itself.[276]

272. No parallels
273. No parallels
274. SC 54; HC 66
275. SC 54
276. No parallels

277   Q. But why does God add visible signs to the Word when he does not offer and confirm for us in them anything different than he does in the Word?

A. First and foremost, because of our weakness, he wants to promise us the same things in different ways and testify that they belong to us, so that he might assure us all the more of our faith, and, as it grows, keep increasing all the spiritual gifts in us. Second, so that throughout our whole life these signs might remind us of the love for God and neighbor to which we obligated ourselves by the covenant established with God. Third, so that they may be marks of the confession that distinguish the church from all other peoples and sects. Fourth, so that the memory of Christ's benefits might be clearer, longer lasting, and publicly celebrated.[277]

278   Q. But since the sacraments are external and physical things, how can they make us more certain of receiving internal and spiritual things?

A. They do not accomplish this by virtue of the act itself, nor by any power infused into or attached to the elements, but because God promises his grace to us by these ceremonies as visible words just as truly as he does by the Word of the gospel, and he wants them to be visible pledges of this promise, given by him publicly to each one who uses them in faith; and because by means of these instruments, as it were, the Holy Spirit confirms faith in the hearts of the elect.[278]

279   Q. Then is God's grace given and sealed to all who use the sacraments?

A. No, only to those who have been born again by the Spirit of Christ and use the ceremonies commanded by God as a mutual testimony of the covenant. But the unholy, by abusing the signs of God's covenant, heap God's wrath upon themselves, give evidence of their ingratitude and dishonesty, and pass sentence on themselves by professing the truth of Christian doctrine.[279]

277. SC 54; HC 66
278. SC 54
279. No parallels

280   Q. But doesn't it detract from divine truth if not all who receive the signs at the same time receive what the signs signify?

       A. Not in the least. For these things were promised and the sacraments instituted for believers only. Therefore, for divine truth and divine institution to agree, believers cannot receive the signs without the things promised, nor can unbelievers receive the things promised with the signs.[280]

281   Q. Can anyone participate in or be certain of the divine covenant and eternal salvation without the use of the sacraments?

       A. Whoever does not use the sacraments when it is possible shows that he has no faith and excludes himself from the communion of saints and the covenant of God. But the promise made to believers is still valid for those who are deprived of the sacraments against their will.[281]

282   Q. Can humans institute sacraments?

       A. No, because testimonies of God's will for us can be given to us by no one but God alone.[282]

283   Q. How many sacraments did Christ institute?

       A. Two: baptism and the Holy Supper.[283]

Baptism

284   Q. What is baptism?

       A. It is the washing done with water in the name of God the Father, the Son, and the Holy Spirit, instituted by Christ, so that it mightbe a testimony that one who has been baptized in this way has been received by God into the covenant of grace, because of Christ, and has been sanctified by the Holy Spirit for eternal life.[284]

280. No parallels
281. SC 55
282. No parallels
283. SC 56; HC 68
284. SC 57; HC 69

285   Q. What does this washing signify?

       A. That just as water removes the dirt of the body, so we are cleansed of our sins by the blood and Spirit of Christ.[285]

286   Q. How are we cleansed by the blood of Christ?

       A. When God remits our sins because of the shed blood of Christ.[286]

287   Q. How are we cleansed by the Holy Spirit?

       A. When we are regenerated by him to new life.[287]

288   Q. What benefit do we receive from this washing?

       A. That in every true conversion to God through our whole life, we are certain of the covenant established with God and of this spiritual washing that happens by the blood and Spirit of Christ.[288]

289   Q. Why does the physical washing make us more certain of the spiritual washing?

       A. Because Christ promised it in the institution of baptism.[289]

290   Q. What is that institution?

       A. At the end of Matthew and Mark the Lord speaks to the disciples as follows: "Going into all the world, make disciples of all nations, baptizing them in the name of the Father, and of the Son, and of the Holy Spirit. Whoever believes and is baptized will be saved; but whoever does not believe will be condemned."[290]

291   Q. What does it mean to baptize in the name of the Father, the Son, and the Holy Spirit?

       A. It means to testify by God's command through this ceremony that the one baptized in this way is received in grace by the eternal Father because of the Son and is sanctified by the Holy Spirit.[291]

285. SC 57; HC 69
286. SC 58; HC 70
287. SC 58; HC 70
288. No parallels
289. SC 59
290. SC 60; HC 71
291. No parallels

292   Q. Is this ceremony then a testimony of salvation to all who are baptized with water?

       A. No, only to believers. For whoever does not believe must be condemned even if he has been baptized, says the Lord.[292]

293   Q. But are infants then rightly baptized since they have not yet been granted faith?

       A. They are. For faith and its confession are required before baptism in adults so that they cannot be included in God's covenant in any other way. But for infants it is enough to be sanctified by the Spirit of Christ in proportion to their age.[293]

294   Q. But why is it necessary for them to be baptized?

       A. First, because God stipulates that whoever he embraces in his covenant be marked with baptism. Children of believers, however, are and remain members of the covenant of grace if, when they come of age, they do not exclude themselves from it by their unbelief. For God affirms that he will be their God also, and Christ affirms that the kingdom of heaven is theirs. Second, because baptism replaced circumcision. Therefore, since infants were circumcised in the Old Testament and the grace of God was not restricted at the coming of Christ but poured out more fully, they now should be baptized also.[294]

The Lord's Supper

295   Q. What is the Lord's Supper?

       A. It is the distribution and eating of bread and wine in the congregation of believers in remembrance of Christ, instituted by Christ so that by this sign he might testify that he most certainly communicates his body and blood for eternal life to believers who partake of this bread and wine, so that the covenant established with God in baptism may be valid for them forever.[295]

292. SC 62
293. SC 63; HC 74
294. SC 63; HC 74
295. SC 64

296 Q. How does the Lord's Supper differ from baptism?

  A. They are signs of the same covenant and grace. Baptism, however, testifies that the covenant has truly been established by God with us, whereas the Supper continually renews the covenant and assures that it will be valid forever. Therefore God wants baptism to be sought once in a lifetime but the Supper to be repeated often.[296]

297 Q. What does the breaking of the bread signify?

  A. That just as that bread is broken for each one of us, so also Christ was torn apart and died for each one of us.[297]

298 Q. What does the partaking of the bread and wine signify?

  A. First, that just as bread and wine sustain bodily life, so also the body and blood of Christ that we eat and drink nourish us for eternal life. Second, that just as the one loaf that we share comes from many grains and the wine that we drink from many grapes, so also believers become one body in Christ.[298]

299 Q. What does it mean to eat the body of Christ and to drink his blood?

  A. It means to believe in Christ and to become a member of the body of Christ through faith and the Spirit of Christ dwelling in us, so that because of that body handed over to death we might receive remission of sins, and so that from that fountain and source, as it were, poured out in us by the Holy Spirit living in him, we might drink of the same eternal life and righteousness that is in him.[299]

300 Q. Does eating Christ mean only that we participate in Christ's merit and in the gifts of the Holy Spirit?

  A. Not only this but also the communication of the person and substance of Christ himself. For his divinity dwells in us, but his body is joined to our bodies in such a way that we are one with him.[300]

296. No parallels
297. SC 64; HC 75
298. SC 64, 69; HG 75
299. SC 65; HC 76
300. SC 65; HC 76

301   Q. How can this be, since the body of Christ is in heaven and we are on earth?

     A. The Holy Spirit, who at the same time dwells in the soul and body of Christ in heaven and in the souls and bodies of the saints on earth, is a bond between the two, joining bodies separated by a very great distance better and more securely than the members of our body are connected to the head, or branches to the vine.[301]

302   Q. Don't all these things come to us even apart from the Lord's Supper?

     A. Yes indeed. Whenever we believe the gospel and are sanctified by the Holy Spirit, it is certain that we receive all these benefits.[302]

303   Q. Then how does the partaking of this bread and wine benefit us?

     A. First, it is a testimony and seal to us of this internal and spiritual eating. Second, this communion of Christ himself and all his benefits increases in us through faith, so that day by day we become more closely united with Christ until we are perfectly one with him in eternal life.[303]

304   Q. Why does this ceremony assure us of communion with Christ?

     A. Because in the institution of the Supper Christ promised believers this communion with him.[304]

305   Q. What is that institution?

     A. It is described by the gospel writers and the apostle Paul in this way: "The Lord Jesus on the night when he was betrayed took bread, and when he had given thanks, he broke it and said, 'Take, eat, this is my body, which is broken for you. Do this in remembrance of me.' In the same way also the cup after supper, saying, 'This cup is the new testament in my blood. Do this, as often as you drink it, in remembrance of me.' For as often as you eat this bread and drink this cup, you proclaim the Lord's death until he comes. For whoever eats this bread or drinks the cup of the Lord in an unworthy manner will be guilty of profaning the body and blood of the Lord. For whoever eats and drinks in an

301. SC 65; HC 76
302. No parallels
303. HC 76
304. SC 67

unworthy manner, without discerning the body, eats and drinks judgment unto himself."[305]

306   Q. How does the Lord say that the bread is his body and the wine his blood?

     A. In the same way that a sign is said to be the thing that it represents and confirms. For in this way a crown or scepter stands for a kingdom, circumcision for the covenant between God and Abraham, the slaughtering and eating of a lamb for the Passover of the Lord, the Levitical sacrifice for the expiation of sins, and baptism for the bath of regeneration. Thus also in general a sacrament is said to be the thing signified and confirmed by God through it.[306]

307   Q. What does Scripture mean when it speaks this way?

     A. That these visible and physical things are signs and testimonies of the invisible and spiritual gifts of God.[307]

308   Q. What then is the meaning of Christ's words when he says that the bread is his body and the wine his blood?

     A. That both the bread that we eat and the wine that we drink are a sign and testimony to believers that the body and blood of Christ were given and shed and are communicated to us through faith, just as surely as we partake of the bread and wine with the bodily mouth.[308]

309   Q. Where is this explanation given in Scripture?

     A. Paul gives it in 1 Corinthians 10. For after he says that the bread is a participation in the body of Christ, he adds this reason: because believers who share in the one bread become one body. And Christ himself also teaches this when he calls the cup a new testament in his blood, which is the remission of sins and the gift of righteousness and eternal life on account of his shed blood. For the Christian faith does not allow this to be understood in any other way than that the cup is a sign and testimony of this testament.[309]

---

305. SC 67; HC 77
306. HC 78
307. SC 69; HC 79
308. SC 69; HC 75, 79
309. SC 67; HC 79

310 Q. But why did the Lord say it this way?

A. First, so that he might teach what these visible signs represent. Second, so that he might impress upon us that as surely as believers experience the use of the external signs, so surely does the communion of his body and blood happen to them.[310]

311 Q. Why did Christ decide to use two signs?

A. To teach us that he is not only our spiritual food but also our spiritual drink, that is, that he gives us everything necessary for our salvation.[311]

312 Q. What does it mean to partake of this bread and cup in remembrance of Christ?

A. It means that by this ceremony we are reminded of redemption through Christ and our union with him, and are shored up by this visible pledge, as it were, to embrace these benefits with a stronger faith and to meditate on, confess, and publicly proclaim them.[312]

313 Q. Is the communion of Christ extended to and sealed in all who partake of this bread and cup?

A. No, only to believers. For since unbelievers are partners with demons, they cannot participate at the table of the Lord.[313]

314 Q. Who are those who eat this bread and drink this cup in a worthy manner?

A. Those who examine themselves when they are about to come.[314]

315 Q. And how will we examine ourselves?

A. By searching out whether we are true members of Christ.[315]

---

310. SC 69; HC 75, 79
311. No parallels
312. No parallels
313. SC 70; HC 81
314. SC 70; HC 81
315. No parallels

316   Q. How do we know that we are members of Christ?

      A. If we experience within ourselves true faith, conversion to God, and love of neighbor.[316]

317   Q. But as long as we find that these things are not perfect in us, shall we abstain from the Lord's Supper?

      A. Certainly not, provided that these things are genuine and not feigned in us. For Christ accepts the weak and instituted his Supper because of our weakness.[317]

318   Q. By whom should the sacraments be administered?

      A. By ministers of the gospel. For administration of the sacraments is part of the public ministry, in which God wants no one to be engaged unless called by him.[318]

319   Q. And who are to be admitted to the sacraments?

      A. In the case of baptism, either adults who rightly profess the basics of the Christian faith and lead a life worthy of a Christian, or infants born to those whom the church recognizes as believers. In the case of the Lord's Supper, however, only adults who are able to examine themselves and give evidence of this examination in confession and life.[319]   ·

320   Q. And what ought to be done with those who lead a life unworthy of a Christian?

      A. They ought to be corrected by church discipline.[320]

Church Discipline

321   Q. What should be the form of church discipline?

      A. Elders should be appointed, who watch over the conduct of the church. Those who are living wickedly should be brought to the attention of the elders after a first and second private admonition, so that the elders too may admonish them. If they do not obey the

316. SC 70; HC 81
317. No parallels
318. No parallels
319. SC 71; HC 82
320. SC 71; HC 82

elders, by agreement of the elders they ought to be excluded from the Lord's Supper until they not only promise amendment of life but also show it by their deeds.[321]

322 Q. How does the discipline of the church differ from the responsibility of the political magistrate?

A. The first and foremost difference is that the magistrate punishes and corrects wrongdoers with physical force, whereas the church only admonishes verbally and excludes from communion. Second, the magistrate is content with the execution of justice through punishment, whereas the church seeks the correction and salvation of those it admonishes. Third, the magistrate proceeds right away to punishment, whereas the church admonishes in a brotherly way, so that magisterial punishment may be avoided by early correction. Fourth, the magistrate does not punish many of the sins that harm the church and must be condemned by it.[322]

323 Q. Why is this discipline necessary?

A. First, because of the Lord's command that sinners be warned several times, and that if they do not listen to us, it be brought to the attention of the church; and that if they do not listen even to the church, they will be treated as publicans and gentiles. Second, so that desecration of the sacraments and the divine covenant might be avoided, which occurs when those who by their confession or life show that they are strangers to God's covenant are admitted to the use of the sacraments with the consent of the church. Third, so that obedience owed to the ministry might be maintained in the church. Fourth, so that to the extent possible, stumbling blocks might be removed among both the enemies and the members of the church, lest the contaminations spread. Fifth, so that nothing that has been instituted by God for the correction and salvation of sinners might be neglected in the church.[323]

321. HC 85
322. No parallels
323. HC 85